Julian's *Against the Galileans*

Julian's *Against the Galileans*

edited and translated
by
R. Joseph Hoffmann

 **Prometheus Books**

59 John Glenn Drive
Amherst, New York 14228-2197

Published 2004 by Prometheus Books

Inquiries should be addressed to
Prometheus Books
59 John Glenn Drive
Amherst, New York 14228-2197
VOICE: 716-691-0133, ext. 207
FAX: 716-564-2711
WWW.PROMETHEUSBOOKS.COM

08 07 06 05 04   5 4 3 2 1

Library of Congress Cataloging-in-Publication Data

Julian, Emperor of Rome, 331–363.
    [Contra Galilaeos. English]
    Julian's against the Galileans / edited and translated with an introduction by
R. Joseph Hoffmann.
        p. cm.
    Includes bibliographical references.
    ISBN 1-59102-198-7 (hardcover : alk. paper)
    1. Christianity—Controversial literature—Early works to 1800.
2. Christianity and other religions—Roman—Early works to 1800. I. Hoffmann,
R. Joseph. II. Title.

BR160.3.J85 2004
273'.4—dc22
                                                            2004009151

Library of Congress Cataloging-in-Publication Data

To the Ancestors
ἐμοὶ διηγοῦ σὺ τοὐμὸν ὄναρ.

CONTENTS

LIST OF ABBREVIATIONS

Abbreviations for ancient works cited frequently in the text. See the bibliography for the full list of ancient authorities and texts.

Abst.	*On Abstinence* (Porphyry)
Adv. Jul.	*Against Julian* (Cyril of Alexandria)
Amm.	*Res gestae* (History) (Ammianus Marcellinus)
Caes.	*Lives of the Caesars* (Suetonius)
C. Cels.	*Contra Celsum* (Origen)
CG	*Contra Galilaeos* (Julian)
Cod. Theod.	*Codex* (Theodosius)
De princ.	*De Principiis* (Origen)
Dial. Tryph.	*Dialogue with Trypho* (Justin Martyr)
Enn.	*The Enneads* (Plotinus)
Ep.	*Epistles* (Julian)
Ep. ad SPQ Ath.	*Epistle to the Athenians* (Julian)
Ep. ad Them	*Letter to Themistius* (Julian)

Frag.	*Fragments* (Eunapius)
Greg., Or.	*Orations*
Hist. Eccl.	*Ecclesiastical History* (Philostorgius)
Libanius, Or.	*Orationes* (Libanius)
Myst.	*De mysteriis* (Iamblichus)
Or. IV	*Hymn to Helios* (Julian)
Or. V	*To [Cybele] the Mother of the Gods* (Julian)
Or. VI	*To the Uneducated Cynics* (Julian)
Or. VII	*Against Heraclius* (Julian)
PG	*Patrologiae Graecae Cursus Completus* (Cyril of Alexandria)
Philos., Hist.	*Historia Ecclesiastica* (Philostorgius)
Socrates, HE	*Historia Ecclesiastica* (Socrates)
Sozomen, HE	*Historia Ecclesiastica* (Sozomen)
Theodoret, Hist. Eccles.	*Historia Ecclesiastica* (Theodoret)
Theog.	*Theogony* (Hesiod)
Zosimus	*Nova Historia* (Zosimus)

INTRODUCTION
JULIAN THE RESTORER

"Time and the gods are at strife; ye dwell in the midst thereof."

Swinburne, *Hymn to Proserpine*

I. THE POLITICAL JULIAN

When Flavius Claudius Julianus, better known to history as Julian the Apostate, died in a poorly planned campaign against Persian forces in Ctesiphon (Mesopotamia) on June 26, 363, he was thirty-one years old. According to one of the many biographies that his brief and eventful reign inspired, he was lanced from behind by an unknown assailant from his own forces. Realizing his wound was fatal, he cupped his hands to gather his blood, flung it toward the sun—which in its aspect as Helios he had once regarded as the presiding god of his rule—and cried, "Galilean—You have conquered."

The words are almost certainly fabricated for effect by the church father Theodoret;[1] Julian was fighting a Persian army, not Christians, but when word of his death reached Constantinople and Rome the interpretation of the event was swift and irreversible. Whoever killed Julian was doing God's work. The man who was killing Christ's church had been put to death by the decree of *Christus imperator*. According to a legend recounted by the Palestinian church historian

---

1. Theod., HE 3.25.3.

11

Hermias Sozomen the omens were in place—the oracle at Bablas
had ceased to utter the prophecies of Apollo, the reconstruction of
the Temple in Jerusalem, ordered by Julian to commence during his
absence, had been disrupted by earthquake and fiery storms spewing
from the foundations, and most portentous of all, a crusading soldier racing to join forces with Julian along the Tigris had received a
vision: a heavenly council of apostles and prophets had been convened and had decided the emperor must die.[2] For Sozomen, the
occlusion of the sun by a dust storm on the bright June day proved
that his death was not due to simple military miscalculation. The
Persians would not claim responsibility for it; no one from among
the Roman soldiery came forward to confess to it; and no conspiracy
was uncovered. Even the most ardent Christian despisers of Julian
profess ignorance in the matter, though Sozomen calculates that the
assassin was probably a Christian.[3] Those who loved or admired
him had other ideas: his bodyguard Callistus, who celebrated
Julian's deeds in a heroic poem known to the historian Socrates
Scholasticus, said Julian had been stabbed by demons,[4] and his
friend Libanius, a Syrian sophist, remained confident that whoever
killed Julian "was neither Persian nor Saracen," but a group of liber-
tine soldiers looking for the right time to put an end to the puritan-
ical regime his religious ideas had brought about.[5]

Julian's inglorious end stands in uneasy symmetry with his early
life and exploits as Constantius's western lieutenant. When he was
nominated Caesar at the age of twenty-two by a vacillating and suspicious Constantius, he was pulled away from a life of philosophical
commitment and personal insecurity. Julian was keenly aware of his
cousin's obsessive readiness to purge the family of conspirators,
would-be usurpers, and rivals,[6] a tendency realized immediately

---

2. Sozomen, HE 5.20, 21, 22; 6.2.

3. Sozomen, HE 6.2 erroneously or misleadingly attributes the suggestion to
Libanius.

4. Socrates, HE 3.21.

5. Sozomen, HE 6.1.

6. After Constantine's death in 337, Constantine II (Augustus 337–40) and
Constantius II (Augustus 340–61) had unequivocal title, while an array of unillus-
trious caesars—Magnentius, Decentius, Vetranio, and Nepotian—failed to establish
their claims to power and were regarded as usurpers.

after Constantine's death in 337 when Constantius targeted the families of Constantine's half-brothers, but spared Julian and his half-brother Gallus because of their age.[7] Born in Constantinople, Julian's father, Julius Constantius, was himself half-brother of the emperor Constantine through Constantius Chlorus, and his mother, Basilina, was Julius's second wife. The half-brothers of Constantine's fold were in fact a paradigm for the uneasy relationships that would later affect the heirs of Constantius; it was only after years of tense relations that Constantine had decided to legitimate his siblings, making Julius Constantius, Julian's father, one of his consuls in 335. Julian was, apparently, especially devoted to his mother,[8] who according to reports by both Ammianus[9] and Libanius[10] was a noblewoman, the daughter of the praetorian prefect Julius Julianus, who had come to win Constantine's always unpredictable favor. Perhaps more relevant for Julian's intellectual development is the fact that his mother had been tutored by the Scythian eunuch Mardonius, and following Basilina's death in 339, Julian was sent away to Nicomedia and to Mardonius's care and tutelage.

To stay for a moment with the foreground of Julian's political biography, the date November 6, 355, was a pivotal one, not only in Julian's life but in the life of the Empire. Recounting the events of that year, Ammianus says that Gaul was in a desperate situation, with every report out of the region bringing worse news than the one before it. Constantius was torn between sharing the imperial power, which could never, his advisers reminded him, be done without risk to the emperor, and presiding over the destruction of Gaul by hordes of unopposed barbarians.[11] (Gallus, Julian's half brother, had been elevated to the purple, accused of treason, and executed as a conspir-

---

7. On the purge, see M. DiMaio and D. Arnold, "*Per vim, per caedem, per bellum*: A Study of Murder and Ecclesiastical Politics in the Year 337 AD," *Byzantion* 62 (1992): 158ff.

8. Or so we may judge from the fact that he founded a city (Basilinoupolis) in her honor; see Lib. XVIII.187–88. It is usually thought that Basilina was an Arian. It is entirely possible that she was a pagan, a fact which makes Julian's being entrusted to Mardonius—almost certainly a pagan pedagogue—more explicable.

9. Amm., 25.3.23.

10. Libanius, Or. 18.9.

11. Amm., 15.7.5.

ator in 354.) Constantius decided on Julian only reluctantly, after the young scholar had spent seven months under protection and observation near Milan, when the emperor's wife Eusebia persuaded Constantius that Julian was too much the hermit to plot intrigue or pose a political threat.[12] In practical terms, however, the purges of Constantine's family had by this time been so effective that Julian was the only viable candidate to restore order along the Rhine frontier.

Ammianus sets the scene: a bright day in November with the emperor taking his place next to Julian "on a high platform surrounded by eagles and standards." In the oration, Constantius praised the bond of kinship which in ordinary life was expendable to him. After receiving the acclamation of the assembled troops, Constantius vested Julian in the purple robe of his ancestors and declared him caesar, to a din of approval—shields being struck against the knee. As though to suggest that the display was not altogether to his liking, Ammianus adds the detail, "Julian stood before [the emperor] dejected and wearing a slight frown."[13] Several days later, to seal the bond of kinship that Constantius had extolled, Julian was married to Constantius's spinsterish sister Helena, through whose physical inspiration, apparently, he found it simple to practice chastity.[14] There followed a progress from Turin to Vienne where he was to take up command of the army. Along the route, Julian learned that Cologne (Colonia Agrippina) had been taken by Alamanni forces after a long siege, which he interpreted as an omen of worse things to come. When he arrived in Vienne, however, there was an outpouring of affection, including one voice, an old woman's, that had a special resonance: "This is the man," she cried out, "who will restore the temples of the gods."[15]

---

12. Julian, Or. III.11 8C and Epistula ad SPQ Atheniarum, 274A–B.

13. Amm., 15.8.10.

14. One of the few references to her by Ammianus (16.10.18), recounting events of the year 357, asserts that Helena was summoned to Rome by Eusebia, the wife of Constantius, who administered a drug to her sister-in-law designed to induce abortion if she conceived. Eusebia is also accused of causing Helena to lose a male child in Gaul, by bribing the midwife to cut the umbilical cord too short. These comments must be assessed in the context of Ammianus's general contempt for the family of Constantius and his desire to extol Julian's reputation for philosophical chastity.

15. Amm., 15.8.16.

The fledgling caesar who took command of an army at Durocor-
torum is described in vivid and conflicting ways by biographers.
Julian had been sent to Athens in 354 after Gallus's execution, largely
for safekeeping, but also for further study with the Neoplatonic
philosopher Priscus.[16] There he came to know the future Christian
bishop who would write tirelessly against him, Gregory Naziazen.
Gregory describes a young man already conniving to "restore the
temples of the gods," but cunning enough to keep his intentions
secret. As Gregory reads the character of his former schoolmate,
nothing good could have come from one so obviously unsuited to a
public role, "a neck seldom steady, a frequent shrugging of shoulders,
an eye always scowling and in motion, together with a frenzied
aspect, a gait irregular and tottering, a nose breathing only contempt
and insult, with ridiculous contortions of countenance expressive of
the same thing; immoderate and very loud laughter, nods, as it were,
of assent and drawings back of the head as if in denial without any
visible cause; speech with hesitancy and interrupted by his breathing,
disorderly and senseless questions, answers no better, all jumbled
together without the least consistency or method."[17] Gregory sees
Julian as an unpromising enthusiast, an unsystematic philosophical
dilettante—an assessment partly born out by the most oblique sections of his works against the Christians and the most effusive passages in his letters to philosophers.[18] But to his admirers, Julian was
a promising and regal figure, whose philosophical works "rivaled
those of the Tyrian old man."[19] Ammianus describes him at his
investiture as having eyes at once "delightful and awe-inspiring and a
face to which animation added charm."[20] What for the Christian

---

16. Ep. V. Julian had met Priscus in Pergamon. His life was written by
Eunapius.

17. Gregory, Or. 5.23.

18. A good example is his approach to the teacher Maximus (Ep. 12, "To Maximus, Philosopher"): "I sleep with your letters as though they were healing drugs of
some sort, and I do not cease to read them constantly, as though they were newly
written and had only just come into my hands."

19. Libanius, Or. 18; Porphyry, with whom Julian was often compared. Cf.
Socrates, HE 3.23.

20. Amm., 15.8.16. The contradictory descriptions have played an important
role in assessments of Julian's character, reign, religious ideas, and achievements.

writer appeared to be a convulsive insecurity in his physical presence was for his Roman biographer a disarming spontaneity.[21]

However he may have appeared to contemporaries, his early skirmishes against the barbarian leaders suggest that Julian had the makings of a good military strategist and administrator. He managed to secure a peace with the local barbarian leaders who were assailing Cologne, wintered at Senoae (Sens), and spent the following spring and summer (357) in operations there and in Lugdunum (Lyons) and Tres Tabernae (Saverne). Then, near Argentoratum (Strasbourg), Julian had his epiphany as a leader against the German forces. Ammianus takes special delight in describing the determination of the barbarian armies, who were willing to thrust themselves headlong at their Roman enemies when it became clear that their early successes had not resulted in puncturing Julian's line. "The enemy, who were willing to squander their lives for victory, tried repeatedly to find weak spots in the fabric of our line. As they perished one after another and the confidence of the Romans who were striking them down increased, fresh hosts took the place of the slain, till the incessant cries of the dying stupefied them with fear. Then at last they gave way under the stress of disaster and put all their energy into attempts at flight. . . . Anyone who was present will vouch that they had more reason to pray than to flee."[22]

By any account the victory was stunning for a young leader, and after the battle, perhaps in awe of their own accomplishments, the soldiers attempted to proclaim Julian *augustus*. He rejected the title, indeed even rebuked the troops for their impetuousness "and solemnly affirmed with an oath that this was an elevation which he neither expected nor desired."[23] The demurer was, however, also pragmatic, since Julian was always aware that Constantius regarded success on the battlefield, even when effected in his name, as a threat to his imperial rule.

---

21. Ammianus acknowledges that his "truthful telling" of the acts of Julian's life result in a panegyric: "He was reckoned to be the reincarnation of Titus, the son of Vespasian, in the glorious outcome of his campaigns very like Trajan, as merciful as Antoninus, and in his striving after perfection and truth the equal of Marcus Aurelius, on whom he endeavored to model his own career and character" (16.1.4).

22. Amm., 16.12.48.

23. Amm., 16.12.60.

The following years saw less spectacular but steady advances against the barbarians. In 358 he managed to pacify mutinous troops who had been put on short rations, subdue Frankish troops along the Rhine, and repopulate a number of cities that had been devastated by years of raids by Alamanni forces. By 359 he was in a position to carry out further strikes against the Alamannic leaders in the Rhine region and to launch guerilla raids across the river near Mogontiacum (Mainz), where their armies were encamped. The effect of these successes, which are attested even by the church father Hilary of Poitiers, is that Julian managed to endear himself to the provincial élites (those who had the most to lose from barbarian incursions) and was seen by them as a savior of the old Roman order. An inscription found near Beneventum Apulia bears witness to his popularity:

> TO FLAVIUS CLAUDIUS JULIANUS, MOST NOBLE AND SANCTIFIED CAESAR,
> FROM THE CARING TOCIUS MAXIMUS, *VIR CLARISSIMUS,*
> FOR THE CARE OF THE *RES PUBLICA* FROM BENEVENTUM.[24]

Popularity came at a price. The contemporary accounts suggest that in the engagements the Romans had lost 243 men, the barbarians more than six thousand—not counting those carried off the field by their comrades. News of such stunning victories could not be suppressed, even though Julian's reports to the emperor were deliberately understated and modest: "The Germans have been defeated." Constantius's courtiers made it their task to find fault, to appease the emperor's vanity by belittling Julian's achievement. The sarcastic word for him in the court was "Victorinus." At the same time they managed to convince Constantius that Julian's victory was only a realization of the emperor's good fortune, "ascribing to his lucky star any success in any corner of the world."[25] Constantius's habit of snatching praise for himself seems to have gone far beyond exagger-

---

24. *Corpus inscriptionum latinorum,* ed. T. T. Mommsen (Berlin, 1883), ix.1562. The phrase *vir clarissimus* suggests Tocius was at the highest level of the social scale in his community and thus that Julian had succeeded in conveying a positive image of himself as Caesar among these strata.

25. Amm., 16.12.68.

ation: "When this battle was fought near Strasbourg," Ammianus complains, "from which [the emperor] was forty days march away, his account of the action stated that he had drawn up the plan of battle, taken his place by the standards, put the barbarians to flight, [and that he alone] . . . had fought and conquered or inclined a merciful ear to the entreaties of native kings. Disgraceful to relate, [Constantius] said nothing of the glorious exploits of Julian."[26] Unknown to him directly, Julian's position in the court was becoming untenable, not for any failures on his part but because, to cite the sentiment put into the mouth of one of his detractors, "his successes are becoming a bore." While the armies were beginning to compare his exploits to the wars against the Carthaginians, though with lower loss of life, his enemies argued that he sought a hero's death in Germany rather than face a traitor's death like that decreed for Gallus.

There were further successes in 358, against the Franks and the Alamanni, while Constantius for his part was barely able to keep Sapor of Persia from his goal of recovering Armenia and Mesopotamia through an extravagant game of correspondence. The symmetry of the events of 358 does not escape Ammianus, who compares Julian's uncharacteristically harsh treatment of the treacherous German kings Suomar and Hortar, prostrate at Julian's feet for defying the terms of a treaty, with the ineffectual scribbling of Constantius, reminding the Persian king that "Rome has never emerged a loser from an entire war."[27] The successes seemed if anything to enflame opinion against him: "Endless silly jokes were bandied about, such as 'He is more of a goat than a man'—an allusion to his wearing a beard—and 'his victories are becoming a bore.' 'Babbling mole,' 'ape in purple,' 'Greek dilettante,' and other such names were applied to him."[28]

By the winter of 360, Constantius could no longer bear to listen either to stories of Julian's successes or to the insincere taunts of the sycophants who despised the young caesar. The punishment was to strip Julian of many of his troops and officers, outwardly because

---

26. Amm., 16.12.68.
27. Amm., 17.10.2–9; cf. 17.5.8.
28. Amm., 17.10.11.

Constantius claimed he needed them for the impending confrontation with the armies of King Sapor.[29] This time, however, Julian was threatened with both adulation and mutiny. The Petulantes did not want to leave their home region of Gaul after receiving orders to march to the east. At Lutetia Julian was again acclaimed augustus. As before he refused the title, but this time his denial was tossed aside. He was raised on a shield, adorned with a neck chain which had formerly been the property of the chief of the Petulantes, twisted in the form of a diadem.[30] Ammianus, at least, suggests that Julian was quick to perceive what would happen if he did not accept the acclamation, saying that Julian did so as much out of fear as resignation. Having accepted the title of augustus, he promised each man a donative of five gold pieces and a pound of silver, then withdrew into philosophical seclusion—a characteristic reaction for him—to reflect on the change that had taken place in his life. He confided to an associate that on the night before his elevation he had had a vision of the *genius* of Rome, who revealed to him that he was destined for greater things than leading armies as Constantius's second.[31] In later correspondence to the Athenians, however, Julian says that he was never more than the figurehead of the armies, and that real power remained with the generals and armies in Gaul, who watched his every move and could have turned coat at any moment if his actions failed to satisfy their ambitions.[32]

Julian's own account emphasizes his reluctance to accept the title of augustus, and records that he did so only after seeking counsel from Zeus. Whatever reaction he expected from the gods, there was little doubt what he could expect from Constantius, and so he addressed the emperor in the hope of finding a peaceful solution and to explain the outcome of events at Lutetia. Ammianus, the lover

---

29. Julian, Ep. ad SPQR Ath., 280D, 283B and Libanius, Or. 12.58; cf. Amm., 20.4.1–5.

30. This event is multiply attested as marking a turning point in Julian's political self-consciousness: Amm., 20.4.10–11; Libanius, Or. 12.57–58; 18.92–93; John of Antioch, Frag. 177; Eunapius, Frag., 14.4. The date is usually fixed at February or March of 360.

31. Amm., 20.5.9.

32. Julian, Ep. ad SPQ Ath. 277D; 278A–B.

of historical symmetry, punctuates his account with stories of Persian advances against the Roman position in the winter of 360 which kept Constantius tied up in Constantinople. Poetically, the historian wants to suggest that Constantius's star is waning and Julian's rising, but Julian himself in his letter to the emperor seems to have believed, or had come to believe, that he was destined to rule as augustus. Julian in the same period was in Paris weighing how best to approach the subject, knowing that backing away from the events at Lutetia was not possible. In his letter he insists on his "fidelity to his undertakings" but he also assumes a chastising tone: "Ever since you sent me into the horrid din of war," he says, "I have been content with the delegated authority you have entrusted to me." But as if to contradict the voices of the sycophants who had slandered him mercilessly, Julian asserts that he "never laid stress on [his] own dangers." If the army has now made its preference known through revolution, "it is because the troops who have worn themselves out without reward in much hard fighting, have carried out a long-standing plan."[33] The letter also berates Constantius for sending the young men in Gaul into a terrible situation and the raw indifference of ordering worn-out troops eastward at the end of a hard struggle. For these and other reasons, Julian implies (and Ammianus makes explicit) the gods have withdrawn their approval of Constantius: he is pictured as unfit to rule, while the armies' choice of Julian make them instruments of the gods' will.[34] Unsurprisingly in the letter addressed to the Athenians, written to refute any suggestion that he was a usurper, Julian stresses that he became augustus at the instigation of the gods. In November 361, recounting his acclamation, Julian wrote to his philosophical mentor, Maximus of Ephesus, saying that while he became augustus against his will, the choice was the gods', and that after the event he had treated his enemies with justice. He also relates that he himself led the troops in propitiating

---

33. Amm., 20.83.

34. Amm., 20.8.5–10. On the authenticity of the epitome of the letter presented by Ammianus, see Michael DiMaio, "The Antiochene Connection: Zonaras, Ammianus, Marcellinus and John of Antioch on the Reigns of the Emperors Constantius II and Julian," *Byzantion* 50 (1980): 163ff.

the traditional gods because it had been revealed to him that his destiny was to revive their worship and receive benefits for doing so.[35]

Constantius received Julian's chiding, accommodating, and mildly threatening letters from envoys in Cappadocia, where he was stuck on the Bosphorus awaiting news of Sapor's advances. After flying into "a passion unusual even for him," he dispatched a messenger to Julian rejecting all of the proposals out of hand and telling the young caesar to stand aside. This message was read out in Gaul, at Julian's bidding, to a throng of soldiers and townspeople summoned for the occasion, to the accompaniment of flourishes. Leonas, the quaestor, made it as far as the passage wherein Constantius condemned the acclamation and ordered Julian to be content with the subordinate office. At this point a general commotion and shouts of "*Julianus augustus*" caused Leonas to hurry back to the beleaguered Constantius, while Julian directed his army across the Rhine to rout a Frankish tribe, the Attuarii, "whom he had no trouble in defeating."[36] During the standoff of 360 Julian devoted his attention to the security of the Rhine and Constantius continued his operations against the Persians. Julian celebrated his quinquennalia in Vienne and obtained for the anniversary a dazzling diadem that contrasted sharply with the "cheap crown, befitting the captain of an athletic meeting,"[37] he had worn previously. Soon after the event, he received news that his wife, Helena, had died—a minor disturbance that he saw to by having her remains conveyed to Rome to be buried in the family estate next to her sister Constantia, the wife of Gallus.

According to his biographers, Julian was torn between wanting a decisive outcome to the stalemate with Constantius and heeding certain augurs that the emperor was near death. Ammianus turns the accusation, later exploited by Christian writers, that Julian was practiced in the black arts into the more congenial suggestion that the emperor was always ready to explore all roads to wisdom. Julian was

---

35. Julian, Epistle VIII.414B; Julian was stationed at Naissa and describes the adulation to the theurgist-philosopher Maximus: "The gods command me to restore their worship in its original innocence and have promised me rewards if I obey them with a good will."

36. Amm., 20.9.10.

37. Amm., 21.1.1.

skilled in the interpretation of dreams, and like his ancestors he set great stock in the divine power of the augurs and auspices, especially the reading of entrails and the flight of birds.[38] Apparently he subscribed to Aristotle's view that dreams are always "certain and reliable" when men are in a deep sleep, and that when signs of future events turn out to be mistaken, it is not the sign but the interpretation of it that is at fault—a maxim of Cicero's.[39] In rallying his troops to fight against Julian, Constantius compared his cousin's treachery to that of Gallus. "Julian . . . has become so madly presumptuous on the score of some trivial victories over half-armed Germans as to recruit from his auxiliaries for an ambitious design against the state a small band of desperadoes who will stick at nothing. He has trampled underfoot the rule of law, the nursing mother of the rule of law."[40] The ploy was meant to trivialize Julian's achievements and to paint him a hubristic interloper, usurper, and coward. But Constantius had received news that Julian's troops had made a lightning-fast march through Italy and Illyricum, had seized the strategically important path at Succi, and would soon be joined by auxiliaries for an invasion of Thrace. The armies drew closer to each other just as Constantius's resolve was melting away. The emperor was haunted by dreams. He dreamed of his father's spirit "holding out to him a fine child, [which he took] and placed on his lap, where it shook from his grasp and threw to a distance the orb which he was carrying in his right hand."[41] In the autumn Constantius rallied his troops once more and moved toward the Antiochene suburb of Hippocephalus, where he saw "in broad daylight the headless corpse of a murdered man lying with his feet towards the west." By the time he reached Tarsus, he had developed a fever, and beyond Mobsucrenae (the last outpost in Cilicia) the fever became so violent that he was often delirious. In a lucid moment, just before

---

38. Amm., 21.1.7.

39. Amm., 21.1.7: This digression in Book 21 portrays Julian as obsessively concerned with omens and the practice of augury, while outwardly still often professing to be a Christian. To conceal his devotion to the old gods he attended church "on the holy day the Christians celebrate in January and call epiphany."

40. Amm., 21.13.4–5.

41. Amm., 21.14.1.

his death, it is reported—but disputed—that he named Julian his legitimate successor.

Constantius had reigned as augustus for twenty-four years. He was forty-four when he died,[42] his wife pregnant with a daughter who would grow up to marry Gratian. Ammianus, always Julian's partisan, nevertheless gives a candid appraisal of the Arian emperor's character, saying he prefers to make a "distinction between his good and bad qualities." Among the good, he lists the fact that Constantius was born to the role: he behaved like a king and refused to court popular opinion—even when it might have done him some good. He was sparing in conferring honors, kept the military in their place, and, in general, was a good judge of character—or at least of the character of opportunists. On the bad side, Ammianus finds Constantius dull-witted, an inferior speaker, pretentious ("when he turned his mind to versifying he produced nothing worthwhile"). His frugality in eating and drinking was accompanied by a sexual moderation for which he was so famous that no one ever accused him of bad behavior. But Ammianus also finds the Spartan athleticism of Constantius (no emperor was a better archer, or more skilled with the javelin) a disguise for cruelty—he calls it a barbarity to rival that of Caligula and Domitian—and suggests that he exhibited all the signs of paranoia that had characterized the reigns of Nero and Commodus. Easily suspicious and driven to extremes of envy by gossip and rumors, especially those planted by his wives or "the shrill eunuchs and court officials who applauded his every word," he was not above inventing evidence in the prosecution of his enemies—making a "mountain of mischief out of a molehill of evidence" and "showing himself the deadly enemy of justice, although his great object was to be thought just and merciful."[43] Constantius is vilified by Ammianus for two further weaknesses: first, his failure to bring the greed of the tax collectors under control, which led to crushing exactions in the provinces and earned him what was perhaps an undeserved reputation for avarice. But the taxing of the provinces paid the bills for foreign wars, and Constantius prided himself on his military

---

42. Amm., 21.15.2.
43. Amm., 21.16.1, 5, 8.

prowess despite humiliating defeats over the course of his reign. Taxes also financed the memorials to his "successes" in civil conflicts—triumphal arches in Gaul and Pannonia, and assorted lesser works and monuments designed to record his deeds for future generations. The second weakness cited by Ammianus was Constantius's understanding of the "simple religion of the Christians" which he "bedeviled with old wive's tales." No better a theologian than he evidently was a poet, he nonetheless took the Arian cause to himself and became its champion—"raising complicated issues that caused much dissension," and transporting "throngs of bishops hither and thither to what they call synods." Ammianus remarks, in language Julian would have applauded, that Constantius's attempts to settle theological disputes "only resulted in clogging the roads."[44]

Julian, now augustus, was eager to usher in a new imperial golden age. Entering Constantinople triumphantly on December 11, 361, he honored the predecessor with the funeral rites appropriate to his station,[45] then set about immediately to pare down the imperial bureaucracy that had grown bloated during Constantius's time. His biographers underscore his naïveté and even acts of injustice in the earliest days of his reign, especially in his choice of interrogators to deal with the unfinished business (as Julian saw it) of his half brother Gallus's execution for treason. Two of the conspirators against Gallus, Apodemius and Paulus Vinculus, were burnt alive and others were forced into exile, under sentence of death, until the end of Julian's reign. In reforming the palace, he is accused even by Ammianus of showing a "lack of concern for the discovery of the truth quite unbecoming in a philosopher,"[46] though for his rooting out corruption and especially his treatment of the eunuchs and the cooks and barbers, the Christian historians of his reign offered a softer assessment.[47]

---

44. Amm., 21.16.18, 19.

45. These are variously described: Amm., 22.2.1–5; Sozomen, HE. 5.1.6–8, Socrates, HE. 3.1; Gregory Naziazen, Or. 5.16–17 and Libanius, Or. 18.120–21.

46. Amm., 22.3.1–12; cf. Libanius Or. 18.130ff.

47. See Socrates, HE. 3.1; Cedrenus 1.532.18ff. Ammianus (22.4.5–6) offers an amusing episode to underscore the need for reform: On one occasion the emperor sent for a barber to trim his hair. When the barber presented himself, splendidly dressed, Julian was astonished and said, "I sent for a barber, not a treasury official."

Traditionally emperors were expected to show clemency at the beginning of their reign; Julian, however, was eager to appease the army and seems to have believed that offers of grace would be seen as a sign of weakness. Ammianus points to the case of Ursulus, Constantius's *comes sacrarum largitionum*[48] as a case in point: When Julian was sent to Gaul as caesar, Constantius had ordered that he should be given only his subsistence and deprived of the means of making gifts to his troops, thereby increasing the chance of mutiny or even assassination. Ursulus had actually ignored the order and arranged for the new caesar to receive whatever he asked for from the treasury; this intervention was remembered by many at court who took Ursulus's execution as a sign of the new emperor's deficient sense of judgement. To cover his embarrassment, Julian circulated a counterreport that he had acted against Ursulus only because the army had demanded his head in exchange for a remark he had made about the incompetence of the Gallic forces after the battle of Amida. Yet this early case of blame dodging and courting the favor of the military and various social élites would characterize the whole of Julian's reign and is one of the few areas severally corroborated by both Christian and pagan biographers. His early reputation for summary justice, however, is as impressive as his attempts to reform the imperial bureaucracy.[49]

The reforms were one way of restoring the prestige of the imperial power, which had suffered considerably from Constantius's encouragement of the sycophants. In pursuing the reforms Julian followed the general pattern of other neo-Flavian emperors in viewing the provincial vicars as intercessors between himself and the general population. In a letter sent to Alypius, the vicar of Britain, for example, he praises the official for his "mildness" and "moderation in the use of force" which characterized the execution of his

---

48. Custodian of the Sacred Largesse, the fund for apportioning military donatives at the discretion of the emperor.

49. For example: Pendatius was charged with involvement in the death of Gallus and threatened with exile, but later acquitted (Amm., 22.3.5); Apodeimus was executed because of his "eagerness" for the death of Gallus and Silvanus, as was Paul the Catena, head of the agents *in rebus*, according to John of Rhodes (*Artemii Passio* 21; cf. Libanius, Or. 18.152); and most famous of all, the eunuch Eusebius was condemned for his complicity in the death of Gallus; cf, Sozomen, HE 5.5.8 and also Amm., 22.3.12.

office. Such characteristics, Julian goes on to say, are the qualities of
the good king, and it is commendable that the emperor is being represented in this way to the provincials.[50] By the same token, Julian
courted the army because it had raised him to power and sustained
him, and the senatorial aristocracy because he required its approval
for legitimacy—a dependence that stemmed from incessant suggestions that he had plotted the ruin of Constantius from the beginning
of his rule as caesar. Of special significance was the consulship of
Claudius Mamertinus, whose speech in praise of the reforms, delivered in Constantinople in January 362, is preserved.[51] Claudius, with
a transparently self-serving interest, presents Julian as *restaurator*—
the inaugurator of an age of renewal that could be compared to the
days of Augustus. Had not Augustus brought in a new order by
forming a partnership with the senate, based upon a system of
honors and benefices given by the emperor to the senators in
exchange for their role as intercessor between emperor and the populace? As Claudius trumpets it, it was this system that Julian was
restoring; indeed, the consulate of Claudius was itself an illustration
of the new triple bond that existed between emperor, senate, and
people.[52] But the perception was not limited to Claudius's grateful
bombast: the municipal senate in Aceruntia (Apuleia) established a
monument on which Julian is commemorated as the "Repairer of
the World," and there is additional evidence of the young emperor's
benefactions to the municipal élites—the pattern he established
when he was still caesar and continued after he became emperor.[53]
To many wealthy pagans, the idea that a new Augustan age was
dawning was not an absurdity.

---

50. Julian, Ep. VII.404A.
51. *Actio Gratiarum* 2.1–2; *Gratiarum actio*, ed. R. Mynors, in *XII Panegyrici
Latini* (Oxford, 1964).
52. Claudius Mamertinus went on to hold a number of offices: prefect of Italy,
Illyricum, and Africa. See note 51.
53. *Corpus inscriptionum latinorum*, 9.417.

II. JULIAN'S RELIGIOUS REFORMS

Ammianus tells this story as a preface to his description of Julian's raids on the Raetian frontier in 361: "While Julian was still at Paris in the position of caesar he was swinging his shield in various field exercises when the pins by which it was secured gave way and he was left with only the handle, which he continued to hold in his strong grasp. There was a general fright among those present at what seemed a bad omen, but Julian said: 'Have no fear; I still have a firm grip on what I held.'"[54] If the omen is taken to mean what Ammianus wishes it to mean, Julian used Christianity as a shield to protect himself from the trouble that only religious suspicion could provoke. The questions that greeted him on his entry to Constantinople were three: Was he Christian or pagan? If a Christian, Arian or Nicene? If a pagan, a tolerant sort like Tatian or a persecutor like Decius?[55]

Julian at the time of his exaltation seems to have harbored no doubts. He was a pagan, neither of the tolerant nor persecuting variety, but a philosopher-soldier who took the title *pontifex maximus* with earnest intent. Comforted by visions of angels reciting hexameters just prior to Constantius's death, Julian was certain that his destiny was to restore the religion of his forefathers to Rome. The date of his "apostasy" from Christianity, if it was that, is unknown; Ammianus's record of the year 361 mentions that his pretense was well established, but that he had given up the faith "some time before." More reason, then, that he should have stayed clear of Constantius, who followed the general neo-Flavian habit of immersing

---

54. Amm., 21.1.14–15.

55. An older view of Julian's "caution" is represented by Bowersock's static notion that Julian came to power resolved to persecute the Christians, but was kept from doing so by pragmatic considerations—a view unfortunately repeated, but with amendments, in Rowland Smith's otherwise excellent study of Julian's religion, p. 215ff. The theoretical basis for Julian's treatment of Christians is summarized in the often overlooked letter to Atarbius (not cited by Smith), one of the few letters written in Julian's own hand, in which he swears an oath by the gods "that [I] do not wish the Galileans to be either put to death or unjustly beaten or suffer any form of injury." Julian's consistent philosophy is that as a "disease" Christianity was to be treated rather than punished.

himself in religious quarrels—which he did not fully understand or have patience with. Few people knew Julian's true feelings about Christianity; fewer appreciated the philosophical and political basis of his devotion to the old gods.

There is some debate concerning how much of the Christian religion he embraced, or rather how much of the religion he knew.[56] Speculation centers on a brief, and inconclusive, passage in Athanasius which gives the name of a certain Basilina as a supporter of the Arian cause, a later source, which names a Basilina who left her property to the church when she died, and earlier references to his mother's relationship to Eusebius of Nicomedia as evidence that Julian's mother was a Christian and saw to it he received "the rudiments of a Christian education," prior to her untimely death when Julian was seven years old.[57] When Eusebius was called to become bishop of Constantinople, Julian was apparently handed over to his dead mother's tutor, the Scythian eunuch Mardonius, to learn the elements of rhetoric and Greek literature, and it was at this point he became infatuated with Greek prose, poetry, and philosophy. While earlier interpreters thought that this ambiguous chapter in Julian's biography was to be explained by the fact that Eusebius and Mardonius were teaching the future emperor at the same time,[58] it seems clear that Julian's education under Mardonius was an unresisted weaning of the boy from the scant catechism he had learned from Eusebius, a "withdrawal into the world that Homer had created [where he] sincerely despised all that lay without its boundaries."[59] His debts to Mardonius were real and consistently acknowledged, though it is doubtful that the teacher played the role in his intellec-

---

56. See G. W. Bowersock, *Julian the Apostate* (Cambridge, MA, 1978), p. 24; A. H. M. Jones, *The Later Roman Empire, 284–602: A Social, Economic and Administrative Survey* (Oxford, 1964), pp. 120–21; and P. Athanassiadi, *Julian: An Intellectual Biography* (London, 1992), pp. 24–25.

57. See Barbara Saylor Rodgers and C. E. V. Nixon, eds., *In Praise of Later Roman Emperors: The Panegyrici Latini* (Berkeley, 1994), p. 1, s.v., "Basilina," and see the brief discussion in Athanassiadi, *Julian: An Intellectual Biography*, p. 18.

58. Thus Baynes, "The Early Life of Julian the Apostate," *JHS* 45 (1925): 251–52 and also J. Bidez, *La vie de l'empereur Julien* (Paris, 1930), pp. 16–21; and cf. R. Browning, *The Emperor Julian* (London, 1975), p. 36.

59. Athanassiadi, 15.

tual biography that one of Julian's more impressionistic modern biographers asserts.[60] For all the circumstantial reporting, it can be doubted that Basilina was a devout Christian, much less a committed Arian like her cousins.

Julian was introspective in youth and later life; in moments of crisis and peril his first instinct was to isolate himself from those closest to him, and he often found consolation or guidance in philosophy or augury. "From my childhood," he writes, "an extraordinary longing for the rays of the god [Helios] penetrated deep into my soul; and from my earliest years my mind was so completely swayed by the light that illumines the heavens that not only did I desire to gaze intently at the sun, but whenever I walked abroad in the night season when the firmament was clear and cloudless I abandoned all else without exception and gave myself up to the beauties of the heavens; nor did I understand what anyone might say to me nor heed what I was doing myself."[61] This might lead us to think that Julian bounced between Mardonius's formulations of Greek ideas and the youth's apprehension of them in frequent philosophical reveries inspired by the work of Porphyry and Proclus. But when he was sent for safekeeping to Macellum after the execution of Gallus, he did come up against (even if he was not notably influenced by) the teaching of George of Cappadocia. It is George's particular brand of Christian teaching that Julian reacts to in the treatise against the "Galileans," even if this is nowhere admitted, and even though George is never acknowledged by Julian as one of his teachers.[62] The most we learn, from an imaginary dialogue Julian

---

60. Athanassiadi, 23.

61. Julian, Ep. XI.130D.

62. In a letter to Ecdicius (Ep. XXIII; cf. XXXVIII) Julian demands that George's library be sent to him intact, "as one who has ever loved reading." Sozomen relates the story of George being attacked by a pagan mob in Alexandria on December 24, 361; cf. Epiphanius, Panarion 76.1 (motives for the murder of George), and below, pp. 40–41. George's influence, to the extent it was significant, seems to have been purely negative, and it is difficult to estimate the extent to which Julian may have regarded the hypocrisy and opportunism of the bishop as representative of elements he thought characteristic of Christianity in general. See Amm. 22.11., and the interesting classic discussion in Gibbon, *Decline and Fall of the Roman Empire*, ed. J. B. Bury (London, 1909), p. 498.

constructs between himself and the murderers of George—the pagans of Alexandria, perhaps with some help from orthodox Christians who despised the old bishop—is that the prelate deserved better than to be torn apart by a mob, though "he might have deserved worse and more cruel treatment [were it] not at your hands."[63] This would suggest that if Julian at the age of twelve endured George's teaching, it was merely that, and that his habit of seeking spiritual sustenance outside the confines of Christian doctrine and its seeming muddle of controversies was well established by this point.

What survives from the period at Macellum suggests that Julian was groping for answers but was largely dependent on periods of "pantheistic exaltation" for deliverance from depression. "Let darkness be buried in oblivion," he says in describing his state of confusion—the same language he uses in his "Hymn to [Cybele] the Mother of the Gods," when he speaks of wandering in the darkness and the goddess helping him to purify himself of desperate thoughts.[64] But, of course, this is not Augustine or Gregory Naziazen praying for conversion; it is Julian praying for deliverance from the errors that he thinks are being thrust upon him from the Christian side. Ammianus makes the point that from earliest childhood Julian was inclined to the worship of the pagan gods but was afraid to profess his beliefs publicly.[65]

This neat assertion is problematical, for the view of Christian writers is the opposite: Gregory Naziazen recalls the young Julian as a lector in the church at Nicomedia and one who revered the martyrs and frequented their shrines—someone who became an enemy of the church and changed faces beyond all recognition—thus an apostate in the specific sense.[66] Socrates Scholasticus and Sozomen agree that Julian became an enemy of Christianity only in adulthood, and that as a young man he exhibited loyalty to the faith. To illustrate the point, Sozomen records a story about the young Gallus and Julian

---

63. Ep. XXI.379D.
64. Or. V, and cf. Libanius, Or. VIII.174c.
65. Amm., 22.5.1.
66. Gregory, Or. IV.97.

building a small monument on the tomb of St. Mamas in Cappadocia. Gallus's work progressed satisfactorily, but Julian's did not—an omen he recounts (without seeing the fundamental contradiction in his argument) to show that even as a boy Julian had no faith.[67] The Christian testimonies concerning Julian's early religious beliefs might be worthless were it not that his apologist Libanius, whose positive assessment of Julian's reign the Christian writers deplored, sees Julian as a convert to Hellenism, a man who was moved by the gods to slough off superstition and embrace the light of day.[68] But withal, the attempts of pagan and Christian writers to see his "conversion" in inverted Pauline terms, the evidence that Julian was ever devoutly Christian (or indeed was baptized)[69] is slim; he seems to have given up any attachment to Christianity and to have adopted the practices of traditional Roman religion, including theurgy, as a natural part of his immersion in Neoplatonic thought prior to being named caesar. In his letter to the Alexandrians written in 363, he states that he had given up the Christian faith when he was twenty years old and had been an adherent of the ancestral rites for a dozen years prior to writing the letter.[70] This corresponds to Ammianus's "official" view that Julian did not openly profess paganism until the threat of reprisal was removed in his thirty-first year.

If there was safety in dissimulation in the matter of religious belief, the death of Constantius changed everything. The Christian church was the one constituency Julian had no wish to court and no reason to appease. At the start Julian gave no one to believe that he intended to discriminate actively against the Christians: he lifted the ban on the teaching of the Arians and permitted various sectarian leaders to return to their sees.[71] But biographers Christian and pagan saw this early expression of "toleration" as more strategic than altruistic. "Julian called the bishops of the sects to him . . . [and told

---

67. Gregory, Or. IV.24.26; and cf. Sozomen, HE V.2.12–14.

68. τὸ σφοδρὸν μῖσος κατὰ τῶν θεῶν ἐπέσχες ὑπὸ τῶν μαντευμάτων ἡμερούμενος, Libanius, Or. XII.34; XIII.11; cf. XVIII.16.

69. Cf. Gregory, Or. IV.52, who thinks that he was, but this is to be able to put him squarely in the apostate's camp as a traitor to the Christian mystery.

70. Ep. XLVII.434D.

71. Amm., 22.5.3–4.

them] to set aside their differences and to live in peace and harmony, knowing that toleration would intensify their divisions and that he would no longer have to fear a unanimous public opinion."[72] Experience had taught him "that no wild beasts are as dangerous to man as the Christians are to one another."[73] When he seeks to explain their intemperance, he not surprisingly points to a lack of philosophical acumen which they share with the Jews, a "second rate race . . . also lacking in *paideia*": "In my opinion, there is no reason why their god should not be a mighty god, even though he does not happen to have wise prophets and interpreters. But the real reason why they are not wise is that they have not submitted their souls to be cleansed by the regular course of study [ἐγκύκλιοις μαθήμασι] nor have they allowed those studies to open their tightly closed eyes and to clear away the mist that hangs over them."

Julian's strategy for dealing with the Christians was threefold: First, he attempted to isolate Christians from the mainstream of Roman society by limiting their rights and abrogating certain benefits to which they were entitled under the law. Secondly, he attempted to circumscribe their influence in a way that does not seem to have occurred to his predecessors: creating a "pagan church" to rival the organization of the Christians—one which would assume some of the charitable functions of Christianity. This reform, or remodeling, of the temples was seen as part of a total religious program designed to make Christianity irrelevant in a social sense. And finally, Julian returned to the custom of conservative pagan intellectuals like Celsus and Porphyry by actively assailing Christian belief in philosophical polemic designed to prove the unoriginality of the faith. In this last effort, Julian wanted to portray Christianity as an apostate form of Judaism which did not remain true to the worthy aspects of a much older religious philosophy. Thus, as a reformed paganism might show the Christians as less beneficent than their pagan countrymen, so the renewed literary attack was designed to point up the inauthentic nature of Christian belief.

---

72. Amm., 22.5.1.
73. Amm., 22.5.2; Julian regarded the Christians as troublemakers (Ep. XXXVII and cf. Ep. XLI.437D).

With respect to the first part of Julian's strategy, a law of the Theo-
dosian code specifies that decurions were not permitted to defer or
avoid compulsory military service on the grounds that they were
Christians.[74] Ammianus tells us that Julian caused legislation to be
passed removing Christian teachers from their posts,[75] a lapse in the
emperor's judgement as he sees it, though Julian's own rescript on
Christian teachers (Ep. XXXVI) provides some insight into the reasons for the action. His view, apparently, was that Christian teachers
should be sacked not for their belief, but because they were poor
models for their pupils—who would not help but notice the
hypocrisy of a rhetoric or grammar master praising the classical stories but believing them impious at the same time, because they also
passed along traditional forms of belief and worship.[76] Other legal
impediments included a law upheld in a statute dated 405 banning
the Donatist sect in north Africa[77] and a law mentioned by Julian to
the Christians of Bostra (Ep. XLI), adjuring them that if they sacrificed to the traditional gods they would hold on to their citizenship,
but that if they persisted in their beliefs, fomenting the factional
strife to which it led, they would be stripped of their legal status.[78]

The rest of Julian's plan fell more easily into place. It would be
too much to say, based on the two letters which serve as the primary
documentation for this phase of his strategy, that Julian (as
Sozomen wants to urge) admired the organization of the Christian
church and wished to emulate it. But its growth, if not the increase
of its factions and disturbances since the days of his uncle, the first
to legitimate Christian proselytizing, was obviously impressive to
the young emperor. In 362 Julian wrote to the high priest Theodorus
to create him archpriest of the diocese of Asia, with the right to

---

74. Cod. Theod. 12.1.50.

75. Amm., 22.10.5. The location of this statement in Ammianus is very puzzling coming at the end of a discussion of Julian's tactical indifference to questions
of religion in hearing cases and doling out punishment. On the issue of the passage,
see Thomas Banchich, "Julian's School Law: Cod. Theod. 13.3.5. and Ep. 42,"
Ancient World 24 (1993): 5–14.

76. Ep. XXXVI, esp. 423A–D.

77. Cod. Theod. 16.5.37.

78. Ep. XLI.437A–B.

appoint all priests to temples in the cities of the region. He takes the opportunity to address a variety of concerns: first, that the customs of the forefathers are being forgotten, with lamentable consequences. Second, he demands certain moral qualifications of the high priest, not unlike those that Christians had long required of their bishops,[79] namely that they lead by example, treating all people fairly, and that they forego luxury in favor of lives of moderation, "since in our day the concern for divine things has been extinguished by the love of vulgarity."[80] Contrasting the apathy of pagans to the zeal of the Jews in matters of religion, he sees traditional religion in a state of dissolution symbolized above all in the moral decline of the priesthood, which then is communicated as lethargy to the people: Where the Jews are fervent about tradition, the pagans no longer observe the religious laws and have forgotten the traditions of the fathers. Late in 362 Julian addressed Arcasius, the archpriest of Galatia, in similar language, wondering how it happens that the sought-after restoration of traditional religious rituals has not led to a renaissance of pagan belief: "The Greek religion still does not flourish as I would like," he begins, "and this is the fault of everyone who professes it."[81] What is missing, he now thinks, is a pagan initiative equal to public displays of Christian benevolence— their kindness to strangers, their care for the graves of the dead, the (alleged, he says) purity of their lives. Julian's solution, however, suggests his desperation; his tactic is to outdo the Christians in displays of generosity. He orders hostels established in Galatia for the benefit of strangers and the poor, who are also to have an allocation of corn and wine. "It is disgraceful," Julian complains, "that no Jew ever has to beg and the wretched Galileans take better care of our poor, as well as their own, than we do."[82]

For Julian the charity and holiness of the Christians is especially cloying because their "atheism" seems to be showing better than the faith of the heirs of Homer. But the political interest in creating these

---

79. See 1 Tim. 3.1–13.
80. Ep. XX.452D.
81. Ep. XXII.429A.
82. Ep. XXII.430D.

charities is close to the surface in Julian's letters on the subject: his real concern is that Christians were looking more and more to the church for their protection and security and less to the emperor. What Christians privately encourage with their benevolence, he suggests, is apostasy from the state, though their practices are not a typical form of sedition. The view that Christianity was a subtle form of rebellion against the legitimate rule of the emperor is something Porphyry had also cited in his books against the Christian sect.[83] At no point does Julian regard Christian charity as genuine philanthropy, but he is willing to fight the errors of the Galileans on the battleground of their own choosing.[84]

A key goal of Julian's reforms was to create a series of social institutions that reinforced his role as supreme patron of citizens and clients. In the letter to Alypius he outlines his desire to have an "intercessory hierarchy" through which the goodwill of the clients and citizens can be maintained through the work of social elites; the panegyric of Mamertinus, already mentioned, emphasizes the same program. His model for religious officials was contrived as the equivalent of the social program: Julian was *pontifex maximus*; as such he viewed himself as the lawful mediator between the Empire and the gods. He regarded himself as having received the gift of prophecy from the apollonian oracle at Didyma (Miletus), and increasingly saw himself as able, in inspired states, to communicate with the gods.[85] It infuriated him that religious leaders over whom he had no practical or moral authority, the Christian bishops, were usurping this role and seeing to their own succession, while the supreme pontiff was empowered only to appoint the archpriests of a diminishing number of pagan dioceses. In a letter to an unnamed official Julian reminds a negligent public servant, who had let an assault on a priest go unpunished, that priests must be respected as much as sacred objects, things set aside for sacred use. He reinforces

---

83. See Porphyry, *Against the Christians*, trans. R. J. Hoffmann (New York, 1996), esp. pp. 39–40.

84. Thus he begins the work against the Galileans as a court case with himself as presiding magistrate: CG 41E.

85. Letter XVIII.451D.

the distinction between priests and laity and insists that the former must be free from the kind of harassment that has, apparently with no public outcry, been visited on members of the pagan orders.[86] The real issue for Julian is less the security of individual priests (he acknowledges some moral laxity within their ranks) than the question of hierarchy and patronage. A man "who strikes a priest is guilty of sacrilege," because he offends at once the priest, the temple, the emperor, and the gods,[87] and an officer of the peace who does not punish the sacrilege is guilty of complicity in the crime. Julian suspects, in any case, that the accused man secretly consorts with Christian bishops and elders over supper, and may even plot with them to harass the pagans—whose gods, Paul had taught them, are not gods but things of wood and stone.[88]

The model of authority to which Julian appeals had already been absorbed by the Christian church; bishops since the time of Ignatius of Antioch had seen legitimacy and authority as extending from God, through Christ, to the bishops, presbyters,[89] and deacons in orderly succession. For Julian, the matter of hierarchy entailed a question about the religious authority of the emperor. The Christian church, in appropriating the imperial model, was guilty of theft on a political level—the same sort of crime Julian accused the Christians of committing, at a religious and theological level, in ransacking the religious traditions of other nations. But if the latter concerned mainly elements of doctrine and practice borrowed from the Jews and pagan philosophy, Julian was genuinely concerned that the theft of Roman political models could be turned against the power of the emperor himself. The reassertion of the emperor's authority over the religious institutions of the empire was thus an essential element of his program.

The third element in his attack on the Christian church was the use of polemic to discredit the religion that had enjoyed freedom from official persecution for forty-eight years prior to Julian's acces-

---

86. Letter XVIII.450D.
87. Letter XVIII.451B.
88. Paul, 1 Cor. 8.4.
89. Ignatius, *Ep. to the Ephesians,* 3.6.

sion. It is perhaps fair to say that of the three sorts of attack, broadside was both the preferred way of dealing with religious annoyances and the least effective. The literary attacks on the Christian church can be traced to the time of Nero; in extensive form, to the time of the slanders and accusations mentioned by Tertullian in the Apology.[90] Celsus, Fronto, Galen, and Porphyry had written tirades against Christianity; Proclus, Plotinus, and Marcus Aurelius were philosophically contemptuous of it as a religion of slaves. The succession of opponents was impressive; but so also were the defenses offered by the Christian fathers, who made the art of apologetics a branch of early Christian theology. It was in the heat of discussion that important doctrines like the nature of the soul, resurrection, the defense of monotheism, and Christian ethical praxis were hammered out.

Julian was thus undertaking to do nothing new when he decided to put pen to paper "in unfriendly Antioch"[91] during the long winter nights of 362–363 against the mischief of the Galileans, and his urgings were the more hopeless because they were not new. It is often suggested that he was indebted to Porphyry's books against the Christians for his arguments, but there are few direct echoes of Porphyry's criticisms, at least in what survives of the treatise, and the influence of the great biographer of Plotinus seems to be more general than specific.[92] Julian was an avid learner but an unsystematic scholar, and the work as a whole lacks the critical acumen of a Porphyry and the originality of Celsus's second-century attack. Like Celsus, he uses Judaism, or rather, the construct of Jewish antiquity, as a point of departure for his own assault, but only in the interest of establishing the familiar argument that Judaism is thousands of years older than Christianity, and thus worthy of respect for its antiquity if not for its strange customs and beliefs. Judaism was to

---

90. Tertullian, *Apology*, II.

91. See Athanassiadi, "The Priest-King and the Philosopher-Priest," *Julian: An Intellectual Biography*, pp. 161–91.

92. As G. Ricciotti has observed, Julian, unlike Porphyry, could "find nothing good at all about Christianity, which he sees only as a bundle of historical absurdities and moral aberrations." *Julian the Apostate* (Rockford, 1999), p. 233. This is clear from the first moment of the treatise Against the Galileans, where he sets out to "prove that the beliefs of the Christians are a fabrication (σκευωρία)," a human invention "wickedly put together."

be preferred, not admired.[93] But it was seen by Julian as the proper interpreter of its original doctrines—not the upstart religion that had been on the scene for less than four centuries, and legitimately so for only a fraction of that time. To the extent that Judaism was at odds with Christian belief—on the question of prophecy, the role of sacrifice, or the identity of the messiah—then the more ancient faith was obviously to be preferred.[94] The doctrine of the resurrection of the body was—for Julian as for all Neoplatonists—an abomination because it taught a grotesque idea of immortality and denied the syzygy between the human (rational) and divine (Intelligible) that had become characteristic of philosophical thought in various and conflicting formats—Neoplatonic, Epicurean, and Stoic.[95]

What Julian seems to have added to the mere polemical thrust, nevertheless, was something his predecessors could not have contemplated: the offer to rebuild the ruined temple in Jerusalem.[96] Julian was savvy enough to know that the exegesis of this event differed in the two communities. For Christians it represented the fulfillment of a prophecy[97] which abrogated Jewish religious authority

---

93. The suggestion that Julian was a "Philo-semite" or a "proto-Zionist" has been largely discredited; but see M. Avi-Yonah, *The Jews of Palestine* (Oxford, 1976), pp. 185–207; F. Blanchetière, "Julien: philhelléne, philosémite, antichrétien," *Journal of Jewish Studies* 33 (1980): 61–68.

94. CG 253A–E; 191E.

95. See Breckinridge, "Julian and Athanasius: Two Approaches to Creation and Salvation" *Theology* 76 (1973): 74–76.

96. Amm., 23.1.7; Julian, Ep. XXV.398A–E. The "Letter to the Community of the Jews," whose authenticity is doubted, may nevertheless represent Julian's intentions accurately (cf. Ep. XLI.369A–398A; and Sozomen, HE 5.22 [Soc., HE 3.20], since a portion of a letter quoted in Lydus, de Mensibus, 4 [Bidez, I.2:197] reports Julian saying, "I will use all my zeal to make the temple of the most high God rise again." The project is also mentioned in the letter "To a Priest" (XIX.295C). The reference to *el elyon* or *theos hypsistos* may have been suggested to Julian by the rabbis and encompasses both the name given to God in the Hebrew Bible (Gen. 14.18ff) as well as the Phoenician theogony known to Philo of Byblos and mentioned by Eusebius (Praep. Evang. 1.10). The language suggests as well that Julian may have regarded the restoration of the Temple as significant to his syncretizing religious program.

97. Mark 13.2 and parallels, especially Luke 21.5–6. It is not clear that Julian was influenced by the famous "documentary" hypothesis of Porphyry concerning the Book of Daniel, but more with the Christian theory of fulfillment, which saw the destruction of the temple as proof of God's election of a new people to replace the

and gave Jewish law and custom, as well as the Hebrew scriptures, a merely theoretical value. For the Christians the destruction of the Temple invalidated Judaism and validated the prophecies of the Gospel, an event of such importance that the earliest gospel writer actually permits himself a glowering anachronism to suggest its physical destruction was augured at the moment of the death of Jesus (Mark 15.38). For the Jews, it was a political catastrophe that signaled the end of their religious hegemony over Roman-ruled Palestine and the loss of their religious center, and the stunning disconfirmation of the sort of messianic and eschatological hopes that saw Jerusalem and the Temple as the locus for the new age. Christians of the fourth century regarded Jerusalem as a city "of Greeks, foreigners, and idolaters,"[98] its association with Judaism a thing of the past. Origen had commented in his treatise against Celsus that the loss of Jerusalem was "eternal," a part of God's judgement on the ejected Jews, "who never before have been cut off from their ritual and worship."[99] For both faiths Titus's devastation of the holy site was a defining moment that formed the irreparable interpretative breach between the two. Julian saw that political capital could be gained by siding with the Jews as a benefactor, in effect making them yet another of his elites and thus enlisting them in his campaign to destroy Christianity.

In 362 he appointed Alypius, formerly the governor of Britain, to begin the work of reconstruction, with the intention of creating a monument to his generosity and religious largesse.[100] Enormous

---

Jews. Cf. Ep. Barn. 4.6–7; the more graphic verdict is Justin's: "The custom of circumcising the flesh, handed down from Abraham, was given to you as a distinguishing mark, to set you off from other nations and from us Christians. The purpose of this was that you and only you might suffer the afflictions that are now justly yours; that only your land be desolate, and your cities ruined by fire, that the fruits of your land be eaten by strangers before your very eyes; that not one of you be permitted to enter your city of Jerusalem. Your circumcision of the flesh is the only mark by which you can certainly be distinguished from other men. . . . As I stated before it was by reason of your sins and the sins of your fathers that, among other precepts, God imposed upon you the observance of the sabbath as a mark." *Dial Tryph.* 16.1.

98. Eusebius, *Commentary on Psalms* 86.2–4 (PG 23.1044c).
99. Origen, C. Cels. 4.22.
100. Amm., 23.1.2.

sums (*immodicis*) were allotted for the project, augmented by contributions from the Jewish patriarch, voluntary offerings, costly garments, and donations of jewels from Jewish women. The work is
said to have begun with clearing the temple site of centuries-old
debris from the valley of the Tyropoeon, which divided the ancient
city into two parts. The basilica built near Calvary during Constantine's time, close to the traditional location of the tomb of Jesus, was
not disturbed during the excavations. If the references in Ammianus's account do not represent an interpolation by Christian edi-
tors, the omens seem to have been bad from the beginning: tremors
and outbursts of "fireballs" made it impossible for the workers to
advance the job of reconstruction,[101] and the project, always a thing
of fits and starts, was abandoned as Julian prepared to cross the
Euphrates en route to his final campaign against the Persians.[102]

*   *   *

One of the persistent themes of Julian's antagonism toward the
Christian church was his belief that they were troublemakers,
causing political discord in any community where they formed the
majority: "they turn everything upside down."[103] The most famous
instance of this is his reaction to a popular uprising in Alexandria,
ending in the violent murder of the Arian bishop George of Cappadocia when he threatened to demolish the temple to the city's
tutelary deity. George is called "a human snake" by Ammianus,
apparently a reference to a poisonous reputation earned by serving

---

101. Ricciotti, *Julian,* p. 225, notes that toward the close of 362 earthquakes
along the Palestinian coast and parts of Syria leveled Gaza, Eleutheropolis (Beit-
Jibrin) and Nicopolis to the southwest of Jerusalem, and that Jerusalem itself was
affected by the tremors.

102. The Christian sources include descriptions by Gregory, Or. 5.3; Socrates,
HE 3.20; Sozomen, HE 5.22.2ff; John of Rhodes, *Artemii passio* 58; Philos., Hist. 7.9;
Theophilus, AM 5855; Theod. HE 3.20.4ff; and see the discussion by Robert
Panella, "The Emperor Julian and the God of the Jews," *Koinonia* 23 (1999): 15–31.
Further, the PhD dissertation by Jeffrey Bross, "Apostate, Philo-Semite, or Syncretic
Neoplatonist: Julian's Intentions for Rebuilding the Jewish Temple" (University of
California, Santa Barbara, 1992).

103. Ep. XXXVII.376C.

as a part-time *chef d'espionage* for Constantius when it served his interests. The bishop miscalculated his popularity on the day he posed a memorable question to the Christian posse that surrounded him, within earshot of the pagan citizens: "How long shall this sepulcher stand?" He was first trampled and then torn apart by an angry mob, the viciousness of which seems to have startled even Julian.[104] In his letter to the Alexandrians, Julian's scolding tone toward the perpetrators leaves no room for doubt that while the method for removing George deserved to be condemned, his fate was not entirely unwelcome.[105] In a second case, Julian writes to Hecebolius condemning the Arian Christians for attacking the small minority of Valentinian-Gnostic Christians in Edessa and disturbing the peace of the city.[106] His response shows Julian at once sarcastic and severe: "Since [the Galilean's] most worthy law tells them to sell what they have and give it to the poor, so that they can attain more easily the kingdom of heaven, I have decided to assist them, and order that all the treasuries of all their churches be confiscated throughout Edessa and distributed to the soldiers; and that such property as they own be assigned to me and converted to public use. This is done so that poverty will teach them a lesson in civility, but also to ensure they inherit the heavenly kingdom for which they yearn."[107] And in a third case (never proved), the Christians were accused of setting fire to the temple of Apollo at Daphne in October of 362, a structure which Julian had sought to aggrandize by erecting a colonnade around the original structure, which had been built during the reign of Antiochus Epiphanes (216–163 BCE).[108] The persistent sense that Christians were reckless, unphilosophical, and disloyal became more intense as Julian approached the Persian campaign, and his

---

104. Amm., 22.11.1–11. Ammianus, however, makes the point that the population of Alexandria was given to frequent outbreaks of violence.

105. Julian, Ep. 21.380A. Julian's primary concern, however, is that the manner of George's death was a desecration of the city reflecting the violent disposition of its people. Ammianus comments on this characteristic of Alexandrian life, 22.11.4.

106. Julian, Ep. XL.

107. Julian, Ep. XL.424D.

108. Amm., 22.13.1–2; the view of Christian writers was that it was destroyed by divine intervention.

earlier dissimulation, if it can be called that, gives way to an unambiguous animosity. Their religious doctrines set them apart from the Greek ideal, and their religious rites—which he regarded as both morbid and uninspired—were further proof of their inferiority.[109] The basic themes of his polemical masterpiece were fixed by the winter of 362.

III. THE FINAL CAMPAIGN

Julian's various strategies to bring the Christian movement under control while advancing the cause of the ancestral faith weakened as he became increasingly involved in planning for the Persian campaign. No one is flattering about his preparations. According to Ammianus, he paid too little attention to those who advised caution because "he interpreted caution as delay." He was "passionately eager to avenge the past," and avoided human counsel out of suspicion. Instead, he resorted, as he had done before battles in the past, to augury and sacrifice. On one occasion he sacrificed a hundred bulls and whole flocks of other animals, and he developed an insatiable need for white birds. Rituals proliferated as needed precautions to win the protection of the gods. His obsessive religious exercises seem to have made no impression on the troops, who are described as lost in an almost constant round of drinking and carousing, especially the Petulantes and Celts, "whose indiscipline at this time passed all bounds."[110] Impatient with traditional modes of inquiry, Julian brought in anyone with a reputation for divination, however shady, and then decided that the time was right to reopen the Castalian springs that Hadrian had closed off after a ritual of reconsecration demanded by the god. The legend of the springs was that Hadrian had closed the prophetic shrine because it

---

109. In the *Misopogon*, 344A, he alleges that the Christian churches were nothing but "loathsome mausolea" built over the bones of their martyrs, a sentiment repeated in the treatise against the Christians (CG 335B, C) when he argues that the Galileans have done nothing "but fill the world with tombs and sepulchers."

110. Amm., 22.12.5–7.

was there he had learned that he was to be emperor, and he feared that other visitors might receive the same message.[111]

*   *   *

Julian immersed himself in a flurry of fund-raising activities to support the campaign against the Persians, with the goal of bolstering his personal prestige and solving once and for all the problem his cousin and predecessor had been unable to put to rest during his reign. As he moved through Asia Minor to Antioch he tried to ingratiate himself to the various communities with gifts and benefactions; but when an earthquake in the region was followed by a severe drought, and Julian refused to divert funds for the campaign in order to offer relief to victims of the disaster, the Antiochian senate became agitated and declined to offer him any additional material support. Ammianus speaks of Julian's "longing" for war, and of his reputation in Antioch steadily declining. He was caricaturized in verse as a monkey, or a dwarf who tried to make himself larger than life by puffing out his chest and squaring his shoulders. The caricature included a standard image of Julian as a goateed imbecile staring down the giants of the east, "taking big strides like a brother of Otus and Ephialtes."[112] The profusion of his sacrifices, including one memorable and frantic search for an Apis bull (thought to be the harbinger of good harvests and success against enemies), earned him the title "axe-man" rather than priest, and tales were spread about the ostentation he displayed by carrying the sacred objects personally rather than leaving it to the members of the lower priesthood. In this respect he was not unlike his uncle Constantine, who took the office of priest very seriously and was given to equivalent outbursts of superstition. Julian kept his temper, then composed a scathing satirical self-portrait, the *Misopogon* ("beard-hater"), enumerating the defects of Antioch and her leading citizens,[113] this while preparations for the war went on.

---

111. Amm., 22.12.10.

112. Mythological giants. Amm., 22.14.4ff.

113. See Friedhelm L. Müller, "Die beiden Satiren des Kaisers Julianus Apostata" (*Symposion* oder Caesares und Antiochikos oder *Misopogon*). Griechisch und deutsch mit Einleitung, Anmerkungen und Index. *Palingenesia* 66 (Stuttgart, 1998).

"I have committed [ ] terrible sins," he ironizes, "for though I was coming to a free city which cannot tolerate unkempt hair, I entered it unshaven and with a long beard, like men who are at a loss for a barber. One would have thought it was some Smicrines he saw, or some Thrasyleon, some ill-tempered old man or crazy soldier, when by beautifying myself I might have appeared as a blooming boy and transformed myself into a youth, if not in years, at any rate in manners and effeminacy of features."

Julian had come to Antioch in the autumn of 361 and stayed on until March 362. Rich and important as the city was commercially, Julian thought her glory depended on two things, the famous shrine of Apollo and its school of rhetoric. Both of these had been neglected by the citizens during the reign of Constantius. A Christian church had been built in Apollo's grove in the suburb of Daphne, and Antioch's most distinguished rhetorician, Libanius, was practically unknown in his home town. As a commentator has observed, "Julian's behavior at Antioch and his failure to ingratiate himself with the citizens illustrates one of the causes of the failure of his pagan restoration. His mistake was that he did not attempt to make paganism popular, whereas Christianity had always been democratic. He is always reminding the common people that the true knowledge of the gods is reserved for philosophers; [yet] even the old conservative pagans did not share his zeal for philosophy. Antioch, moreover, was a frivolous city. The Emperor Hadrian three centuries earlier had been much offended by the levity of her citizens, and the homilies of . . . Chrysostom exhibit the same picture as Julian's satire. His austere personality and mode of life repelled the Syrian populace and the corrupt officials of Antioch."[114]

The Sassanid Persians and before them the Parthians had been natural competitors for hegemony in Mesopotamia since the days of the late Republic. Yet it is often pointed out that Julian had no reason, other than to settle an old score, to renew hostilities in the east. There is also the possibility that he needed to win back the respect and allegiance of his armies, since relations between Julian

---

114. W. C. Wright, *Julian*, vol. 2, *Orations 6–8. Letters to Themistius, To the Senate and People of Athens, To a Priest. The Caesars. Misopogon* (Cambridge, MA, 1923), p. 89.

and his officers had reached a low point. Victory over the Persians would bring Julian the respect he craved and glory to the army, and fighting a traditional enemy, rather than the Germanic intruders to the west, would bring a special sweetness to any victory.

In early March 363 Julian set out on his final campaign. Ammianus is careful to mention that he began his journey under an auspiciously sunny sky. When he entered Heliopolis a colonnade suddenly collapsed, with its beams and timbers crushing fifty soldiers and wounding many others who were encamped around it. Julian accelerated his pace towards Mesopotamia, intending to take Assyria[115] by surprise—his trademark strategy of striking quickly and where least expected. He crossed the Euphrates on a flotilla of boats and entered the town of Batnae, where he encountered another omen: a hayrick loaded with fodder collapsed under the weight of groomsmen, burying fifty of them under its weight. Entering the market town of Carrhae, the scene of a memorable disaster for the Roman army during the time of Crassus, Julian performed sacrifices in accordance with the lunar customs of the region, and for a small space, between March 19 and March 29, the emperor's mood began to clear; the signs had improved. After an especially restful night, when he ordered his horse "Babylonius" to be brought to him, the animal rolled on the ground in a fit of colic and dumped its jewel-encrusted harness. Julian announced triumphantly, "You see: Babylon has fallen, stripped of her finery."[116] After performing a sacrifice to the Magna Mater to confirm the omen, he is reported to have been in good spirits and full of confidence that his armies would triumph. Even a desperate letter from his friend Sallustius, the prefect of Gaul, urging him to defer the campaign made no impression on him.[117]

The omens in April turned dark again, and on April 7, toward sunset, a small cloud "suddenly spread out over a darkening sky" and with it flashes of lightning and thunder. One lightning bolt

---

115. For Ammianus, the region of Assyria encompasses Babylonia and Assyria.
116. Amm., 23.3.6.
117. On this, see A. D. Nock, ed. and trans., *Sallustius, De diis et mundo* (Cambridge, 1926).

struck and killed a groomsman by the name of Jovian and two of his horses (the irony of his name was not missed by later commentators), and the interpreters decreed the lightning bolt had been "advisory"—a warning from the gods to desist. But in this case the Etruscan soothsayers were ignored by the emperor who consulted the philosophers who, contemptuous of the diviners, conveniently turned the omen on its head: it signaled, they said, the gods' high regard for Julian and the propriety of his battle plan.

And there were successes. Julian's forces took the fortress of Anatha and received the surrender of several local princes along the way. He continued surprise attacks throughout Assyria, ravaged the countryside between the rivers, and sensibly avoided the well-guarded fortresses of Thilutha and Achaiachala.[118] The cities further to the south, Diacira and Ozogardana, were sacked and burned by the Roman army, as was the better-defended city of Pirisabora after a brief siege.

With the battle for Pirisabora the Romans got their first taste of a sustained Persian resistance, and as they moved southward local inhabitants became increasingly aggressive, flooding and otherwise impeding their route. Just before reaching Ctesiphon, the Romans came first to a deserted Jewish settlement and then to Maiozamalcha, a sizeable Persian enclave with strong fortifications. Julian must have imagined that in taking this city he would have driven the Persian army to panic, since he had begun to feel the enterprise was under the protection of a god.[119]

The battle of Maiozamalcha was Julian's last major victory in the Persian campaign. Many Persian troops had escaped by stealth and retreated to Ctesiphon, where the Persian army was entrenched and waiting. As the Persian resistance grew stronger, increasingly using guerrilla tactics against the Romans, and as Roman supplies dwindled, Julian began for the first time to consider the possibility of defeat. A sizeable number of troops was lost; Julian himself was almost killed a few miles from Ctesiphon, and as they approached the city the enormity of their miscalculation must have been clear. They had relied on the cumulative effect of previous battles to

---

118. Amm., 24.2.3–4; Libanius, Or. 18.227–28; Zosimus, 3.151–52.
119. Amm., 24.4.1–31; Libanius, Or. 18.223–27; Zosimus, 3.20.2–7.

damage Persian morale, but after preliminary skirmishes with Persian advance troops it became evident that the battle would be a long one—and one for which the troops were not equipped. Ammianus, who witnessed the events, is reflective about the deceptiveness of early Roman successes: "No star relieved the darkness of the night, which we spent as one does in moments of doubt and difficulty; no one dared to sit down or close his eyes for fear."[120] Julian ignored the caution of his generals that the army was unprepared for a protracted battle—"enraged by the possibility of defeat," Libanius says. But by this point the omens were unequivocally evil:

> At dead night Julian after a short period of restlessness and troubled sleep had roused himself, as was his habit, and was writing in his tent, after the example of Julius Caesar. He was a lost in the profound thoughts of some philosopher when he saw in the gloom . . . the shape of the genius of the Roman people, which [had] appeared to him in Gaul when he rose to the dignity of Augustus. Now it was departing in sadness through the curtains of his tent with its head and horn of plenty veiled. For a moment Julian remained in a state of stupor; then he rose above all fear and committed the future to the will of heaven. The night was far spent and he was fully awake, so he left his bed, which was on the ground, and betook himself to prayer, using the ritual appropriate to avert evil. Then he thought he saw a blazing light like a falling star, which clove its way through part of the air and vanished. He was horror struck by the thought that the star of Mars had appeared to him in this manifestly threatening form.[121]

Haunted by the certainty of failure, Julian chose retreat and ordered his fleet burned, as he had decided to march through the province of Assyria and allow his troops to live off the land as they moved westward.[122] The Persians had the upper hand. Outflanking

---

120. Amm., 25.1.1.

121. Amm., 25.2.10–20.

122. The failure of Julian is attested by a number of pagan as well as by Christian writers. Libanius emphasizes that the boats would have been useless in the circumstances (Or. 18.262–63), and see also Ephraem Syrus, *Hymns,* 2–3; Gregory Naziazen, Or. 5.12; Theod., HE 3.25.1. Further on the boatburning, see Michale diMaio, "Infaustis ductoribus praeviis: The Antiochene Connection," *Byzantion* 51 (1981): 502.

Julian's forces, they harassed the troops and burned crops along the way, effectively starving them out before they could replenish their supplies. The men suffered from fatigue and burning sun; scores died of exhaustion. Ammianus, ever reluctant to call the emperor's motion a retreat, suggests that the Persians had decided against pitched infantry battles and preferred ambush to direct encounter, keeping watch over the progress of the Roman troops from the surrounding hills. In one such ambush, Julian, who had moved forward to reconnoiter, was dismayed to learn from a scout that the army had been attacked from the rear and rushed to join the beleaguered troops without his breastplate and armed only with his shield. In fact, the Roman forces were under attack on all sides, and Julian went about frantically in an attempt to shore up the defenses, "flying from one danger spot to another."[123] In this reckless and confusing moment a cavalry spear struck Julian solidly, piercing his ribs and lodging in his liver. There are various reports about what came next: according to some, the blow was enough to knock him from his horse. In another, he tried in vain to extract the lance from his body. Encomium has it that he insisted on being returned to his horse so that he could continue the fight, "after the manner of the great general Epaminondas." Ammianus's version of Julian's deathbed oration, one worthy of Socrates, is basically an exoneration of his policies and a rebuttal to the charges of rashness and immoderation that greeted news of his failure in Mesopotamia: "I have enjoyed imperial power. This came to me as a gift from the gods to whom I am kin, and I have kept it, to the best of my belief, free from stain, showing moderation in the conduct of civil matters and waging war, whether offensive or defensive, only after mature deliberation."[124] He died on June 26, 363.

---

123. Amm., 25.29–16.
124. Amm., 25.3.18–25.

III. THE RELIGION OF JULIAN

Julian tells us in his letter to the Alexandrians that he shared the faith of the Galileans until he was twenty, but had not practiced it for a dozen years.[125] However many interpretations this remark may invite, it is clear that Julian's agenda to restore the ancestral religion of his pagan predecessors was formulated specifically to underscore his rejection of Christian doctrine and practice. His attack on the "creed of the fishermen" and the "carpenter's son,"[126] was also his way of purging himself of a teaching which he persistently refers to as the "disease" of the Galileans—the name he imposed on the Christians to emphasize the geographical and social obscurity of their origins.[127]

Despite the barely repressed desire of certain Christian commentators to see Julian as a new Decius—or a would-be Nero but for his untimely death—there was in fact a more sinister aspect to Julian's program than earlier apologists had confronted in doing battle with impatient emperors and pagan critics. It is the simple fact that the persecutors before Diocletian not only had *not* been Christians, but also had known very little about the religious enemy at the door. The juridical way in which Christians were handled from the time of Trajan (98–117) suggests nothing so much as disinterest in the Christian church at an intellectual level, and the processes and sporadic persecution directed against them were targeted against associations, not specific ideas or practices. The latter were, of course, the fodder for the attacks of variably informed critics such as Celsus and his intellectual successors, who seem to have relied on rumor and report, especially calumnies circulated by Jewish teachers and lapsed proselytes, for their information. Julian, by contrast, less than two generations after the legitimation of Christianity in the Empire, found the religion philosophically defective, doctrinally unoriginal,

---

125. Ep. XLVII.434D.

126. Ep. XLV (To Photinus, preserved only in a Latin version of Facundus Hermianensis, dating from around 564), where he refers to "the whole mistaken folly of the base and ignorant creed-making fishermen."

127. Gregory, Or., 4.76; but even St. Jerome was troubled by the geographical beginnings of the Church: Ep. 129.4.

and liturgically impoverished. If Julian had not been reputed to be the most philosophical emperor since Marcus Aurelius, or if his information about the faith had been second-hand, like that embedded in Celsus's treatise, then his apostasy might have been seen as unimportant, a caesura in the succession of faithful (more or less) heirs of Constantine. But Julian's devotion to the vocation of philosophy was famous, acknowledged (if belittled) even by the staunchest of his Christian opponents and attested by his tireless correspondence with teachers, former schoolmates, dabblers, and hangers-on, even in the midst of war.[128] As newly appointed caesar, in the heat of the Gallic campaigns, he wrote to Eumenius and Pharianus, two Athenian students, "Let your whole effort be to understand the teachings of Aristotle and Plato; let this be your only vocation, the foundation, the base, the house, the roof."[129] He combined this philosophical commitment, moreover, with intense personal piety, devotion to the cults, an interest in the rituals and theologies of towns and cities throughout the empire, a genuine concern for the physical integrity of shrines and holy places, a desire to reinvigorate local ancestral traditions he thought had been squandered through impiety—disloyalty—and lassitude, and an almost naïve religious optimism that his loyalty to a cause imposed on him by the gods would be rewarded by the gods.[130] Above all, he did not think or write in disgruntlement as a pagan threatened by a new and unapproved form of superstition (though he is keen to see Christianity as something new) but as a former member of a religious association about which he is knowledgeable, whose holy books he can quote, often from memory, and whose theologians, still battling among themselves as "homoousians" and "Arians" he can refute intelligently. These factors combined to make Julian a new kind of enemy for the Church—an apostate—and this accounts for the energy spent on his vilification following his death in 363.

His unpopularity among Christians seemed increasingly to tor-

---

128. G. W. Bowersock, *Julian the Apostate* (1978), p. 88, suggests that Julian's correspondence was the result of an inability to relate to his countrymen at a social level.
129. Ep. III.441D.
130. Cf. Ep. XXXVII.376C and especially Ep. VIII415D.

ment Julian just prior to the Persian campaign, since, perhaps inno-
cently, he expected their gratitude for following what he regarded as
a fair and even course concerning their right to practice their rites in
public.[131] He boasts that he has exercised leniency when he might
have been severe, and even Sozomen catalogues Julian's "persecution" as a program of artful maneuvering rather than an assault on
the fabric of the church and its teachers.[132] The most that can be said
of the disabilities suffered by Christians during his brief reign—
restrictions on teachers, revocation of military commissions, and
(doubtfully) threats to strip recalcitrant proselytizers of citizenship—must all be assessed against the perception of many church
leaders that Julian was always guided by appearances: to be rash
would be seen to be unphilosophical—imprudent and intemperate—and his confidence that it was the Christians who were truly
unphilosophical would finally be shown up in the kind of chaotic
displays and social unrest that accompanied their doctrinal disagree-
ments. Sozomen notes that however intent Julian was in promoting
the pagan cause, he was "equally intent in refusing to employ violent means [against the Christians] which might prove embarrassing
or seem tyrannical."[133] This accounts for the sense felt by many
writers that the true measure of Julian's opposition to Christianity
was unknown at the end of his reign, and that his death intervened
between a set of tactics that had not succeeded in bringing about the
restoration of "the Hellenic faith,"[134] and more direct measures that
would have suffocated the Church if he had returned victorious
from the Persian front. Theodoret, Gregory Naziazen, and John
Chrysostom all register certainty that Julian would have unleashed a
violent persecution if he had returned a victor.[135]

---

131. See the letter to Hecebolius (Ep. XL.424C) and to the Bostrians (Ep.
XLI.436A), where he expresses unhappiness with the response of the Galileans to
his leniency.

132. Sozomen, HE 5.16–17. But Sozomen also makes the point that by his
actions Julian encouraged even if he did not instigate persecution.

133. Sozomen, HE 5.17.

134. Ep XXII.429C.

135. Theod., HE 3.16; Greg., Or. 5.9; John Chrysostom, Contra Julianum, 22.
The most famous defense of the thesis that Julian was a persecutor in disguise,
biding his time and weighing his means before a fully fledged campaign against

*   *   *

JULIAN'S NEOPLATONISM

All of this speculation leaves unanswered the fundamental question: What elements of Julian's religious and moral faith led the normally pragmatic emperor to take the side of a dying religious cause? During the period he was caesar, and an object of Constantius's suspicion, Julian is characterized by observers, both Christian and pagan, as a soul in turmoil. There are traces of enthusiasm and excess in his letters, especially those to philosophers and former teachers.[136] Certain letters are little more than panegyric, and others have the superficial quality of stoic extemporations on the difficulty of suppressing human love. "Where will I find a loving friend like you," he writes on learning of the departure of his friend Sallustius, "who will sustain me, counsel me with wisdom, correct me with love, support me in

---

the Christians, is Bowersock's *Julian the Apostate* (London, 1978), which sees him as an implacably intolerant persecutor. A more nuanced view is that of Smith (*Julian's Gods*, esp. pp. 214–16), which sees a change in attitude in Julian's approach to the Church, partly as a response to provocation. On this reckoning, it is argued that once he became confident that he could act with impunity against the Christians, Julian decided on "the eradication of Christianity as a social force in the Empire." Smith cites in favor of his assessment the fact that Julian punished Palestinian Constantia for its Christian associations (it was merged with pagan Gaza) and when the Caesareans destroyed the last temple in their city "there was not only a fine but civic demotion and higher taxes to boot." The information comes from Sozomen, 5.3. While there should be little doubt about Julian's mindset against Christianity, the question of his intentions remains open. Like his predecessors he regarded Christians as troublemakers at a social level; hence most of the penalties assessed were social penalties designed to make the profession of Christianity an expensive choice. An example is the confiscation of the Church's wealth in Edessa, which he says is generous in view of what they might have deserved by presuming on his *philanthropia*: "sword and exile and fire" (Ep 40.425A). A balanced assessment of the evidence would suggest that Julian's policy hinged on challenges to an official policy of repressing the growth of the Church and advancing the growth of the temples; to the extent he was frustrated in this effort, his policies toward Christianity varied, but did not become violent.

136. Libanius comments on this trait, as does Ammianus (27.7.3–4), who deplores that when Julian greeted his former teacher, Maximus of Ephesus, his enthusiasm was "unbecoming to an emperor."

doing noble deeds humbly, speak freely to me taking the sting from his words."[137] But this apparent effusiveness is a philosophical pose. As a Neoplatonist, though of a decidedly eclectic variety, Julian seems to have felt a constant pressure for purification of the emotions that impeded the soul's ascent to the One, and he gives literary vent to this struggle in his epistles to intellectuals, priests, former schoolmates, and teachers. For Julian the use of language in this way is a form of exercise, marking his attempt to cultivate the cathartic or purifying virtues of his philosophical caste. "Write, and do not cease writing to me continually," he implores his "philosophical" mentor, Maximus. "No, rather come to me by heaven's intercession, and know that while you are away from me I cannot be called alive—except insofar as I am able to read what you have written."[138]

In the system of Plotinus, the ultimate goal of ethical asceticism was godlikeness, or "assimilation to God,"[139] and Julian relied more than averagely on the assistance of professional philosophers, teachers, and charlatans as guides on his journey. At least a part of the enthusiasm incipient in his letters to teachers is familiar from the "love-language" of Plotinus's system, one which freely employed words like intercourse (ὁμοίωσις), rapture, ecstasy, and nakedness to convey the accessory levels of "undressing," "entering," and "uniting." The concept of the lover journeying to his beloved was often construed[140] in language which was frankly sexual, and the master-pupil relationship which Julian cultivated with teachers such as Maximus and most explicitly, perhaps, in relation to the sophist philosopher Priscus[141] frequently and deliberately exploits the Neoplatonic idiom.

---

137. Or. VIII.243c. The language is analogous to Augustine's lament over a friend's loss: *Confessions*, 4.8.13–9.14, also steeped in the Neoplatonic idiom.

138. Ep. XII 383B; and cf. Or. VII.235A; *Letter to Themistius* 264D. Julian's effusive admiration for Maximus is also recorded by Ammianus (27.7.3), who says that on hearing word of the teacher's arrival, Julian suspended a meeting of the Senate. Maximus was with Julian at Constantinople in 362 and at his deathbed on the Persian front. According to Ammianus (29.1), he was executed at Ephesus under Valens in 371, having been implicated in a conspiracy against the emperor.

139. Plotinus, Enn. 5.3.7: ἄφελε πάντα.

140. Enn. 6.9.11.

141. Ep. V.425D.

Yet there was an unavoidable contradiction in the Neoplatonic system for Julian—at least in the unextrapolated and drier forms developed by Plotinus and Porphyry. Carried to its logical extreme, the system of Plotinus was not for the masses but for a philosophical élite. Julian may have had no misgivings about belonging to this caste, but its religious aspect "was so inward and so abstract that it rejected on principle anything so material as temples and formal worship, the very things which were the chief foundation of ordinary pagan religion."[142] Plotinus himself had been contemptuous of religious externals and rituals ("It is for the tokens to come to me, not for me to go to them," he is reported to have said about religious ceremony)[143] and therefore contemptuous equally of the accoutrements of pagan, Jewish, and Christian liturgies.[144] These were for the weak-minded, the hylic (earthbound) men who were not able to move beyond the world of appearances to the intelligible (divine) world. Plotinus or perhaps his teacher, Ammonius Saccas, had already found a clientele among some Christian sects, especially the Egyptian and Syrian Gnostic schools, but where the system attained the status of a theosophical creed, as in the Gnostic cults, it tended to quarantine itself from the worship and life of ordinary believers. It was exclusivist, hierarchical, and élitist rather than, as some have claimed about the Egyptian Gnostic communities, proleptically democratic.[145]

Within the system, God (τὸ ἕν) is the source of a dizzying profusion of beings or emanations (the πρόνοδος) constituting the entirety of the existing universe, while the emanations, through a process of "reconversion" (ἐπιστροφή), move toward the One by fits and starts. For the Platonic demiurge or creator, Plotinus inserts the concept of Intellect (νοῦς) and for the Platonic notion of a world-soul he offers ψυχή or soul-in-itself. The intelligible world thus consists of Mind (intellect) and Soul as emanations of the One; while through a further outpouring of emanations comes the material

---

142. Ricciotti, *Julian the Apostate*, p. 31.

143. Porphyry, *Vit. Plot.* 10.

144. The ambivalence of Julian toward Mithraism must also be regarded in this context.

145. See, for example, the work of Elaine Pagels, *The Gnostic Gospels* (New York, 1978).

world and material beings, including man—a mixed creature comprising the hylic or material element as well as a spiritual element that "directs" him by degrees back to the true source of being, often imaged as the "fatherland" (πατρίς).[146] Most popular understandings of Plotinus's philosophy, unlike the starkly metaphysical Gnostic renderings, chose to emphasize the practical means of reconciling the two "motions" of emanation from the One and return or epistrophe, by envisioning levels or grades of attainment, roughly equivalent to the grades of perfection known in religious circles through the mystery cults, especially Mithraism. Julian, like many of his soldier-comrades, would have seen no inconsistency in being both a Neoplatonist and an adherent of the Mithraic and Cybeleian mysteries, except the high symbolic content and private pursuit of the latter contrasted with the public display of political, social, and contemplative virtues that Neoplatonism demanded.[147]

---

146. Julian either misses or is uninterested in the Christian adaptation of certain Neoplatonic themes, especially those in early writers like Paul (e.g., 1 Cor. 15.35–49).

147. Cf. Or. IV, the Hymn to Helios, and further on the subject, David Ulaney, "Mithras and the Hypercosmic Sun," in *Studies in Mithraism*, ed. J. R. Hinnells (Rome, 1994), pp. 257–64, and the popular treatment of Julian's Helios-worship, M. Clark, "The Emperor Julian and Neoplatonism," *Sunrise* (October/November 1996; December 1996/January 1997). Starting with Plato's notion that the universe itself "came into being as a living creature possessing soul and intelligence," Julian enunciates the doctrine (Or. IV, the Hymn to King Helios) of the hierarchical nature of the universe and all its parts, wherein the One Supreme Cause sends forth from itself gods or powers that rule over lesser and lesser degrees of living beings, until everything is included in the cosmic embrace. The sun and moon and the heavenly bodies "are only the likenesses of the invisible gods." The same oration contains Julian's allegorical description of the constitution of the universe, its substance, origin, powers, and energies which are the sun's gift to its domain, including the mysterious "fifth substance, aether" (after Aristotle) which binds the whole together. Following Plotinus he describes a chain of being, emanating from the "uncompounded Cause": Helios, the god behind the visible Sun, is lord of the intellectual worlds, not only "the common father of all mankind," who "continually revivifies [the substance of things generated] by giving it movement and flooding it with life," but also "the mind of the universe" bestowing through Athena "the blessings of wisdom and intelligence and the creative arts." Helios gives to the "divided souls" (mankind) the faculty of judgment, and bestows on all nature the generative power. Julian emphasizes that Helios brings about the various activities of his solar realm, not directly to the beings, but through the means of countless other gods, angels, daemons, heroes, and others. Referring to the Phoenicians, he cites their teaching that "the rays of light everywhere diffused are the undefiled incarnation [embodiment] of pure mind."

Plotinus had emphasized the significance of "aloneness" (*ut solus cum solo uniaris*) as a perquisite of the soul's journey, beginning with the acquisition of wisdom (prudence, justice, fortitude, and temperance—political virtue) with respect to one's relations with others, but ending with a self-mastery which required abnegation and self-denial of a more austere nature. While Julian is known to have demonstrated levels of mastery in regard to the political virtues, he is also criticized for falling short in each category: imprudent in the Persian campaign and in relation to his paganizing agenda; unjust in his attempts to curry favor with the army and the social élites when first elevated as augustus; excessive in his final hours; intemperate in his craving for augurs, omens, priests, soothsayers, and sacrifices. His widely reported philosophical withdrawals were partly meditative, partly, as Ammianus reports, laced with experiences of dreams and visions such as one might expect of any religious zealot of the era.[148]

But the strands of Julian's attachment to Neoplatonism must be understood in terms of a philosophical tradition that winds from the early disputes over the "true" interpretation of Plato's philosophy in the work of Plotinus and Porphyry to the more radical reformulations of Iamblichus of Chalcis and the Syrian schools, which developed an increasingly radical view of the separation between the One (ἡ πάντη ἄρρητος) and the sensible world, configured as links in a tortuous chain of intermediaries. The artificial complexity of Iamblichus's thought resembled the Syrian gnostic schools, which doubtless took ideas from and gave notions back to the impulsive mystics who propagated Iamblichus's doctrine. Central to this teaching is the subdivision of the sensible world into an upper level, the home of gods, heroes, angels, and demons, and a lower, material

---

148. Amm., 25.2.10–21. In the Hymn to King Helios, Julian recalls that these periods of withdrawal began in childhood: "A vehement love for the splendors of this god took possession of me from my youth; in consequence of which, while I was a boy, my rational part was ravished with astonishment as often as I surveyed his ethereal light; nor was I alone desirous of steadfastly beholding his diurnal splendors, but likewise at night, when the heavens were clear and serene, I was accustomed to walk abroad, and, neglecting every other concern, to gaze on the beauty of the celestial regions with rapturous delight."

level inhabited by mankind. Uniquely, man mediates between these worlds, since he alone among sensible creatures has intimations of the gods as well as a vague aspiration for the supreme good. Yet in his natural state, as in classical Platonic thought, he is bounded and inhibited by the "prison house of creation." The theosophical implications of the system take us beyond Plotinus to a world where "the divine element is echeloned, and scattered throughout the whole range of being,"[149] and where all phenomena must be scrutinized as broken fragments or images possessing a reflection, however dim, of the divine. The unusual, the quaint, the horrific, the surreal, and the ambiguous might contain information channeled from the realms of all-seeing power: a calf born with two heads—or in Julian's instance, a collapsed hayrick or a dyspeptic horse—might reveal as much about the outcome of events as the predictions of soothsayers or the contemplations of an enlightened conscience. There is something to be said for the claim that this phase of Neoplatonic teaching, because of its rejection of reason as a way of knowing the intelligible Good, represents the end of Neoplatonism as a philosophy and its transformation into a form of theurgy and magic. Iamblichus himself seems to have avoided vulgar displays of magic, though he is presented as a magician on several occasions by the biographer Eunapius.[150] In fact the term "theurgy," which is much debated in relation to Julian's own religious conspectus, is greatly misunderstood:[151] it does not relate to a subclass of magicians or hierophants, but simply to men and women from a variety of religious and philosophical castes[152] who claimed to be god-evokers. Iamblichus himself had proclaimed that

149. Ricciotti, *Julian the Apostate*, p. 33.

150. Eunapius presents Iamblichus as being challenged by his earliest followers to do ever greater feats of magic. His demurer on one occasion ("It is irreverent to the gods to give you this demonstration, but for your sakes it shall be done.") has significant cognates in the reticence of Jesus, according to the gospel tradition, to perform miracles: cf. John 4.48; 2.4; Mark 1.40–43; 6.5, etc. Eunapius, *Lives of the Philosophers*, 459, in W. C. Wright (trans.), *Philostratus and Eunapius: The Lives of the Sophists* (London, 1922), pp. 368–73. See also R. J. Penella, *Greek Philosophers and Sophists in the Fourth Century A.D.: Studies in Eunapius of Sardis* (Leeds, 1990).

151. See Rowland Smith, *Julian's Gods*, pp. 91–113.

152. The Chaldean and Iamblichan "theurgies" discussed by Smith, pp. 91–113, provides a good theoretical framework for understanding Julian's milieu, if not specific aspects of his own practice.

"it is not by thinking that men are linked to the gods, but . . . by the efficacy of unspeakable acts performed in the appropriate manner, acts which are beyond all comprehension, and by the potency of the unutterable symbols which are comprehended only by the gods."[153] These symbols or "tokens,"—herbs, salves, signs, and displays of necromancy—"accomplish their proper work without intellectual effort by their own virtue." In this sense the tokens of theurgy are efficacious, a moment of revelation made available to those trained in interpretation. Other ancient forms of divination and prophecy envisaged a relationship with the divine through the divine being's, or the gods', immediate self-disclosure. Without challenging—indeed, taking for granted—the legitimacy of the Hebrew and Apollonian modes of revelation, θεουργία, as it was understood by the later Neoplatonists, was a bringing of divinely hidden truths to light by a sort of detective work: θεαγωγία. The difference, while significant, is essentially one of emphasis; in the theurgic system of Iamblichus and his disciples much less integrity can be accorded the divine being than in the ancient prophetic systems, where the divine will is known through revelation or λόγος.[154] Thus in his discourse on theurgy, Iamblichus discusses the marks of "true" theurgy in relation to physical and mental states involving possession, dreaming, and rapture, and certain visible tokens of genuine (as opposed to fraudulent or deceptive) divination, such as healing powers, levitation, orgiastic purification, the invocation of spirits, and visions of specters.[155] Similar theological calculuses were developed by Iamblichus and his school for the study of numbers and harmonics.[156]

153. Iamblichus, *Myst.* 2.11.

154 Without stretching the analogy, which the church fathers almost unanimously rejected prior to the theosophical reworkings of the Pseudo-Dionysius, Nicene Christian theology offered a reductionist soteriology, emphasizing the savior as "consubstantial" and *sui generis* (*unigenitum*). Gnostic Christianity, on the other hand, conformed to the Neoplatonic model.

155. Iamblichus, *Theurgia* III.7 (*Theurgia, or The Egyptian Mysteries,* trans. A. Wilder, London, 1911).

156. The "break" in the Neoplatonic tradition is sometimes thought to consist in the dispute between Iamblichus and Porphyry over the role of religious symbols and the place of liturgy and ritual in the attainment of philosophical truth, as the following exchange, composed from Porphyry's *Letter to Anebo* (Epistula ad Anebonem) and Iamblichus's *De mysteriis*, a refutation of Porphyry's critique

Essentially, however, theurgy in the Neoplatonic context, whether primarily mystical (mystagogic), or thaumaturgic-liturgical, was a form of soteriology: the goal of theurgy is not merely the understanding of the cosmic order but clarifying the relationship between individual destiny and the noetic (the origin of all: ἡ πάντη ἄρρητος ἀρχή) through special rituals and techniques. In its practical aspect, it seeks to answer the Platonic question, How is one saved from the world of appearances and brought into the light of the One; reciprocally, how can flashes of the noetic illuminate everyday existence, so that the future becomes decipherable rather than mysterious and

---

(addressed ostensibly to an Egyptian priest) suggests. (Page numbers refer to respective sections in the two epistles):

Porphyry's Questions: (Section 3) Since the gods are unlimited, undivided, and uncircumscribed in power, how does it happen that religion and ritual treat them as allotted to different spheres of influence?

Iamblichus's Replies: The differences do not lie in the gods, but in the recipients and their varying capacity to receive different types of divine power (30–33: cf. n.3). (I, 9)

Porphyry's Questions: (Section 4) Why are shocking and obscene events and language used in the Mysteries?

Iamblichus's Replies: (a) Because this is the correct way of worshiping the generative forces (38–39), (b) because it "inoculates" those elements in matter seeking order, showing them the better by demonstrating the worse (39). (c) Repressing emotions makes them more destructive, moderate release is cathartic (39–40). (I, 11)

Porphyry's Questions: (Sections 4 and 5) Why are so many things at sacred rites performed as though they were directed to beings who are swayed by emotions?

Iamblichus's Replies: Prayer and invocation do not mean that the gods are persuaded to come down to us, but rather that by their means we adhere to and become like them (42, 46–49). The "anger" of the gods is not their turning away and desertion of us by them. The situation is rather that we render ourselves incapable of receiving their beneficence. And the same argument holds true for expiatory sacrifices (43–44). (I, 12–15; VIII, 8)

Porphyry's Questions: (Section 6) How is it that some (planetary) gods are givers of good things, but others of evil?

Iamblichus's Replies: These things arise from a misunderstanding of astrology, which talks of benefics and malefics. All the gods are good, but material conditions may distort that which emanated from the divine in a state of harmony and lead to conflict (53–57). (1–18)

Porphyry's Questions: (Section 8) What is the difference between gods and daemons?

Iamblichus's Replies: The governance of the gods is all-embracing and unrestricted. That of the daemons is limited in time and place; daemons do not completely transcend that which they rule (63–64). (1, 20)

unknown: "You must look toward the light and toward the rays of the
Father, whence your soul was sent to you clad in much *nous* . . ."; "Do
not look upon nature; the name is enmeshed with fate"; "Let the
immortal depth of the soul be opened up; spread out your eyes
strongly and upwards."[157]

Following his initiation into the "entrance to philosophy" by
Maximus, Julian seems to have been attracted to the rites of the so-
called Chaldean Oracles, the "canonical" text of Neoplatonic
theurgy, or so we may judge from a letter written to Priscus from
Gaul in 358, asking the philosopher to bring with him a copy of
Iamblichus's commentary on the Oracles. In fact, Julian says little
about theurgy or the Oracles as such in his writings, but there is evidence to suggest that he remained attached to theurgic praxis
throughout his career as a military commander and emperor.[158]
According to Ammianus, the practices, now intertwined with traditional augury, intensified throughout his period in Illyricum, just
prior to the show-down with Constantius in 361, when Julian
seemed to undergo periods of depression if confronted with
ambiguous portents or forced to deal with charlatans.[159]

Julian's letters addressed to Iamblichus are without doubt for-
geries,[160] but the emperor's inclination to Iamblichan doctrine cannot
be seriously doubted. He describes Iamblichus as "a truly godlike man,
the third after Pythagoras and Plato," and one "who has reached the
highest wisdom that man can attain . . . so that no one can be anything
more perfect than he."[161] The most important names associated with
Iamblichus's school are those of the Pergamese teacher Edesius[162] and

---

157. Chaldean Oracles, 115, 102, and 112, and Smith's discussion, *Julian's
Gods*, p. 101. On the Oracles generally, H. Lewy, *Chaldean Oracles and Theurgy: Mys-
ticism, Magic and Platonism in the Later Roman Empire* (Paris, 1978).

158. Some of the evidence for this is arguable (cf. Smith, p. 91), but Julian
does petition for perfection in theurgy in his Hymn to Cybele, Mother of the Gods.

159. Amm., 22.2.1; 22.1.2–3.

160. Eps. LXXIV–LXXIX. Or—in view of their innocuous content—letters
written by another admirer and wrongly ascribed to Julian by virtue of the latter's
professed admiration for the philosopher's doctrine: see Wright, III, xlix.

161. Hymn to Helios, Or. IV.157C, D.

162. According to Eunapius, Edesius for either political or intellectual reasons
refused to accept Julian's lavish gifts at Pergamon with the retort, "You have heard
me teach many times but are still ignorant of my soul."

his pupils Chrysanthius, Eusebius of Myndus, Priscus, and Maximus—all of whom had associations with Julian, as did Eunapius, the biographer of Iamblichus, and the philosopher and mysteriously influential rhetor Eustathius, a hierophant and sage who impressed the Persian king Sapor with his oratory, if not with his magic.[163] Of these, Maximus occupies the preeminent position, especially as an arbiter and judge in philosophical discussions: "αὐτὸς ἔφα."[164] On his arrival in Pergamon, the aged Edesius's reticence toward Julian (or perhaps toward his potential as a philosopher) left him in the care of Chrysanthius and Eusebius, Priscus having gone to Greece and Maximus having been called to Ephesus. Eunapius makes the point that Julian was torn between Chrysanthius's irrationalism (his devotion to the occult was famous), and Eusebius's quiet pursuit of dialectic "when Maximus was not present to correct him." The picture of Maximus, Julian's "twin soul," that emerges is not flattering: on the one hand a sycophant and a power-broker, on the other hand someone whose eloquence and personal magnetism made him impossible to ignore. Eunapius speaks of his "grand nature," but at the same time as one who despised rational proofs, dialectical reasoning, and was completely devoted to magic, "even to the point of playing the madman." Julian's devotion to the old teacher may have been encouraged by a tale told him by Eusebius involving a scene at the temple of Hecate,[165] who had a special role as prophetic intercessor in the Neoplatonic theurgy, especially that represented in the cosmogony of the Chaldean Oracles.[166] In the tale told by Eusebius, Maximus convinced a number of his friends that he could demonstrate to them how far he surpassed ordinary mortals; he then burned a single grain of incense before the statue of Hecate in their presence, whereupon the goddess began to smile, then laugh out loud, until at last "the torches she held burst into flame." The element of fire was especially significant as "proof" of Maximus's semi-divine stature, because of its symbolic centrality in Neoplatonic, especially the

---

163. Amm., 17.5; cf. Julian, Eps. XLIV and XLV.

164. "He has said it." Ep. 16.452B.

165. Libanius observes (13.11) that a "certain spark of the mantic art" caused Julian to lose his hatred of the ancestral gods and become docile to the oracles.

166. See the excellent discussion of this subject in Rowland Smith, *Julian's Gods*, pp. 99–104.

Chaldean, theurgy. "The fire . . . which has occupied a vessel above the heavens . . . is infinitely in motion, a boundless eternity. It is not within the grasp of the blessed gods unless the mighty father should plan his purposes so that he himself might be looked upon."[167] On hearing the story, whatever Eusebius may have wished its effect would be, Julian kissed Chrysanthius on the forehead and set out for Ephesus in pursuit of Maximus.

According to his adversary and former schoolmate, Gregory Naziazen, Julian was initiated into the mysteries at Ephesus by Maximus and became an adept in theurgy under his tutelage.[168] As one modern commentator has observed, the "conversion" of Julian in 350–351 owes a great deal to his "human exemplar" and the distinctive color of his Neoplatonism is probably best sought in Maximus's teaching.[169] Julian does not seem to have been converted by the cool truths of Neoplatonic doctrine but by the thaumaturgic displays that almost unexceptionally impressed all of Maximus's disciples—even those not able to duplicate his feats. This is not to suggest, as an older school of interpretation claimed,[170] that Julian's conversion was totally without a philosophical motive or interest,[171] but that it was as much a devotional need as intellectual commitment that sealed his loyalty to the pagan cause and the ancestral rites, and inevitably shaped his attitude toward Christianity thereafter. Gregory tells the story of the initiation in a detail that calls attention to its basis in hearsay and Christian legend, though the essential outline of the event is plausible. Accompanied by a hierophant, Julian

167. Translated by Smith, p. 98.
168. Gregory, Or.V.34; Eunapius, 475.
169. Smith, *Julian's Gods*, p. 186.
170. See Arthur Darby Nock, *Conversion* (Oxford, 1933), pp. 14, 185, 218–19.
171. The Epistle to Themistius is the primary source for Julian's understanding of politics. His primary model is the optimus princeps of Plato's Laws, especially where Plato discusses the "more divine nature" of the king ($\phi\acute{\upsilon}\sigma\epsilon\omega\varsigma$ $\delta\epsilon\tilde{\iota}\sigma\theta\alpha\iota$ $\delta\alpha\iota\mu\omega\nu\iota\omega\tau\acute{\epsilon}\rho\alpha\varsigma$). While admiring the examples of Solon, Pittacus, and Lycyrgus, Julian remarks that he "has been assigned by God the same position formerly occupied by Heracles and Dionysus, who being at once philosophers and kings purified almost all the earth of the ills infesting them" (253c–254B). Julian's refusal to play an active role in politics, preferring the "Socratic" to the "Alexandrian" style, is based on the conviction that $\theta\epsilon\omega\rho\acute{\iota}\alpha$ exceeds $\pi\rho\tilde{\alpha}\xi\epsilon\iota\varsigma$. See further on this period the discussion of Athanassiadi, pp. 56–58.

entered the mithraeum in fear, "greeted by strange sounds, revolting exhalations, fiery apparitions, and prodigies." Comforted by the words of his guide ("We loathe but no longer fear [the demons]"), Julian emerged from the abyss reconciled to his future and "from that day on was possessed."[172]

The basic accuracy of Gregory's final comment on Julian's pagan "baptism" is borne out in the events of his subsequent life as caesar and emperor, as well as by the testimonies of Libanius, Ammianus, and Julian himself. In his Hymn to King Helios (Oration IV), composed over three days, and only six months before his death, Julian rehearses the episodes that brought him to the worship of Helios and the proofs he feels secured and justified his faith in the god's sovereignty. "From my youth I have longed for the rays of the god to embrace me; from early days my mind was enthralled by light ethereal (τὴν διάνοιαν ἐξιστάμην) such that I not only wanted to gaze at the sun without stopping but I wanted as much to walk alone at night, beneath the clear and luminous sky, giving my whole soul to the beauty of Heaven, having no regard for anyone nor anything that was said to me."[173] Claiming to be ignorant of the science of astrology, Julian records that even as a child, and lacking the "proper" tools of interpretation—the Platonic view of the divinity of the cosmos—he sensed the natural affinity of the sun and enlightenment, and revered the sun as the medium that dispelled the clouds of ignorance, now associated in his mind with Christian doctrine.

The association between "darkness" and Christianity would become more pronounced in Julian's mature work, especially in an oration delivered against the teaching of the cynic Heraclius (Oration VII). In it Julian recalls a spiritual crisis that he seems to have undergone close to the time of his initiation into theurgy. What provoked the crisis is anyone's guess—a delayed reaction to the slaughter of his relatives during his childhood may have been responsible[174]—but the language of the oration seems also to sug-

---

172. Greg., Or. IV.55–56; Theod., HE 3.1.

173. Or IV.130B–131A.

174. "Having been so tormented by the death of my kinsmen as to want to hurl myself into the bowels of Tartarus" (Or. VII.229D).

gest that he had come to believe that the religion of Constantine's sons, and especially that exemplified by Constantius himself, was not passively offensive but actively repugnant. He prays to Zeus "that this wicked zeal for impiety should not overtake all men," and urges Helios "to take care especially of your child Julian and cure him of this sickness, for you see how he is infected with smoke and filth and darkness, and there is a risk that the fire you sowed in him will be extinguished."[175] Notably, the sickness and disease to which he refers make Christianity and error indistinguishable, and Julian rhetorically favors the epithet "disease" as a way of describing the Christian faith in his letters. The devotion to Helios finds its closest approximation in the pre-Christian devotion of Constantine himself to the Sol Invictus, but Julian's mystical conviction—that he was in direct relationship with the god, and that the god not only guided but admonished, chastised, and befriended him in time of need—is distinctive. Thus Julian records that Helios himself recognizes the divine particle—the splinter of light—within him, and that the god preserves him from danger.[176]

The sense of divine favor is consistent in Julian's orations and letters, if somewhat fluctuating from moment to moment. In his letter to the Athenians, he claims that he sought divine guidance "with outstretched hands" when nominated to be Caesar by Constantius, and saw the goddess Athena atop the Acropolis, "who sent guardian angels to my side from Helios and Selene."[177] In a similar episode, he sought divine counsel about whether to send an embassy to the Empress Eusebia in Milan, and was warned by the gods that if he did so he would be killed.[178] These visions are mentioned also in reports from Ammianus, who says that the emperor was in the habit of telling his closest friends about his dreams and apparitions, and that the night before he was proclaimed Augustus he was visited by the *genius publicus*—the guardian spirit of the

---

175. Or. VII.228B, 229B, D.
176. Or. VII.229D. Julian comments that he was saved from his wretchedness through the intervention of Helios and Athena.
177. Ep ad SPQ Ath. 275B.
178. Ep ad SPQ Ath. 275C, D.

state—who upbraided him for his recalcitrance and threatened to abandon him forever if he declined the dignity.[179]

Julian's composite Neoplatonism, his reputation as a mystic of sorts, a visionary given to philosophical rhapsodies and the practice of theurgy, yields an uncertain portrait of his religious faith. If he was a Christian until his twentieth year, what sort of Christian was he?[180] If his acknowledgement of the principality of Helios predated his "philosophical" conversion under Maximus, as he seems to suggest in the concluding section of *Against Heraclius*, does this nascent paganism nullify the outward attachment to Christianity during his youth? Libanius suggests that Julian's religious hypocrisy was so well developed, "that if Aesop wanted to tell a new fable, it would not about the ass that hid under the skin of a lion, but of the lion that hid under the skin of the ass." The lion is Julian; the ass, the ancient symbol of opprobrium for the ignorant Christian.[181] At another level of interpretation, however, Julian's religious "hypocrisy" conforms to the eclecticism of his age. One sees repeatedly in his letters and orations the syncretism that characterized the religious melting pot of late antiquity: the supreme God or ruling power can be addressed as Helios, or as Zeus, invoked solely, or in combination with Athena. In the Hymn to the Mother of the Gods, addressed to the Great Mother

---

179. Amm, 20.5.10.

180. The many attempts to answer this question can perhaps be put aside in favor of the following: Julian's mother, Basilina, was, if a Christian, an Arian; his first guardian, Eusebius of Nicomedia, was a defender of the Arian theology; Constantius himself, who controlled the fate of both Julian and Gallus, professed the heresy; and both George of Cappadocia, whose library Julian inherited, and Aetius, who had once tried to convert Julian to Christianity on learning of his pagan inclinations, were Arians. In his writings Julian does not distinguish between Arians and orthodox Christians, but does seem to know of the doctrinal disputes dividing the two contingents. The extent to which the confusions of the post-Nicene period in Christian theology may have contributed to his abandoning Christianity cannot be assessed; however, Ammianus "represents" Julian's attitude in the following: "[He knew from experience] that there are no wild beasts so hostile to mankind as are most Christians in their hatred for one another" (Amm., 22.5.4).

181. Libanius, 18.19; on the ass image, in addition to the famous graffito from the second (?) century, cf. Tertullian, Apol. 1.16 ("Nam et somniastis caput asininum esse Deum nostrum" etc.); Ad nationes I.11, 14; Minuc. Felix, Octav. 9. Tertullian traces this absurdity to Cornelius Tacitus, who uses it against the Jews (Hist. V.4).

Cybele, the focus, if there is one in this meandering tract, is on the redemption of Attis by castration as an allegory of the soul's epistrophe to the One; yet it is possible that the hymn itself is impregnated with allusions to the Mithraic zodiac and cultic astrology.[182] The double and triple aspects of gods (trimorphism) made it possible for Julian to mix and match deities according to need, or the severity of a crisis: one such moment was the call from Constantius for Julian to return to Constantinople when he had been in Athens for less than three months. His prayerful approach is to Athena, regnant on the Acropolis, though underlying his appeal is the notion that Athena acts as intercessor between himself and Helios, an aspect often associated with Cybele.[183] It should be stressed, however, that this does not represent a "confusion" of names in Julian's theology,[184] but is rather an essential feature of the Iamblichan system, reflecting the provisionality of all revelations of the divine nature. In the same way, Julian can speak of the God of the Jews, without irony, as the Most High God,[185] who under any other name is a revelation of the One. In the Hymn to Helios, he intones his conviction that the many names of the "intellectual" (intermediate) gods are always to be associated with the source of their power, and hence are modes of knowing the supreme god: "We say that [Helios's] royal establishment among the intellectual gods, from his middle order between the planets; for if we perceived these, or as many other properties, belonging to any other of the apparent gods, we should not ascribe the principality among the gods to the sun. But if he has nothing in common with the rest, except that beneficent power which he imparts to all, we ought to rely on the testimony of the Cyprian priests, who raised common altars to Jupiter and the Sun; or, indeed, prior to these, we should confide in Apollo, who is the attendant of this god; for thus he speaks: Jupiter, Pluto, Serapis, and the Sun, are one. And thus we should consider that there is a common, or rather one and the same principality, among the

---

182. Smith, *Julian's Gods*, p. 161.
183. Ep. SPQ Athen. 275A.
184. Thus against Ricciotti, *Julian the Apostate*, p. 64.
185. Ep. LI.398A.

intellectual gods."[186] When Julian addresses Maximus shortly after the death of Constantius, he invokes Zeus, Helios, and Athena as a trinity of powers who have revealed to him that his master would come to no harm.[187] Similarly, he invokes Apollo as the "coregent of Helios"[188] whose rule binds Rome, Constantinople, and Athens together in a community (the *oikoumene*) of shared values.

In the oration Against Heraclius,[189] Julian alludes to his consecration as "soldier" in the Mithraic mystery. It is sometimes supposed that this initiation took place during his governorship of Gaul.[190] In another passage Julian is reminded by Hermes, the formidable symbol of mystagogic gnosis, of his responsibilities to the cult. The depth of his involvement in the cult of Mithras is widely debated. On one reckoning, Julian can be seen as a good *miles Mithrae* [soldier of Mithras], whose devotion to the cult was intensely personal and entailed keeping its secrets.[191] The argument for this view is chiefly from silence, since in his most extended religious tractate, the Hymn to Helios, Julian does not mention the Mithraic rituals and makes no allusion to its doctrine. On another reckoning, the silence is more telling; Julian does not mention Mithras, except fancifully, because he was more interested in promoting the well-established gods of the Empire as a part of his political agenda to restore the ancestral cults of Rome. Thus Zeus, Apollo, Cybele, Athena, and the tutelary gods of cities are mentioned frequently, and to a certain extent coalesce, as is typical within Neoplatonic theurgy. Perhaps because of its origins, its special association with the guardian caste, and Julian's sense that "philosophical" rulership demanded virtues not altogether patent to Mithraism,[192]

---

186. Or. IV; T. Taylor's translation (1793), pp. 49–50.

187. Ep. VIII.415A, B.

188. Ep. XI.152D.

189. Or. VII.234A.

190. Thus Athanassiadi, "A Contribution to Mithraic Theology," p. 38.

191. Rightly challenged by Smith, *Julian's Gods*, p. 162, as being "impossible to verify or refute." Cf. Cumont, *Les mystères de Mithra* (Paris, 1913), p. 146.

192. Smith (p. 170) calls attention to Julian's emphasis on *philanthropia* and *civilitas*, the cultivation of civic virtue and justice. By contrast, Athanassiadi (p. 41) stresses the moral code of Mithraism would have been appealing to Julian. Or. VII.233D–234A presents Helios as prescribing four commandments for Julian:

he may have seen contradictions between promotion of the latter and his commitment to Iamblichan doctrine.

By the same token it is possible to exaggerate the incompatibility of the two systems. The Pergamese and Anatolian schools of Neoplatonism represented by Julian's teachers were not themselves closely identified with the traditional gods of Roman religion, so the "foreignness" of the Mithraic system was not in itself a decisive mark against it for Julian, whose ability to syncretize gods within his theological calculus is attested by all available literary and epigraphic evidence. In fact, it is Julian's religious inclusivism that distinguishes his philosophical opposition to Christianity from the largely intellectual opposition of Celsus. While Celsus speaks with the voice of a conservative second-century intellectual, opposed to new and unapproved cults—especially those associated with the lower classes—Julian speaks as a religious syncretist and takes the arrows for his quiver from a variety of religious and philosophical traditions, domestic and foreign. For all this, it is questionable whether Julian was initiated into the Mithraic mysteries as early as 351[193] or that it was Mithraism, as opposed to Neoplatonic theurgy, which provided that "flash of light" that lifted him from his period of depression at the age of twenty. The most that can be said is that there is no good reason to doubt that Julian found *some* elements of Mithraic doctrine compatible with Neoplatonic theurgy, and in the typical pattern of his day regarded Mithras as a mode for understanding the revelation of Helios. In the biographical portions of the Oration against the cynic Heraclius, often thought to reflect Julian's attachment to Mithraism, a tearful prince receives instruction from Helios that "initiation" does not provide security against the demands and commitments of the real world.[194] This very advice

---

worship of the gods, loyalty to friends, philanthropic love of his subjects, and impassibility in judgment and service. The extent to which these are commonplaces having no particular role to play in Mithraism or are importations into the system based on Julian's natural tendency to syncretize Mithraic and Neoplatonic thought would have significant bearing on deciding the nature of his adherence to the cult.

193. Athanassiadi, p. 39, generally supports Bidez' emphasis on the centrality of Mithraism to Julian's religious ideology, but with qualifications regarding the Paris "coup d'état" (1992, pp. x–xv).

194. Or VII.231C, D.

should perhaps be seen as Julian's manifesto concerning the cult, whose basic rituals were mirrored in the ladder of ascent Julian had already come to know from Iamblichan doctrine,[195] especially with respect to "solar piety"—the belief that the cosmos is shot through with divinity and thus to be venerated in its own right for the revelatory function it serves as mediating between the One and its hypostases. If Mithraism did appeal to Julian, it would have been in connection with the corollaries he saw between it and his broader philosophical commitment to Neoplatonism: the concept of continuous progress through a ladder of ascent; the movement of the soul from the confinements of passion to purification; the sloughing off of greed, private ambition, sensual desire ($\chi\iota\tau\acute{\omega}\nu$), and sloth.[196] The political virtues to be cultivated in the system of Plotinus were the positive corollaries of the Mithraic levels of divestiture—the shedding of the garments of the flesh through the seven levels of the cosmos. Porphyry himself speaks of the apogenesis of the soul, liberated from the cycle of birth and rebirth and fully "saved,"[197] and it would have been no great leap for Julian to have seen Mithraic ascent as the cultic equivalent of what was a cardinal doctrine of Neoplatonic theurgy.

For all this, it is doubtful that Julian's profound silence about Mithraism throughout an eleven-year period can be interpreted as secrecy or obedience. Other than conflational tendencies in the Hymn to King Helios and the oration against the cynic Heraclius, there is little to suggest deep commitment to the cult at any time during his life.[198] It must also be admitted that Julian never wholeheartedly embraced the darker aspects of the mysteries. He is acknowledged to have been repulsed by the "stygian symbolism" of his initiation,[199] and his tendency to associate Christianity with

---

195. See R. Turcan, *Mithras Platonicus: Recherches sur l'héllenisation philosophique de Mithra* (Leiden, 1975).

196. Cumont, *Les mystères de Mithra*, p. 146.

197. Abst. 4.16.

198. See the useful review of Rowland Smith's speculation by Thomas Banchich, "Julian's Gods: Religion and Philosophy in the Thought and Action of Julian the Apostate," *Bryn Mawr Classical Review* (1997): 238–39.

199. Gregory, Or. 4.55–56; recognizing Gregory's use of invective to describe the scene, it is worth quoting the following portion: "He had descended into one

graves and sepulchers would seem to suggest a general aversion to the use of darkness and death as religious *topoi*: His intellectual preference to "keep separate the things of Helios . . . and the bright Olympians" from the things of the night, associated with ignorance and death, must not only have influenced his view of Christianity[200] but determined his attitude toward Mithraism as well.

Julian's devotion to the great mother Cybele cannot be doubted. It can be traced to his time in Bithynia and several trips to Phrygia,[201] where he encountered "the marvelous woman [called] Arête." According to Gregory Naziazen, Julian's real "apostasy" dates from this period of discipleship when "through impious blood he washed away the waters of his baptism."[202] If the pattern outlined in Julian's correspondence and Gregory's diatribe can be given credit, then it was Arête, who may have been a pupil of Iamblichus herself, who explained the meanings of the Phrygian mysteries to Julian and arranged for his initiation. It would be ten years later, in March 362, that Julian would visit Phrygia again, this time as emperor, where he composed the exegetical Hymn to the Mother of the Gods. Word of his strange activities must have reached Gallus, and may have reached Constantius. At any rate, Julian, apparently to quiet reports, became a lector in the Christian church in Nicomedia, "reading scripture with great feeling and causing everyone to admire his

---

of those sanctuaries [the Mithraic cave] inaccessible to the multitude, and feared by all (as would that he had feared the way leading unto hell before proceeding to such extremities), in company with the man that was as bad as many sanctuaries put together, the wise in such things, or sophist more rightly to be called; for this is a kind of divination amongst them to confer with darkness, as it were, and the subterranean demons concerning future events: whether that they delight more in darkness, because they are darkness, and makers of the darkness of wickedness, or that they shun the contact of pious persons above ground, because through such they lose their power. But when, as my fine fellow proceeded in the rites, the frightful things assailed him, unearthly noises, as they say, and unpleasant odours, and fiery apparitions, and other fables and nonsense of the sort, being terror-struck at the novelty (for he was yet a novice in these matters), he flies for help to the Cross, his old remedy, and makes the sign thereof against his terrors, and makes an ally of Him whom he persecuted. And what follows is yet more horrible."

200. This separation is clearest in the language of Ep. LVI, the edict on funerals.

201. Ep VI.259C, D.

202. Greg., Or. IV.52.

Christian devotion."[203] On hearing of his behavior, a distressed Gallus then commissioned the Arian theologian Aetius to go to Bithynia and question Julian about his true religious feelings. Whatever the outcome of these interviews, the two men seem to have struck up a friendship—probably because Aetius was a passable philosopher, and arguably because his theology, that of the radical Arians (Anomoeans), taught that the substance of the son is unlike that of the Father, thus making Jesus decisively inferior to the supreme God. Julian was similarly forgiving of the theology of the Photinians.[204] Philostorgius relates that Aetius was careful to tell both Julian and Gallus what they wanted to hear.[205] Julian therefore continued his life of religious dissimulation in Nicomedia[206] without interruption, developing a cadre of friends and philosophical dilettantes around him.

If the nature of Julian's attachment to Mithraism, especially as it is made available in the Hymn to King Helios, is fraught with ambiguity,[207] the theology of the Hymn to Cybele is far more clear. There are similarities in the theology of the hymns: Like Helios, the *Magna Mater* is polymorphic: she is Athena, Rhea, Ceres, and Dio. Like Helios she permeates the cosmos as "the source of the intelligible gods,"[208] while Attis becomes the mediator between the Great Mother and the material world. In her generative aspect, she "produces" emanations in the same way that the Sun produces its light in the form of solar rays—an image which was common not only to Neoplatonic philosophy and Gnostic thought, but even to the

203. Socrates, HE 3.1.20.

204. CG 262C; on the theology of Photinus, condemned by both the Nicene and Arian parties, cf. Sozomen, HE 4.6.

205. Philos. 3.27 and Julian, Ep. 15.

206. Lib. 18.19.

207. In her introduction to the 1992 paperback edition of *Julian: An Intellectual Biography*, first published as *Julian and Hellenism* in 1981, Polymia Athanassiadi confessed that she had "overemphasized Julian's Mithraism . . . and distorted the balance of Julian's religious belief, especially in his imperial years by making him lean heavily on the cult of Mithra" (p. xiv). By the same token she is undoubtedly correct in her assessment that Julian's "was a personality fraught with more contradictions, tensions and inconsistencies than the average man" (p. viii).

208. Or. V.166A, B.

Nicene fathers who appropriated the image to symbolize the procession of the son from the Father, φῶς ἐκ φωτός. Julian's contribution to the interpretation of the Cybele myth—the castration of Attis—is his application of Neoplatonic exegesis to the story of Attis's desertion of Cybele (as noetic principle or principality) in favor of sensuous passion, the love of a nymph. Attis's treachery represents the soul's confusion and entrapment in the material world in contrast to the divine Cybele's apathetic or passionless love. His castration interrupts the process of diremption—the potentially endless rupture of the perfection of the divine being—and sets in motion the process of redemption: the reversion of the soul from error to truth, from many to the One. Because it was unthinkable to Julian that a god could die, he rejected the received version of the myth which centered on the death of Attis. Like Porphyry and Celsus before him, Julian will make this point again in his diatribe against the Galilean belief that Jesus, a god, could die and rise again from the dead.[209]

Julian is at pains to link the origins of the Phrygian cult to Rome—"the friend of divinity"—a measure of respect notably absent in his tepid references to Mithras. Cybele's history was clearly linked to Rome's history, whereas for all the links between Helios and the Mithraic religion, Mithras himself, at least in Julian's theogony, remained curiously Persian rather than Roman, astral rather than cosmic, and literal rather than allegorical. As a modern commentator has observed, Julian felt that it was not through the bloody mysteries of Mithras but through the intellectual patronage of Cybele that "the Empire would be cleansed of the stain of atheism."[210] Her worship provided the most immediate paradigm, a central myth, for the Iamblichan theurgy he sought to cultivate.[211] She was the patron deity of his political program to propagate the teaching of his ancestors and pagan worship throughout the empire.

---

209. In what is either an odd or a gratuitous denial, Julian claims he had not read a work by Porphyry on the same myth, almost certainly *On the Cave of the Nymphs* (Or. V.161C), and asks that any similarity be charged off to coincidence. *How* he might have anticipated the similarities argues strongly in favor of the unoriginality of his interpretation.

210. Smith, *Julian's Gods*, p. 178. Cf. Or. V.180B.

211. Smith, *Julian's Gods*, p. 162. Smith catalogs the influence of the Chaldean Oracles on Julian's exegesis of the Cybele myth.

It is widely thought that the reference to "the stain of atheism" in the Hymn to Cybele[212] refers to Christianity, though the context of the reference is broad: despite the fact that atheism was an epithet often applied to Christianity by pagan intellectuals, the term had a far less restricted meaning. Julian's own understanding of atheism embraces all forms of impiety, especially the kind of negligence that had led to the moral dissolution of traditional cults and rituals. If Christianity is the irritant and the Church the seducer of people away from pagan tradition, Julian is clear that those who abandon the gods do so at a risk, and paraphrases Homer to document his displeasure: οὐ γάρ μοι θέμις ἐστὶ κομιζέμεν σουνδ᾽ ἀποπέμπειν ἄνδρα τὸν ὅς κε θεοῖσιν ἀπέχθηται μακάρεσσιν.[213] In the letter to Arsacius, written in July 362 from Antioch, Julian complains that the lassitude of his subjects has angered the Mother of the Gods, and that they must become her suppliants to win his favor. Christianity is always in Julian's purview as that form of "disease" or "ignorance" that most impels to atheism, but atheism itself in Julian's view is the rejection of the "Hellenic faith," whether through acceptance of Christianity or failure to return gifts to the gods.[214]

IV. THE GALILEAN PROBLEM AND THE CONTRA GALILAEOS

The issues that encircle Julian's hatred of the Galileans have already been surveyed briefly: To what extent is Julian to be accounted a "convert" (or apostate) from Christianity? Are his later recollections or "glimpses" of the Hellenic faith in his childhood and adolescence, in the words of modern reviewer, nothing more than "the retrojections of a would-be born-again pagan"?[215] Was his apostasy provoked by "exemplars" such as Eusebius of Nicomedia, Constan-

---

212. Or. V.180B.
213. Ep. XXII.432A; paraphrasing *Odyssey* 10.73: "It is not lawful for me to love or pity men who have made themselves enemies of the immortal gods."
214. Ep. XXII.430D.
215. T. Banchich, Review of R. Smith, *Julian's Gods* (London, 1995), *BMCR* (1997): 22.

tius, Eusebia, George, and (even) Gallus, on the Christian side, in contrast to the example of pedagogues and friends such as Mardonius, Maximus, Priscus, Eustathius, and Arête? Put in that way, the question leaves little doubt that the Christian religion for Julian represented his dark night of the soul and was associated by him with superstition and the rejection of the Hellenic worldview.[216] The bishops' unproductive struggling for a narrow orthodoxy based on texts he found unoriginal and philologically poor stood in sharp contrast to the beauties of Homer and the wisdom of Plato: "[My pedagogue Mardonius said to me] 'Do you long for horse races? There is one very cleverly described in Homer. Take up the book and study it! . . . Moreover, in Homer there are so many more plants more pleasant to read about than those we see; even so near the altar of Apollo on Delos did I once see a date palm burgeoning. And there is the wooded isle of Calypso, and the caves of Circe, and the Garden of Alcinous. Know that you will never see anything more delightful than these.'"[217] In contrast to his memories of life as Mardonius's pupil, his allusions—and there are few of them—to a Christian childhood are brusque and painful: "Let that darkness be forgotten," he says in the hymn to King Helios and in almost identical words in his Letter to the Alexandrians.[218] "When I groped all alone in darkness," he says in the Hymn to the Mother of the Gods, referring to the days before his initiation into the Metroac mystery.[219] Julian's references to his sense of isolation—loneliness, blindness—in childhood must refer, on one level, to the family purges being carried out by his cousin when Julian was only six years old. At the

---

216. There is enough evidence in Julian's writings cumulatively to suggest that he was conscious of having been a Christian in his youth, though this formulation would be slightly different from Athanassiadi's view that Julian was never "consciously a Christian" (*Of Julian and Hellenism*, pp. 24–27 and *Julian: An Intellectual Biography*, p. xii). Bowersock's efforts to show that Julian's attachment to Hellenism can be explained in the light of an exclusively Christian upbringing are, in my view, unconvincing; cf. G. W. Bowersock, *Hellenism in Late Antiquity* (Cambridge, 1990), pp. 6, 26, and does not reflect an adequate grasp of the religious and theological context in which Julian's religious ideas were shaped.

217. *Misopogon*, 351C–352A.

218. Helios, Or. IV.131A; Ep. XLVII.434D.

219. Or., V.174C.

same time, these dynastic atrocities were the work of Christians; they were performed under the nodding gaze of self-serving bishops like George of Cappadocia, a "poisonous" man whose arrogance outstripped even that of the orthodox Athanasius whom he would later come to despise.[220] Julian seems to have felt that his escape into the beauties of Hellenic thought were also an escape from the darkness of his Christian family.

Julian came to believe, not in a flash but as a cumulative matter, that Christianity was a cancer on the polis, and that he had been entrusted by the gods to remove it. Before his departure for Persia he decided to ventilate his animosity for the Christian faith in a long diatribe against the followers of "the carpenter's son." The project is either outlined, or at least alluded to, in a letter written soon after Julian arrived in Antioch in July 362, addressed to Photinus, bishop of Sirmium.[221] In it, Photinus is congratulated for his view that "a god can by no means be brought forth from the womb," in contrast to the muscular defense of the divinity of Jesus put forward by the Nicene theologian Diodorus of Tarsus, who was in Antioch during Julian's time in the city, "whose false myth styles [the Nazarene] eternal." "If only the gods and goddesses and the Muses and Fortuna herself will lend me aid, I shall show that [Diodorus] is a weakling, a perverter of the law and order of the pagan mysteries of the god of the underworld, and that this upstart Gaililean god of his, the one he calls 'eternal' by employing a lie as a myth, has been stripped of any divinity Diodorus ascribes to him by virtue of his humiliating death and burial."[222] Julian's plan, then, was to demonstrate to the "base and ignorant creed-making fishermen" the folly of their ways. Libanius is even more direct: the purpose of the work, he said, "was to refute those writings which make a god and a son of God of the man from Palestine."[223]

---

220. Cf. Ep. XLVII.

221. Ep. LV, preserved in Latin fragments by Facundus Hermianensis (546?); cf. Neumann's partial reconstruction, Contra Christianos, p. 5. According to Sozomen 4.6, Photinus was tried, deposed, and banished by Constantius for his heretical views on the divinity of Christ, which seem to have run afoul of both the Nicene and Arian parties equally.

222. Ep. 55.

223. Libanius, Or. 18.178.

A modern biographer of Julian has suggested that in judging the merit of Julian's *Contra Galilaeos*, "we are in the position of a sailor who has to describe a boat sunk at some distance from the shore, with only the mast and a few other pieces of the rigging rising above the surface."[224] Byzantine Christianity had no interest in archiving the remains of the Church's most vicious opponents, and with the fifth century ban on anti-Christian teaching[225] the remaining copies of Julian's book, along with the polemical writings of Celsus and Porphyry, were destroyed or began to disappear. Julian's work is known to us, like the fragments of his anti-Christian predecessors, from the refutations of his opponents, mainly the *Against Julian* of Cyril of Alexandria (written around 440),[226] and a few quotations in the writings of Theodore of Mopsuestia, Aretas, and Jerome. Cyril's refutation ran to twenty books, of which ten have survived, together with "scraps" in the anthologies of later church writers. Cyril's surviving chapters deal almost exclusively with the first of Julian's three books against the Christians, with a very few quotations from book two being preserved in the anthologies. Not only has nothing survived of Julian's third book, but Cyril says that he has passed over "those passages injurious to Christ and repugnant to Christians." Cyril regarded the work of Julian especially threatening to Christian belief "and greatly to be feared" because "he alone was worthy of holy baptism and was trained in the holy scriptures." That Julian was baptized can be doubted; that he was passably versed in Christian and Hebrew scripture is beyond question. Indeed, Cyril's purpose in dredging up Julian's arguments against the Church nearly eighty years after the emperor's death was to show that despite his impressive command of the biblical writings and his rhetorical skill, "he did not understand what [the texts] meant": "[The pagans even in our day] reproach Christianity up and down, arraying Julian's writings against us, saying that they are beyond compare and saying that none of our [Christian teachers] has the skill to refute him."[227]

---

224. Ricciotti, *Julian the Apostate,* p. 231.

225. Presumably under Theodosius II in 448 CE. The ban was aimed chiefly at the works of Porphyry.

226. *Pro Christiana religione adversus Iulianum Imperatorem* (PG 76).

227. Adv. Jul. 76.809C.

Cyril's comment is evidence that even in the fifth century Julian was seen as a champion of the pagan cause, and feared as a potential threat to weak-minded Christians who might be swayed by the power of his rhetoric. The same fear accounts for the heavy-handed way in which Cyril edited out those passages "injurious to Christ and repugnant to Christians."

What can be claimed for the remnant is that it represents a bowdlerized selection of passages from the first of Julian's three books, enough to give us the thrust of his argument but not enough to permit us to form a judgment of the whole. If, as suspected, the subject matter of books two and three formed a more direct assault on Christian doctrine than the matter of book one, it is no wonder that the existence of Cyril's refutation itself was thought to be dangerous and that the refutation needed to be suppressed.

Despite suggestions that Julian was more attuned to the anti-Christian polemic of Porphyry than to that of Celsus, the general pattern followed by Julian reflects the argumentative approach of the earlier critic. The thesis is that Christianity has no connection with Judaism, a religion not to be admired for its practices but recognized for its antiquity. On the one hand the God of the Hebrews can be apprehended, at least, as a national god,[228] even though his partiality and jealousy make him less than the important gods of the Hellenic faith. Julian elsewhere pays what may be ironic tribute to the "most high God" of the Jews,[229] or he may simply, in this case, be citing the famous passage from Genesis 14.19–20—Melchizedek's blessing of Abraham in the name of *el Elyon*. However we are to understand Julian's vacillating understanding of the God of the Hebrews, he finds it a crime that the Christians have abandoned this deity and proclaimed a new revelation. Both the Jews and Christians err in thinking that God reveals himself in paltry ways—writing, prophecy, and magical tricks—when he can be known in the depths of the soul and through the order of nature. With Celsus, he finds it offensive that a god thought to be supreme would limit knowledge of himself to an insignificant tribe and race—the Hebrews first, the much inferior Christians thereafter.

---

228. CG 106E.
229. Ep LI.398A.

The direct purpose of the books against the Christians was to demonstrate that the Christian scriptures are a fable and to prove that there is no truth in the doctrine "that that fellow from Palestine is a god or a son of a god."[230] In short, the Christians had fallen into the error of worshiping a man as a god—a lapse scarcely to be defended even by reference to their own scripture, where only the evangelist—John—dared to call Jesus a god, and even he "did not do so clearly and distinctly."[231] By contrast, Paul, Matthew, Luke, and Mark say nothing about the divinity of Jesus, though Paul is "guilty" of being the first to entice the Greeks away from their ancestral faith.

Julian was aware that the Christian teachers of his day were fond of arguing their case on the basis of prophecy. Whereas Porphyry would claim that these prophecies were fulfillments of particular historical conditions and predictions applicable to their own day and region, Julian appeared to believe that the prophecies themselves were fables. He ascribes the belief that Jesus was a god to the followers of Jesus and not to Jesus himself; but in so doing, he does not find Jesus better than "the company of abject and ignorant apostles" who followed him. He finds no basis in scripture for teaching the divinity of Jesus, since "Moses taught that there is only one God. The belief that the Word was the first born-son of God is one of the ideas falsely constructed by you Christians later."[232]

The main points of the surviving portions of *Against the Galileans* can be summarized simply.

First, the God worshiped by the Jews is a tribal God, a fact Julian thinks is supported by a careful reading of their scripture. "The God of the Hebrews did not create the whole universe and has no sovereignty over the whole; his rule is limited and we must think of him as one god among the many."[233] Julian supports this point with the familiar Neoplatonic axiom that the God of All is not the "property" of a particular race, since to restrict his acts to a chosen people would also be an admission of his limitations. The human race possesses its knowl-

---

230. Libanius, Or. 18.178.
231. CG 213B; cf. 327A.
232. CG 290C.
233. CG 100C.

edge of God by nature—by a natural "yearning" for the divine—and not by teaching.[234] In this absurd notion of "particular revelation," Julian finds the Christians and Jews equally culpable, since the Hebrew idea was simply taken over by Paul ("of all magicians and deceivers the worst") and imposed on Christianity. Echoing Celsus,[235] Julian asks the Christians, in his role as prosecuting attorney, why God would limit his attention to Judaea rather than extending it to Greece and Rome: "[Why] to us no prophet, no anointing with oil, no teacher, no messenger to announce his love for man. . . . If he is god of all and creator of all, why did he neglect us?"[236]

Second, Julian hopes to profit from comparison, not simply from pointing out absurdities in Christian and Jewish teaching. He does this by contrasting the creation accounts of Genesis and the Platonic myth recorded in the Timaeus. It is not that the Greek myth is superior to the Hebrew myth, Julian maintains, but that the Jews and Christians fail to recognize the myth as an allegory, whereas the "Hellenes" are not content with the ridiculous picture of God and the universe that emerges if the accounts are taken literally. The story of the creation of man and woman in the Garden is especially perplexing to Julian, who finds it ridiculous that a god worthy of the name would create man and woman without the power of moral discrimination. Like certain Gnostics, Julian holds that the serpent must be regarded as the benefactor of the human race, since through him a knowledge of good and evil came into the world;[237] yet Christian teachers regard this knowledge as the source of evil. Julian sees such a god as morally irresponsible. In this section of the work can be found Julian's fundamental objection to Christian doctrine: it exalts obedience and suppresses the exercise of reason, making ignorance virtue and mindless submission the only source of happiness. For Julian the Genesis myth is "blasphemous" on three counts: first, in teaching that "the Woman who was created to be a helpmeet would be the cause of the fall," it makes ridiculous the idea of an all-knowing god. Second, it is a blasphemy against the Platonic

---

234. CG 52B; cf. 100A.
235. C. Cels. 4.7.
236. CG 106D.
237. CG 93D, 94A.

teaching that knowledge is the "principle" through which men become godlike by making knowledge a form of rebellion. Worst of all, it teaches that God is by nature envious and grudging, in teaching that the punishment for desiring immortality (the tree of life) is for the soul to be cut off from immortality and to become mortal. In every one of these ways Julian saw not only contradiction, but opposition between the Hebrew and Platonic cosmogony. The Hebrew God was petulant, fickle, jealous, grudging, and spiteful— qualities Julian says that we would abhor in a man, "but, in the Christian account, they are regarded as divine attributes.[238]

In the third place, Julian argues against the completeness of the Christian myth. The doctrine of the Neoplatonists saw the universe as a plenum, full of spiritual beings of every grade and variety. The Christians too, Julian says, believe in a "spirit," but they cannot make up their minds whether this being is "ungenerated" or "generated." He refers of course to the great theological debates of the post-Nicene period concerning the procession of the Holy Spirit. But he fails to find anything in the writings of Moses that would help them out of their dilemma, since the spirit Moses refers to does little more than "move upon the face of the waters." This points to another weakness in the Christian teaching about creation, since Moses teaches "that God is the creator of nothing incorporeal," in other words, is not the creator of spiritual beings but essentially the fashioner or organizer of preexisting material substances.[239] By contrast, Plato's description is full of references to the creation of invisible beings and the noetic principles that proceed from God—the intermediate grades between the unseen or intellectual world and the created order.

Fourth, Julian finds the teaching of the Christians incoherent. This is an old charge, dating from before the time of Celsus, but by Julian's day it had become clear that the more of Greek philosophy the Christian writers imbibed the more inconsistent their theological positions became. He finds it ludicrous that a man, born in

---

238. CG 155C. Julian's claim that in the Greek myths God "is never shown to be angry, resentful, wroth, oath-taking, fickle or turned from his purpose" (160D) is probably meant to be interpreted strictly in relation to the Timaeus.

239. CG 99C.

Palestine to a mortal woman and a carpenter, should be regarded as
the preexisting logos of God, a teaching attested by only one gospel,
and even there in a completely unconvincing way.[240] But even if it
could be maintained that Jesus was a god or the son of a god, "what
about other saviors—those worshiped by the Hellenes, including
Asclepius, Dionysus, and Heracles?" In some cases the incoherence
does not extend to soteriology but simply to etiology: the Christians
seem to take literally the wholly fabulous story of the tower of Babel
as an explanation of the variety of languages in the world;[241] but
they refuse to credit Homer's story of the Alodac (*Odyssey* 11.316),
who tried to scale heaven by setting three mountains one upon the
other. Why should one myth be preferred to another, when both tell
the same tale?[242] It is clear, Julian argues, that the Christians have
abandoned the Hellenic faith and adopted certain teachings of the
Jews.[243] But here too they are vulnerable to the charge of incoherence, for while they twist and turn the prophecies of the Hebrews to
suit their own ends, they reject some of the "praiseworthy" customs
of the Jews such as the offering of sacrifice—a tradition Julian ostensibly wished to restore to the Jews through the rebuilding of the
Temple, while in the process invalidating the Christian prophecy
ascribed to Jesus, "No stone [of the temple] will be left standing on
another" (Mark 13.2). It is a double apostasy of the Christians, as
Julian sees it, first to reject the myths of the Greeks and then to rebel
against the religion of the Jews.

Julian cites a number of passages to point up the inconsistency
of Christian interpretation of Hebrew prophecy. Moses taught that
all humankind should worship one God; the Christians have made
Jesus into another god.[244] The Jews possess the prophecy that "a

---

240. CG 213B.

241. CG 134D.

242. The myth of the giants is preserved in the story of the *nephilim* in Gen.
6.1–4, which has been conjoined to the story of the flood and its aftermath
(6.5–10.32). The story of the tower "resumes" the narrative of human challenges to
God by providing an aetiology for learning to use bricks in place of stone for the
construction of temples.

243. CG 235D; 207D.

244. CG 253C.

young woman shall conceive and bear a child" (Isaiah 7.14), but there is nothing unusual about this. The Christian translation of the passage, "A virgin shall conceive and bear a son," had been used since Matthew's day to underscore the extraordinary event of Jesus' birth. But applying his own brand of literal exegesis to the passage, Julian argues that it says nothing about a "god" being born of a virgin or the "firstborn of creation" being born of a young woman.[245] So too, the prophecy of Deuteronomy 18.15–16, "The Lord God shall raise up a prophet like me," ascribed to Moses[246] and applied to Jesus does not suggest that the prophet will be divine. Then there are the references to Jesus' links to the House of David which ceased to exist in the time of Zedekiah: how, Julian wonders, can this be relevant to Jesus when "[their books teach] that he was not born of Joseph but of the Holy Spirit?"[247] Jesus did not come from Judaea, Julian reminds his opponents, and the genealogies of the gospels disagree and do not establish a coherent family pedigree for him.[248]

A final area of concern for Julian is the fact that Christians, who make so much of obedience to the will of God, disobey the tradition that brought them into existence. Christians boast of abolishing the law or being set free from the requirements of the law. Does this make them good Greeks or bad Jews?[249] He stresses that the law of Moses was supposed to last for all time, and cites Deuteronomy 4.2 (also cited by Jesus in Matthew 5.17–20) to show that nothing could be added or subtracted from the law.[250] Yet the Christians neglected the practice of circumcision, and defend their negligence by invoking Paul's view that it was a circumcision of the heart and not the flesh that was given to Abraham as a covenant. Julian has little use for this strategy; as he sees it, this is a simple case of Paul playing the charlatan to win converts from among the Greeks. It is also proof that Jesus himself was relatively closer to the Jewish position on the ques-

---

245. CG 262D; in this section Julian also shows some awareness of arguments over the status of Mary.
246. Acts 7.37.
247. CG 253C, 261C.
248. CG 261C.
249. CG 305D.
250. CG 320A.

tion, since he had said himself, "Whoever relaxes one of these commandments and teaches others to do so shall be called least in the kingdom of heaven."[251] A related issue is the Christian intolerance of sacrifice. Here Julian will argue that the Jews continue to sacrifice in the privacy of their homes and in symbolic ways, by eating consecrated meats, praying, and "giving the shoulder [of the lamb] to the priests as the first fruits." Julian is aware of the technical impediment to the older sacrificial practices, namely the destruction of the Temple,[252] but the Christians do not sacrifice because they are in active rebellion against the Jewish law and tradition; they have "invented a new sacrifice which does not need Jerusalem."[253] Their practice has no claim to validity because it is not grounded in antiquity, whereas the Greeks, at least, "have temples, sanctuaries, altars, purifications and precepts," making Judaism and Greek religion closer to each other than either is to Christianity. Julian's argument was intended to be painfully clear: religion is defined by adherence to ancient tradition. The true Hellenic faith demands such adherence, as does the law of Moses. Consequently, the true Greek will offer sacrifice and worship the gods; the Jew will obey the law of Moses. The Galileans repudiate both and thus have no claim to legitimacy.

*   *   *

While the effect of Julian's work is difficult to assess, the emperor himself probably assumed it would have a devastating impact on the Christians. There is some reason to think, judging from contemporary references, that its immediate influence was on those who supported Julian's political and religious ideas and programs. Libanius knew the work, and the heretic Photinus had probably read it. With the accession of Julian's Christian successors and the general malaise that greeted the pagan cause thereafter, Christian intellectuals developed a greater interest in the treatise and seem to have used the work as a compendium of accusations against the Church. Theodore of

---

251. Matt. 5.10.

252. CG 306B.

253. CG 306B. Julian does not seem to associate the Eucharistic celebration, if that is the intended reference here, to Jewish Passover ritual.

Mopsuestia and Philip Sideta composed refutations, both lost, as did
Cyril, who decided on a response following renewed pagan hostility
against Christians in Alexandria in the early fifth century. It comes as
some surprise that neither Basil of Caesarea nor Julian's schoolmate,
Gregory Naziazen, mention the work in their invectives against
Julian, nor is it mentioned by western theologians.

It is easy to lose sight of the fact that Julian's literary attack on
Christianity was only one part of his larger program to restore the
cults and breathe new life into a dying, or rather suffocating, tradition. His personal example in this regard was energetic and impressive: he is celebrated by Libanius as someone who has never neglected his religious duty, but has taken the gods as allies in the cause:
"Hermes, Pan, Demeter, Ares, Calliope, Apollo, the Zeus of the
Mountain and the Zeus of the City."[254] With so many friends and
allies among the gods, Julian scarcely needed the Palestinian carpenter to complete the side. His idea of restoration was as comprehensive as the creed of the fishermen was exclusive.[255] As the Christian church had become the locus for a shrinking vision of divine
revelation and the divine presence, Julian's world was fully inhabited: "[It] was full of ever-present helpers, manifest gods, and they
lived in the cities' temples as much as in the caverns of the theurgists.
They had been neglected. . . . Temples had closed and oracles had
failed; to restore them was his duty to the Empire and the gods."[256]
For Julian, this was a tragedy in which the Christians were complicit:
their refusal to worship the ancestral gods was clear; their tendency
to cause social unrest—to profit from religious confusion—was also
clear. If the Galileans could not be corrected through reasonable
argument or the acceptance of "true paideia" perhaps they would
succumb to ridicule; thus the strident and prosecutorial tone of his
writing. For all that, it is not clear that the *Contra Galilaeos* shows
Julian at his best. Like the Christian apologists or the invectives of
his more famous predecessors, Celsus and Porphyry, Julian is determined to win his case without subtlety. Unlike Porphyry, he has

---

254. Libanius, Or 12.87, 91; cf. 15.79.
255. See Smith's excellent summary, *Julian's Gods,* pp. 215–17.
256. Ibid., pp. 217–18.

nothing at all good to say about Jesus; unlike Celsus, he is unwilling to grant his opponents even a notional foothold in Judaism. He seems to have been sensible of the fact that the battleground on which he fought was a different one and that the methods he used against the church needed to be rhetorically unsparing. The result is a hodgepodge of accusations, specious arguments, sarcasm, unargued propositions, adventitious allusion, and special pleading—all quite normal in the religious debates of the third and fourth century, and not only in pagan-Christian interchange, but in Christian attacks on the heresies as well. Tertullian's contempt for Marcion and Irenaeus's hatred of the Gnostics are rhetorical cousins of Julian's narrative assault on Christian teaching. What "heresy" was for the Church's apologists, Christianity was for Julian. To tolerate it would be the death of faith, the leveling of Olympus, the plunging of the halls of heavenly light into the stygian gloom.[257]

---

257. Cf. Eunapius, frag. 28.

A NOTE ON TEXT
AND TRANSLATION

The earliest independent reference to the *Contra Galilaeos* is Libanius's comment (Or. 18.178) that in his books "Julian has made the doctrine of the Christians look ridiculous." The Council of Ephesus meeting in 431 does not mention Julian's work but condemns Porphyry's to be burned, and an order of Theodosius II dated 448 similarly condemns the works of Porphyry without alluding to Julian. An edict of Justinian in 559 envisages a more comprehensive destruction of anti-Christian books, but here again only Porphyry is named. The invective of Gregory Naziazen already discussed[258] may have relied on a knowledge of the *Contra Galilaeos*, but does not name or quote the treatise. Cyril's refutation, written perhaps between 429 and 441, was provoked by a resurgence of pagan activity in Alexandria and by a worry that the earlier antagonists of Julian had been, by his reckoning, heretics themselves.[259] It cannot be known how widely circulated the treatise was, but judging from the measures taken by Julian's successor Jovian beginning in 364 to reestablish religious toleration, there is no reason to think that the work was equally well known in all parts of the empire. It cannot have been as widely known as Porphyry's work, and its prominence in Alexandria should be explained in the context of local political and religious tensions.

---

258. See note 219 above.
259. He seems to have Theodore of Mopsuestia and Philip Sideta in view.

The letters of Julian were collected and published before the end of the fourth century; Eunapius (346–414) knew them and used them in writing his history.[260] Among pagan collectors, Libanius, Aristophanes of Corinth, and Zosimus (450–501) had key roles to play in the preservation of the epistles and in deciding which were safe for keeping. It is likely that the church historians Socrates, writing in Constantinople ca. 440, and his contemporary Sozomen, who quotes from ten letters and mentions fourteen that have not survived, possessed a "mixed" collection of Julian's writings. We would doubtless have a fuller vision of Julian's view of Christianity if certain letters had not been suppressed by their owners, as being too dangerous for circulation in the religious environment of the fifth century. Others doubtless were destroyed by Christians who would have regarded them as disrespectful to Christianity. By the same logic, certain letters (e.g., Ep. XLI) would have been preserved as showing Julian in a bad light (Ep. LXXXI, a forgery) or as an imitator of Christian practice (e.g., Ep. XX). Because some letters were mutilated, others expanded, others preserved in handbooks as models of the epistolary style, the question of authenticity has been a constant feature in Julian scholarship.

The modern collection of Julian's letters begins with the 1696 Leipzig edition of Spanheim (Latin translation) which also included the *Contra Iulianum* of Cyril. The canon of letters expanded from an original inventory of 48 in 1499 (the Venetian corpus) to 63 by 1630 (the Paris corpus of Martinius, Rigalt, and Petau). The more recent editions of Julian's complete works are those of F. C. Hertlein (Leipzig, 1875–1876) and J. Bidez, Rochefort, and Lacombrade (Paris, 1924–64). The partial reconstruction of the *Contra Galilaeos* by K. J. Neumann (*Contra Christianos*, Leipzig, 1880)[261] which sup-

260. See R. Blockley in *Fragmentary Classicizing Historians of the Later Roman Empire* I and II (Liverpool, 1981–83).

261. *Juliani imp. Librorum contra christianos quae supersunt.* Neumann's textual commentary is included in the Latin prolegomena. Amendments are provided by Gollwitzer, *Observationes criticae* (Erlangen, 1886) and by Asmus, *Julians Galiläerschrift* (Freiburg, 1904). See also the occasional corrections provided in W. C. Wright, *The Works of the Emperor Julian*, 3 vols. (London, 1913–23), and E. Masaracchia, *Giuliano imperatore Contra Galilaeos* (Rome, 1991). Neumann's choice of title is inexplicable, considering Julian's consistent use of the more disparaging term.

ports the present translation relied on Spanheim's pagination. Textual numeration in this translation of the *Contra Galilaeos* refers to that edition. References to the letters and orations of Julian appear according to Hertlein's standard pagination in his edition of the complete works. In cases where the Greek is uncertain or where a hypothetical reconstruction is warranted to complete the sense of a statement, insertion brackets < > have been used.

In the critical notes I have followed the standard practice, unless otherwise dictated by context, of referring to the works of Julian by citing only the source (thus, Or.VII.161 or Ep. XXII.356B). References follow the Loeb edition numeration, for ease of reference, with cross reference, in the case of the letters, to Hertlein. The edition of the letters edited by Bidez and Cumont (*Epistulae, leges, poematia, fragmenta varia*, Paris, 1922) is the standard for questions of textual accuracy.

R. Joseph Hoffmann

JULIAN'S *AGAINST THE GALILEANS*

39A–42E:[262]

Themes time has come for me to say for the benefit of all how I discovered beyond any doubt that the stories of the Galileans[263] are the inventions[264] of deceivers and tricksters. For these men seduce people into thinking that <their> gruesome story is the truth by appealing to the part of the soul that loves what is simple and childish.[265]

I propose therefore to deal with what they consider their primary teachings. And I should say at the start that if my readers wish to refute me, the way to do so is to proceed as though this were a case at law. Moreover, as it is their views that are on trial, their countercharges (and whatever other trivialities they may wish to raise) must wait until they have defended themselves. It will be best all

---

262. Marginal numbers in the English text refer indicatively to the pagination of Spanheim's 1696 edition of Cyril of Alexandria's polemic against Julian, *Pro Christiana religione*, as rearranged by Neumann in his 1880 reconstruction of Julian's treatise.

263. Γαλιλαῖοι: Julian's, like Epictetus's, designation for the Christians is designed to stress the insignificance of the founder. See Gregory Naziazen, Or. IV. 76 (115).

264. Here σκευωρία, the equivalent of κατασκεύασμα, implying malicious design.

265. See Paul, 1 Cor. 13.10–12.

round if they hold their fire until they have answered for themselves:
So, for the present, let us leave these countercharges[266] to one side.
   43A–52C

The best way forward is this: First, to consider briefly how we
came to have a conception of God. Then, to compare what Greeks
and Hebrews have to say about the divine being; and finally, to ask
those "who are neither Jews nor Greek,"[267] namely the Galileans,
why they chose the belief of the Jews above our own, only to
abandon Jewish belief to follow that strange path of theirs.

<These Galileans> have accepted not a single admirable or
important belief from those that we Greeks hold; <nor any> from
those imparted by Moses to the Hebrews.[268] They have instead taken
on the mold that has grown up around these nations like powers of
evil—denial of the gods[269] from Jewish recklessness;[270] <and from
us> laziness and superstition as a consequence of our way of life.[271]
This, they say, should be considered the most excellent way of
revering the gods.[272]

---

266. While it is not clear what Julian may mean by the term ἀντικατηγορεῖν,
he alludes to the general pattern of Christian polemic against pagan practices.

267. Οὔτε ῞Ελληνος οὔτε Ἰουδαῖος. 1 Cor. 24. In the *Ad Nationes* Tertullian
rehearses a number of derogatory names for the Christians originating in pagan circles, including the designation "third race": "If you attach any meaning to these
names, tell us what are the first and second races so that we can know something
of this 'third'" (*Ad Nat.* 1.8). Julian's polemic harkens back to the charge common
in Diocletian's time: that Christians were officially stateless persons and thus lacked
an ἔθνος.

268. On the ambiguity of the origins of Christian beliefs, see Celsus, *C.Cels.* V.33.

269. ἀθέστης: see Tertullian, *Apology* 10.

270. Julian's complaint is repeated in the *rescriptus* on Christian teachers,
written from Antioch in 362. On the tradition that Julian assisted the Jews materi-
ally in the rebuilding of the Temple in recognition of Yahweh's stature as a tutleary
God: Amm., 23.1.2.

271. In addition to Julian's own defense of his asceticism in the *Misopogon*,
Libanius in the *Epitaphios Iuliano* comments on austerity measures introduced in the
imperial court, which included the expulsion of barbers, cupbearers, cooks, and
jugglers. So, too, Amm., 22.4.2–5; 23. Even Christian historians such as Socrates
(HE III.53) were approving of Julian's correction of "dissolute morals" while
deploring his policy toward the Christians. See further the discussion in P. Athanassiadi, *Julian: An Intellectual Biography* (London, 1992), p. 97 and note 40.

272. θεοσέβεια.

It is not by teaching[273] but by nature that humanity possesses its knowledge of God, as can be shown by the common yearning for the divine that exists in everyone, everywhere—individuals, communities, and nations.[274] Without having it taught to us, all of us have come to believe in some sort of divinity, even though it is difficult for all to know what divinity truly is and far from easy for those who do know to explain it to the rest.

Besides this notion of divinity which all people seem to have in common, there is another: all of us are naturally dependent on the heavens and the gods that appear there, so much so that even if someone imagines a god beyond these he invariably assigns him a place in the heavens. In so doing he is not separating him from the earth but elevating him to "kingship of the All"[275] in the heavens as being the position of honor; and he thinks of him as seeing from <heaven> all that happens in the world.

What is the use of calling Hebrews and Greeks as witnesses to this? Is there anyone who does not stretch his hand toward the heavens when he prays? Whether he professes one or many gods, if he has any idea of the divine, he looks to heaven. This is natural, this feeling that men have, because in the heavenly sphere they see stability and order, unchanged and undiminished. <They see> harmonious movement unaffected by discord—the regularity of the illuminations of the moon or of the rising and setting of the sun, completely regular and in accordance with definite seasons of the years.[276] And so naturally they considered that heaven was a god, indeed, the throne of a god.

A being of the sort they conceive is <likewise> free from change, decay, alteration; not subject to increase by having something added

---

273. διδακτός: He does not mean to imply Christian revelation but the interpretations of Christian teachers.

274. Julian's acceptance of this trademark Neoplatonic idea is attested by Firmicus Maternus, *De errore* VII–VIII. Julian argues the essential unity of Hellenistic religion on the basis of the dispersal of the divine logoi and innate apprehension of the divine. In Ep. XLVII.434C, D, Julian argues that the true logos—the living, animate, and beneficent image of the intelligible father—is Helios. Cf. Or. IV.133C.

275. Cf. Plotinus, VIII *Ennead* 17. A faint echo can be found in Eph. 4.5–8.

276. II *Ennead* 3.5.

to it, or to decrease by having something taken away; beyond every impurity, every possibility of stain.[277]

This all-moving being is eternal, as we comprehend it: traveling in circuit around the majestic creator, perhaps motivated by a sublime and rarefied soul existing within <it>, as our bodies are animated by the soul existing within us; or perhaps receiving its motion from God himself as it moves in unstopping spiral through its unending course.[278]

44A: Of course, the Greeks concocted their stories about the gods, those incredible and terrible fables. They held, for instance, that Kronos swallowed his children and then vomited them out.[279] They told tales of illicit couplings, Zeus bedding his own mother, having a child by her, marrying—rather, not marrying her, but lying with her and then handing her over to someone else. There is a story about how Dionysus was torn in two and his body reassembled again.[280] And this is the sort of thing we get from the myths of the Greeks.

75A: Compare with this the Jewish teaching:

A garden was planted by God, and Adam was made, and afterward, for the sake of Adam, woman was created. God said, It is not good for a man to be alone; let us then make a helper resembling him.[281] And yet, she was no help at all. She deceived him and caused the fall from a life of pleasure in the garden.[282]

75B: This is complete fable. Is it likely that God would not know that a creature designed to be a helper would be a curse rather than a blessing to the one who accepted her? And then—what language

---

277. V *Ennead* 8.11.

278. Plotinus had maintained that the existence of souls in diversity was educed from the primal unity of the soul: IV *Ennead* 9.3–5.

279. Hesiod *Theogony*, 453ff.; Apollodorus, I.4ff.

280. Dionysus, in a poem by Nonnos, is identified with Osiris. In the ancient tradition known to Euripides (*Alcestis*), it is Pentheus who is torn to pieces for spying on the votaries of the god.

281. Gen. 2.18ff.

282. Because Julian wishes to stress a resemblance between Greek myth and Hebrew fable, he sees the story of the fall as a repetition of the Pandora-Prometheus story (Hesiod *Theog.* 535–70). He sees Eve ("all mother") as equivalent in deceit to Pandora ("all-gifts"), though he stops short of saying that Eve was sent deliberately by the gods to foil the progress of the human race.

would the serpent have used when speaking to Eve? 86A: Was it the language spoken by human beings?

Furthermore, how do fables of this sort differ from the myths made up by the Greeks? Is it not extremely odd, for example, that God refused to the beings he created the power to tell the difference between good and evil? Can anyone imagine anything more absurd than such a being, one unable to tell what is acceptable from what is wicked? It should have been evident that <left to himself> man would not avoid the latter, I mean evil things, nor pursue the former, I mean good things. The heart of the matter is that God refused to let man taste of wisdom,[283] even though nothing could be more important to mankind.

89B Even the fool recognizes that wisdom includes the power to tell the difference between the good and what is less good, and so considered it emerges that the serpent <was really acting as> benefactor of the human race.[284] Moreover: their God is to be called malignant,[285] for when he perceived that man had obtained a bit of the wisdom he once had been denied, and to prevent him tasting the tree of life, God casts him out of the garden saying something like, "Aha! Adam has become just like us, knowing good from bad; forbid him to stretch out his hand and take from the tree of life, eat from it, and thus live forever."[286]

94A: Hence, if it is not the case that every one of these tales possesses some secret meaning, as I think must be the case, then they are full of blasphemy against God. First, in suggesting <God's> ignorance, that the one made to be a helper would be the cause of calamity; second, to withhold from mankind the very knowledge which might have made his mind complete; then to be jealous lest man eat from the tree of life and turn from mortal to immortal: this would be petulant envy of the worst kind.

96C:

---

283. Gen. 2.16–17.
284. This platonizing interpretation of the serpent's activity is also a feature of certain gnostic exegesis; cf., for example, the Testimony of Truth, IX.3147: 14–30; 48.4–13; 50.3–5.
285 βάσκατος or jealous.
286. Gen. 3.22.

I turn now to consider the true opinions of the Jews and the ideas handed on to us <Greeks> from the beginning by our fathers. <Whereas> our account[287] specifies an immediate creator of this universe, Moses says nothing at all about gods who may be superior to this creator. 96D Nor has he anything to say about the nature of angels. Even though it is often said, in various ways, that they serve God, it is not clear from what he says whether <angels> are begotten or unbegotten, or begotten[288] through one god and made to serve another, or something still different. <Moses> does tell us clearly how heaven and earth and their contents were ordered: he says, for instance, that God commanded things such as light and the firmament to be; and again, he says God fashioned certain things—the heavens, the earth, sun and moon—and that things which already existed but had been buried such as dry land was then separated from <encircling> water.

Beyond this <Moses> says nothing about the begetting or making of a spirit, merely that "the spirit of God moved above the face of the waters," but nothing at all about the nature of this spirit, whether generated or ungenerated.

49A Compare if you will the statements of Plato,[289] namely what he says about the creator at the time of creation of the world,[290] and see how it fits the picture of creation painted by Moses. In this way we can judge whose conception is nobler: 49B Plato, who did justice to the eternal images, or Moses, of whom it is written that God spoke to him face to face.[291]

"In the beginning God created the heavens and the earth. And the earth was unseen and without a form; and over the face of the abyss, darkness was. And over the face of the abyss God's spirit

---

287. There is an amount missing from Cyril's discussion at this point, no doubt a reference to the Platonic cosmogony in the Timaeus.

288. εἴτε δὲ γεγονότες εἴτε ἀγένητοι. Julian has in view the silence of Hebrew scriptures on the question of whether the spirit of God is begotten or unbegotten. His general view was that Christian theology was lost in unproductive theological controversies which were insupportable in scripture.

289. See Julian, Ep. XIX and Or. IV. The doctrine quoted is a paraphrase of Timaeus 41, A, B.

290. κοσμογενεία.

291. Num. 12.8; Exod. 33.11.

moved. And God said, let there be light, and there was light. And God saw the light was good; and God divided the light from darkness. And God called the light Day and darkness he called Night. And the Evening and morning were the first day.

"And God said, let there be a vault in the middle of the waters. 49C<> And God called the vault heaven. And God said, let the waters under heaven be gathered into one place, and let dry land appear; and it happened. And God said let the earth bring grass for feed and fruit tress bearing fruit. And God said Let there be lights in the vault of heaven to illuminate the earth. So God set them in the vault of heaven to govern the day and the night."[292]

In no place does Moses say that the abyss was created by God, nor the darkness, nor the waters. 49E And yet it would seem that after ordering the light to be, and after it was, <Moses> ought to say something of the night and also of the abyss or the waters. But even though he often refers to them, <Moses> says nothing to avoid the impression that they already existed. Nor does he describe the birth or fashioning of the angels or how they were brought into being: he treats only the created things in heaven and on earth. As Moses tells the tale, God is creator of nothing *without* a body; he merely organizes and shapes the stuff that already exists—since the words "And the earth was unseen and without form"[293] must mean that <God> thought of wet and dry stuff as original matter, and <this means> that God is simply the shaper of this matter.

57B–C But Plato must be heard concerning the universe:

"Now the whole of heaven or the universe—or whatever other name it may be appropriate to call it (for so should we name it)— did it exist eternally? did it have no beginning? <Did it have> no point of origin?—or does it indeed have a beginning? It had a beginning. It is seen, manipulated, has a body, and like all objects known to the senses and made perceptible to us through sensation, being those which had a beginning <the universe too> has come into

---

292. Gen. 1.1–17; abbreviated.

293. ἀόρατος καὶ ἀκατασκεύατος. Julian's point is that the Hebrew myth incorporates an older mythology, in which preëxistent matter is shaped by the demiurge. God is the molder of material things that come into being through him.

being, and thus as we can see, had a beginning.[294] Logic dictates that this universe came into being, just as a living creature does: ensouled and truly full of intelligence through the foreknowledge of God."

57D–E We only need to compare <these accounts> point for point: What kind of speech does the god of Moses make? And what does the god of Plato say?

58A: "And God said, let us make man in our image and likeness. And let <them> have governance over the fish in the sea and the birds in the air, over cattle, and everything on earth and every thing that crawls upon the earth. So God created man. In the image of God he created him. Male and female he created them. And he said, Be fertile, multiply, and stock the earth and subdue it. 58B Take command over the fish of the sea, the birds in the air, over the cattle, and over the earth.[295]

Listen now to the words which Plato attributes to the demiurge:

"Gods of gods—What things of which I am the fashioner and father will endure unchanged and indestructible forever, so long as it is my will. Observe, everything that has been established can be uprooted. But to will to uproot what is soundly planted and harmonious: that is the work of an evil being. And so, since you have been brought into being, you are not altogether indissoluble nor immortal. 58C But you have found through my will something stronger to establish you than when you first came to be; accordingly, you will not, by any means, be uprooted or undergo death. Listen now to the word that I say to you: Three sorts of mortal beings are yet unborn: and the heaven is incomplete unless they are given birth, as <heaven> would not <then> have within itself all kinds of living things. If these, however, come into being to receive a share of the life that is in my power to bestow, they should become equal to gods. And so, that they may be mortal, and that the All may truly be All, busy yourself with the fashioning of living things according to your nature. Imitate the power that I demonstrated in fashioning you. 58D And the part of them suited to receive the same name as the immortal beings—that which is called divine and beckons to those who follow you in the ways of justice—this power which I have sown and begun, I will deliver to

---

294. Plato, *Timaeus* 30A.
295. Gen. 1.26–28 (LXX).

you. As for the others, in fashioning the blend of mortal and immortal, create living beings and give them birth, support and increase,
receiving them back again when they perish."[296]

65A–B But before considering whether this <narrative> is purely
a fable, learn something of what it means.

Plato calls those things which are visible <by the name of> gods:
sun, moon, the stars, and the heavens—but <he regards them>
merely as images of the invisible gods. The sun which we see with
our eyes is a likeness of the intellectual principle, the invisible sun;
and so the moon we see with our eyes, and the stars: these are likenesses of the intelligible. Clearly Plato knows of intelligible and
unseen gods who are immanent within and exist alongside the creator, and proceeded or originated from the creator himself.

Accordingly the creator in Plato's narrative speaks of "gods" when
he means invisible beings, and when he means the visible gods he
speaks, apparently, <about that which comes> "of-gods." And the creator of both is the one who made heavens and earth and the sea and
stars and begot archetypes of these within the intelligible world.

Notice the excellent saying which follows this:

"There are <yet> three kinds of mortal things," namely, human
beings, animals, and plants, and to each of these he gives its own
particular definition. 65D "Now if each one of these," he continues,"
should come to exist through me, it would be, through necessity,
immortal." And it is certain that in the case of the intelligible gods
and the visible world, the cause of their immortality is solely to be
sought in the fact that they were brought into being by the creator.
So, when he says, "The part of these which is immortal must be
given to them by the creator," he refers to the reasoning soul. 65E
"For the rest, blend immortal with mortal." It is clear, therefore, that
the creating gods [297] got from their father the creative power <which
gives us> all living, mortal things on the earth. For if there were no
difference between heavens, man, and animals, by God, right down
to the little colonies of crawling things and fish that swim in the sea,
then there would surely have had to be one single creator for all of

---

296. Plato, *Timaeus* 41A–C.
297. οἱ δημιουργικοὶ θεοί.

them. But <as it is>, there is a great divide between immortals and mortals. And this cannot become either greater through adding to it nor less by taking something away; nor can it be combined with what is mortal and hence subject to fate; 66A and so it follows that the group of gods who were responsible for mortals is different from the group of gods who were the cause of immortal beings.

Now, as Moses seems to have failed to give a thorough rendering of the creator of the universe, let us compare further the opinion of the Hebrews and the views of our <true> fathers concerning the two nations. 99E Moses says that the shaper of the universe selected the Hebrew people, indeed <says> that only to this people did he show care and concern, and he takes responsibility only for it. Where other nations are concerned, and by what sort of gods they are ruled, he says nothing—that is, unless we take the sun and moon[298] as their allocation. But more of that a bit later: 100A Here I want only to suggest that Moses himself and the prophets after him, and the Nazarene Jesus, and that magician and deceiver, surpassing all others of every place and time, Paul <all these> say that he is the God of Israel and Judaea alone and that the Jews are his chosen people.

Listen to their very words, first of all to those of Moses:

You will say to Pharaoh: Israel is my son, my firstborn. And I have said to you: Let my people go in order that they might serve me. But you refused to let them go.[299]

100B And further on:

And they <said> to him: The God of the Hebrews has summoned us. Therefore we will go three days' journey into the desert to sacrifice to the Lord our God. [300]

He soon speaks again in a similar vein:

The Lord God of the Hebrews sent me to you to say, Let my people go, in order to serve me in the wilderness.[301]

---

298. Deut. 4.19.

299. Exod. 4.22.

300. Exod. 4.23.

301. Exod. 5.3. Missing from Cyril's text are the words of the prophets and Jesus promised by Julian. While Paul's religious exclusivism is undermined by specific passages (e.g., Rom. 11.1–11), Julian may have been less taken with the structure of Paul's argument than with specific passages showing Paul's debts to Judaism as in Rom. 11.2. Similarly, Jesus' words in Matt. 6.31 or 8.4.

106A, B Moreover, that God from the start cared only for the Jews and chose them for his own has been clearly stated not only by Moses and by Jesus but also by Paul, albeit it is an odd thing coming from him. He changes his ideas about God according to his situation—just as a polypus changes its colors to match the rocks.[302] So that here we find him saying the Jews alone are God's, and here in an effort to get the Greeks to join sides with him, saying "Don't think he is the God of the Jews alone, but the God of the gentiles also."[303]

106C Thus we are justified in asking Paul why God, if <he is>the God of the gentiles and not only of the Jews, <would send> the sacred gift of prophecy to the Jews in a bounty, as well as Moses and the chrism [consecrated oil] and the prophets and the Law—along with their puzzling and banal myths.

For you hear them crying, "Man eats the food of angels."[304]

At last God sends Jesus to them as well: but to us <Greeks> he sends no prophet, no chrism, no teacher, nor any messenger to announce 106D <God's> philanthropy which, though it come late, would someday extend even to us. Even so, he stood by for innumerable, or if you'd rather, thousands of years, <during which time> mankind in its ignorance served idols, to use your expression; and from where the sun rises to where he sets, and north to south in its compass <God saw> only the tiny tribe which had settled some two thousands years previously in a corner of Palestine.

Yet, if he *is* the God of all alike, the shaper of everything, why did he overlook us? 100C Is it not preferable to think that the God of the

---

302. Theognis; cf. *Misopogon* 349D.

303. Rom. 3.29 and Gal. 3.28.

304. Psalm 78.25: [ἀκούεις γὰρ αὐτῶν βοώντων], ἄρτον ἀγγέλων ἔφαγεν ἄνθρωπος: Literally in Hebrew, "bread of the mighty ones." Julian perhaps has in view the whole myth envisaged in Psalm 78, whereby God takes pity on the tribes in the desert by opening the doors of heaven (a phrase found only in 78.23) and providing manna (cf. Exod. 16.1–36; Num. 11.1–35). It is called "bread of angels" only here in the Old Testament. Early Christian exegetes doubted on the basis of Mark 12.25 whether there was eating and drinking among the angels; cf. G. F. Moore, *Judaism* (Cambridge, MA, 1927), 1:405. The Christian fathers referred to the eucharist as the angelic bread or bread of angels in conjunction with John 6.50, 58; see John Chrysostom, *Commentarius in sanctum Ioannem apostolum et evangelistam*, Hom. 46. It is not clear whether Julian means to imply that the Christians echo the Jews with this cry, or refers simply to Jewish claims on behalf of their status.

Hebrews is not maker of the whole cosmos with power over it all, but only, as I have suggested, a god of the limits, whose dominion is bounded on all sides 106D–E—a god who should be thought of as one of a club of other gods?[305] Or are we to pay special attention to you because you or one of your kind thus pictured the God of the universe, even though your picture is only the vaguest hint of him? Is this not pure partiality? God is a jealous God,[306] you say—but <of what has he> to be jealous, so much that he settles the score for the sins of the fathers with their children?[307]

115D But regard now what we teach in opposition to your doctrine. Our authorities maintain that the fashioner <of the universe> is both the common father and lord of all that exists, while the gods of nations and the gods who protect cities have been delegated specific responsibilities by him. Each has been given a role to play in strict accordance with his character. 115E. So it is that in the father all things are complete and the all is unified, while in the distribution of gods one trait or another <tends to be> dominant: so Ares rules contentious nations; Athena those who are wise as much as warlike; Hermes those that are more cunning than daring; and, to be brief, each nation ruled by a god exhibits the character of its own god. If common experience is not adequate witness to the truth of our teachings, we will allow that ours are the fictitious traditions and the wrong doctrines and, if so, 116A that we really ought to be persuaded and embrace the teachings you hold to be true. But if the evidence is on our side, and if history teaches through experience that our account is the true one, and does not support your accounts, why continue this endless game of make-believe?

Here, tell me why it is that the Celts and Germans are violent while Greeks and Romans for the most part are humane <in their

---

305. ἄλλοις νοεῖσθαι θεοῖς: be conceived as one among other gods.

306. Θεὸς ζηλωτής.

307. Exod. 20.5. The principle of vengeance is particularly alien to Julian's platonic conception of the divine artificer and is strictly speaking "incomprehensible" within his system: see Plato, *Timaeus* 27, 28, and esp. 29b: The creator makes the world of generation because he is good, "and the good can never have jealousy." The implicit point of Julian's play on this theme is that jealousy requires a rival and the use of the term in reference to God is tantamount to an admission that the Hebrew God shares power with other gods.

laws> and political life, even if courageous in waging war. Or <why is it that> the Egyptians are clever at crafts while the Syrians are womanish, hot-tempered, quick to learn, and quick to flee from danger? 116B If you maintain that there is no good reason for these differences among peoples, or that <though the differences exist> they occur by dint of chance, how then will you maintain that the universe is governed by a foreknowing power?[308]

If, however, anyone should say that reasons exist for these differences, then let that person explain them to me and teach me in the name of the creator himself. 131B As for the laws of men, these obviously have been created by men in conformity with their natural inclinations.[309] 131C I mean to say that civil and moral laws were established by those in whom civilized instincts were dominant above other instincts, <while> those of a different inclination fashioned vicious and inhuman laws. And the shapers of laws have scarcely been successful in shaping the characters of men or improving by law what is <inherent in> their essential disposition. So it was that the Scythians refused to accept the religious rantings of the possessed Anacharsis.[310] Nor will you find that Gauls and Iberians have any knack for geometry or philosophy or pursuits of <an intellectual> kind, fields in which the Roman hegemony has long been established. 131D Likewise, those whose gifts are for discussion and argument refrain from studying anything else: so decisive is nature's power over us, it appears.

And where do these differences of character and of laws originate?[311] 134D Moses for his part gives a preposterous explanation for differ-

---

308. Προνοία. Julian repeats the conventional wisdom concerning the character of nations; cf. Herod. 4.76; Lucian, *Anacharsis*, and Julian, *Misopogon* 359B.

309. φύσις οἰκείνους.

310. Julian refers to a story told by Herodotus (4.48) designed to show antagonism between cultures, especially Scythian dislike of Greek ways. Anacharsis encounters the cult of Rhea-Cybele at Cyzicus, makes a vow to the Mother of Gods, and attempts to introduce the cult into Scythia on his safe return there. He is shot with an arrow and killed by King Saulinus when the king discovers the illicit night procession and the raising of sacred images. Julian tells the story to reinforce his point concerning cultural diversity, and perhaps also to suggest the novelty of Christian worship within the context of Greek and Roman religious observances.

311. See Herodotus, 4.76.

ences in <customs and> languages. For he explained that the sons of men convened with a plan to build a great city with a tower at its center, but that God decided he would <foil their plan by> confusing their languages. So that no one can accuse me of fabricating this to slander him, let me cite specifically the following from the book of Moses:

"And they said, let us go and build a city with a tower with its pinnacle touching high heaven. And let us make a reputation for ourselves before we are scattered over the face of the earth. And the Lord came down to see the city and the tower which the sons of men had built. 135E And the Lord said, See: this people is one and they all have a single language; and this they have done, such that now nothing that they propose to do will be impossible for them. Let us then go down and in that place confuse their language so that no man should be able to understand his neighbor's speech. So the Lord God scattered them over the face of the earth and they ceased building the city and the tower."[312]

And you <Galileans> insist that we ought to believe this account while you refuse to believe Homer's story of the Aloadae, where <it is recounted> that they planned to build three mountains, one on top of the other "so that the heavens might be scaled."[313] From my point of view, one tale is like the other. But say, if you credit the <story of Moses>, why in the name of the gods do you reject Homer's myth? I guess that to people as ignorant as you it goes without saying that even if men the world over had but one language they still would be unable to build a tower to heaven, even if they turned the whole surface of the earth to bricks! 134C Because a tower of that sort would need innumerable bricks, each brick as large as the earth itself, even if they are to succeed reaching <merely> the orbit of the moon. Imagine, for a moment, that everyone came together speaking one language, one tongue, and that these <very>

---

312. Gen. 11.4–8.

313. *Odyssey* 11.316. This section of the epic includes the story of illicit unions between the Olympians Zeus and Poseidon and the mortal women Leda and Iphimedeia, the latter of whom bore the giants Ephilates and Otus who threaten to make war on the gods by stacking mountains to reach the heavens. They are killed by Apollo. Julian attempts a connection between the Greek myth and the legend of the nephilim in Gen. 6: 1–4 and the legend of the beginnings of technology in Gen. 11:1–9.

people decided to dig stones and turn earth to brick; and even though they stretch it finer than thread, when would <such a structure> reach up into high heaven?

Or do those of you who hold this fiction to be the truth believe also that God trembled before the threatened violence of mankind? Is it for this reason he had to 'come down' to confuse their languages? 135D And I ask: do you still dare to boast of your knowledge of God?[314]

137E I shall return to the question of God's confusing the languages. Moses explained the reason as follows—namely, God was afraid of <men> having one language or a common way of thinking, lest they find some way to build a 138A road leading up to heaven, and there do something perverse against <God>. Precisely how God caused this to happen is not recounted: <we are told only> that God came down from heaven—because apparently the deed could not be done while on high, without <God> coming down to earth. But neither Moses nor anyone else[315] has given insight into the origin of differences between characters and customs—this despite the fact that political constitutions among nations differ, as do their traditions, in ways far greater than than differences among languages.

138B What Greek would tell us that a man should marry his sister or his daughter, for example? But this is thought to be a virtuous <practice> among the Persians. Why, however, go through the list of characteristics—or recall the German love of freedom and lack of self-restraint; the docility and the mildness of the Syrians, Persians, Parthians—and, to be brief, all barbarians east and south, and all peoples who are happy with the rule of despots of some sort. If, then, these greater and more important differences <of national character> emerged in the absence of a greater and more godlike providence,[316] why should we worry about—and why worship—<a god> who cares nothing for us?

138C Indeed, is it right that the one who cares nothing for the way we live, our customs, lives, good government, political structure,

---

314. γνῶσις θεοῦ?

315. οὔτε ἄλλος: That is, no biblical writer or Christian teacher.

316. πρόνοια: Julian seems to mean that important differences can be assigned only to a foreknown purpose: the God of the Jews behaves reactively and out of φθόνος [jealousy], hence without foreknowledge of consequences.

should demand veneration from our hands? It is not. See to what absurdity your teaching leads! For among the blessings that we see in the life of a man those which pertain to the soul are primary, and those which concern the body are secondary.

Thus <I conclude>: if <the God of the Jews and Christians> gave us nothing in the way of spiritual blessings[317] nor any thought as to our material welfare, 138D and if, in addition, he sent no teachers to us, no lawgivers to us as he did to the Hebrews—Moses and the prophets after him—for what, precisely, are we supposed to thank him?[318]

But think, has not God given us gods as well: kind protectors never acknowledged by you, but not the least inferior to the <God> revered by the Hebrews as first among the Jews of Judaea <who allege>, as Moses taught, that they and those after them are the only ones he cared for. For even if the God worshiped by the Hebrews is none other than the demiurge, yet our beliefs about him are better[319] than theirs, even as he has given us greater gifts than he has given them, both spiritual and material. Of these I will speak further, but reiterate here that he sent many lawgivers who were not Moses' inferior; and many were far better.

143A

As I have suggested, if it is not the case that the differences in laws and peoples are the work of the god holding precedence over a separate nation and thereunder his angel, demon, hero, or order of beings working for the whole pantheon and obeying them in all respects, you must show me what other power brought such differences about. It is clearly not proof of your case to say simply, "Well, God spoke and it happened as he said." For the commands of God must harmonize with the nature of the things he has created.[320] To put it more precisely: Was it chance that God established that fire should rise up and earth should sink down? To complete the ordinance, wasn't it necessary that <fire> be light and <earth> heavy?

And is this not also true of other sorts of things: <if differences in language and political constitutions exist, must not these be

---

317. ἀγαθῶς ψυχικῶς.
318. καλῶς εὐχαριστεῖν.
319. In the sense of being more virtuous.
320. See Oration IV.140A; Plato, *Laws* 713D.

attributed to the preexisting conditions of the nature of the people who create them?>[321]

143C

And so too with the things of the gods; for just as mankind is ordained to die and perish, so also his works are by nature destined to perish—changeable, subject to every permutation. But as God is eternal it follows that his ordinances are unchanging. This means that they comport with the nature of things and constitute the nature of things. Nature cannot be at variance with nature, that is with the will of God. How could it depart from harmony?[322]

So I conclude that if <God> ordained the confusion of languages and the lack of harmony among us, and consequent differences in our political institutions, then it was not that he did this by a particular or special ordinance, as if to make lack of agreement a feature of our natures.[323] Indeed different natures must have been a part of everything that stood to be distinguished, nation from nation. Just look at the physical difference between Germans and Scythians from Libyans and Ethiopians. Is this due simply to God willing it, without <the preexisting cause> of climate and geography having a joint influence, as it were, with the gods in the determination of skin color?[324]

---

321. Based on Cyril's paraphrase; Julian seems to compress this point, which is worked out fully in Oration IV.

322. Julian here expresses one of Porphyry's criticisms of the Christian faith, particularly the emphasis on revelation as "interruption" or discord of the created order: see Hoffmann, *Porphyry's Against the Christians*, p. 35.

323. Wright's gloss of this passage is puzzling: "<Julian means> if there were to be differences of speech and political constitution they must have been adapted to pre-existing differences of natures in human beings" (III, p. 357, n. 2). Julian's point is more acute: Once having established difference of character and language as part of the nature of humanity, with the result that there should be differences of political order, there was no further need for God to differentiate by further, particular revelations (e.g., as to Abraham or Moses). Like an earlier generation of pagans, Julian would have understood "superiority" of these political ordinances in a pragmatic way: Rome's difference from the Hebrews and Christians could be demonstrated by its superior political status in the world. The argument reaches back at least to the time of Celsus, who enunciates it in a less philosophical style.

324. This is a good example of Julian's "cooperative teleology" which depends on a principle of noncontradiction between the nature of things and the role of God in maintaining harmony. In Julian's view, things move toward differentiation, or evolve, partly because they are disposed to do so through natural process, partly

146A–B

And yet Moses deliberately drew a veil[325] around this kind of reasoning when he fails to attribute the confusion of languages to God as the sole cause.[326] For he says[327] that God did not descend <to earth> alone but that others descended with him, although he does not say who these were. Obviously those who descended with God were godlike; and indeed it was not God who acted alone to disturb the languages but others with him—evidently the same beings who, acting with God, served to create the divisions in the human race, each with its distinguishing marks.

148B

You may wonder why I have gone on for so long when I wanted merely to say a few words. It is this: If, as you say, the direct creator of the world is none other than the God proclaimed by Moses, then <I say> we hold a truer belief in him. We consider him to be the ruler of all things in a universal sense: but <we believe as well> that there exist the gods of nations who are like him—just as governors, each having power over his province, are like a king, but subordinate to him. And we hold that <God> is not the fractious rival of these lesser rulers.[328] But if Moses gives his allegiance to a lesser god, and then makes leadership of the world contrast with his power,[329]

---

because of preexisting factors (climate, geography, etc.) which positively encourage change and difference.

325. ἐπεκάλυπτε τὸ τοιοῦτον ἐιδώς . . . Cf. Exod. 27.31: Moses was instructed to make a veil to draw around the Ark containing the law. Julian here interprets the passage to refer to the obscurity of the Hebrew account of the origin of language.

326. The phrase τῷ θεῷ μόνῳ seems to require this construction as dealing with God as cause of the world's languages.

327. Gen. 11.7.

328. A slightly different view of the familiar pagan argument that Christian exclusivity in having no gods but the God of Moses is a form of intolerance that diminishes true religious feeling, patriotic fervor, and proper veneration of the gods.

329. The point is somewhat oblique, but Julian probably has in mind the Christian teaching (see Eph. 2.1–5) that the kingdom of this world has a lord other than the Creator and that these archons, led by the "prince of the powers of the air," may have been the agents described in Gen. 11.7. The antipathy between the creator-god and the ruler of the age (aeon) was a fundamental starting point in Christian exegesis of the fall; see Origen, De princ. 3.2.1. The point is also made by Porphyry, *apud* Macarius Magnes. Julian's larger, and politically nuanced, point is that the world would reflect no harmony if it were caught between the rival purposes of

surely it would be better to believe as we do: for we recognize the God of All[330] though with due regard also for the God of Moses.[331] It is far better, I think, not to substitute the worship of one who has been given <only> his small portion for <the worship> due the Creator of all.

152B

What a surprise is this law of Moses—I mean the famous decalogue. "Thou shalt not steal," "Thou shalt not kill," "Thou shalt not bear false witness." Let me write down each of these commandments which he says were written personally by God:

"I am the Lord God who brought you out of the Land of Egypt," and then the second,

"Have no other gods over me."

'Make for yourselves no graven image," followed by this explanation:

"For I the Lord God am a jealous God, visiting the sins of the fathers upon children to the third generation."

"Take not the Name of the Lord your God in vain."

"Remember the sabbath day."

"Honor your father and your mother."

"Commit no adultery."

"You shall not commit murder."

"You shall not steal."

"You shall not bear false witness."

"You shall not covet anything that is your neighbor's."[332]

I ask you in the name of all the gods, with the exception of "You shall worship no other gods" and "Remember the sabbath day," is there any nation that does not think it ought to keep the other commandments? So true is this that there is a price to pay for anyone

---

a "national" God, such as he imagines the God of Moses to be, and those seeking to extend their dominion at his expense.

330. Lit., the God with hegemony over all.

331. This is Julian's clearest statement of the belief that the God of Moses is a deity worthy of honor as a national god, but whose revelation as recorded in the books of the Christians and Jews puts him on a par with the *mythoi* of other national gods—i.e., as the creator of the Hebrew nation.

332. Conflating passages from Exod. 20.2–3, 4, 13–17; Deut. 4.24.

who decides to break <any of the commandments>—in some cases more severe penalties than those ordained by Moses, but often more humane.[333]

Now as to the commandment, "You shall not worship other gods," <Moses> attaches a monstrous 155D untruth about God: "I am a jealous God," he is made to say, or later, "Our God is a consuming fire."[334] Now if a man is jealous or covetous you consider him immoral, but if it is God—you call the attribute divine? But how can this obviously false contradiction be at home with reason? For if <God> is indeed jealous, it must follow that all other gods who are worshiped receive honor to spite him, and all people who worship these other gods defy the will of God. Well, then, how is it that he is not able to restrain the nations if his jealousy demands that other gods, besides himself, should not be worshiped? 155E Perhaps he was not able to do it, or perhaps at the beginning he did not wish to deny these gods their due reverence. As to the first suggestion: it is impious to say that he was unable to do it. As to the second, it is exactly what we ourselves say. Spare us such nonsense and avoid incurring the charge of blasphemy!

159E Further, if it is God's will that "no other god" should be worshiped, why is it that you worship this so-called son of his, whom he has never yet recognized or acknowledged as his own? I shall prove this to you, while you, for mysterious reasons, insist on giving God a false son.[335]

160D

Nowhere <in the Greek books> is God shown to be angry, spiteful, petulant, oath-bound, or fickle, leaning now to one side and now to the other, and suddenly front face again, as Moses tells us happened in the case of Phineas. Any of you who have read the book called Numbers know what I mean.[336] For when Phineas had seized

---

333. φιλανθρωποτέρας, or of benefit to the human race.

334. Deut. 4.24.

335. Cyril suggests that Julian here launches into a discussion of Christian abuse and misunderstanding of Greek accounts of the gods.

336. In Num. 25.10–13, Phineas, son of Eleazar, is said to have turned back God's consuming anger (expressed as fire and earthquake in 26.10f.) as an agent of his jealousy and wrath.

and slain by his own hand the man consecrated to Baal—Peor, together with the woman who persuaded him, dealing her a shameful and excruciating wound to the stomach, the God of Moses is made to say, "Phineas, son of Eleazar, the son of Aaron the high priest, hath turned my wrath away from the children of Israel, for he was jealous with my jealousy among them, and in my jealousy I devoured not the children of Israel."[337] Can you imagine a more trivial reason for the inane anger of God than that concocted by the writer of this passage? What could be more irrational than this—even if there had been ten or fifteen, or for argument's sake even a hundred (no one would suggest a thousand, I think), but let them say as many as that had defied one of the laws laid down by God, would that then make it right—if these thousand had transgressed, that 600,000 should be annihilated by God?[338] In my view I think it might be better in every case to save a bad man along with a thousand virtuous ones than destroy a thousand because of the one! Indeed, if the wrath of a single hero, or one insignificant demon, is hard for countries and cities to withstand, who could be expected to endure the anger of such a powerful God, whether directed against demons, angels, or men?

168B

It is useful to compare <God's> behavior with the grace of Lycurgus, or the tolerance of Solon, or even the mildness and benevolence of the Romans toward those who have done some wrong. And mark, too, how much superior our teachings are to these others, for the philosophers advise us to imitate[339] the gods as best we can and tell us that this imitation is achieved through the contemplation of ideas; and this sort of study has nothing to do with passion—in fact, as I must say at the risk of saying the obvious, it is grounded in freedom from passion.[340] Only to the degree that we have been successful in the duty of contemplating these realities,[341] and learn freedom from passion, do we become like God.

---

337. Num. 25.11.

338. According to the census concluded after Korah's rebellion, the total number of the people of Israel threatened by God was 600 and 1,730 (Num. 26.51).

339. μιμεῖσθαι.

340. ἀπαθεία.

341. θεωρίαν.

But what sense does this "imitation of God" make to the Hebrew people? Anger, wrath, hateful jealousy—the God who says, "Phineas has turned away my wrath from the children of Israel, because he was jealous with my jealousy among them." In other words, God found someone as petulant as himself and aggrieved as much as he was, and so was made to keep his petulance at bay. This sort of utterance and other, similar words are seen frequently in relation to the God of Moses in the sacred writings.

176A–B

It is also to be marked that God does not in later times show concern only for the Hebrews, and that while caring for all nations he gave the Hebrews no special privileges or gifts, while giving us benefits far surpassing theirs. Consider the example of the Egyptians, who manage to count a few wise men among their ranks, claiming proudly the successors of Hermes—that Hermes who visited Egypt in his third epiphany.[342] The Chaldeans and Assyrians take pride in the successors of Oannes and Belos,[343] while the Greeks boast of the many successors of Cheiron.

Out of it all the Greeks developed a reputation for the sacred mysteries and theology—much in the same way, as you know, as the Hebrews, <who> claim to be uniquely gifted in this area.[344]

178A

But has God commissioned you to start a <new> science or philosophical movement? Well, then—what may it be? For the charting of celestial bodies was advanced by Greeks, who built on the theories first made by the barbarians in Babylon. So too the study of geometry, which originated among the Egyptians during the course of surveying the land and has since become of immense importance <to all nations>. Arithmetic was begun by Phoenician

---

342. The "third great Hermes," identified with Thoth, who had special status among the Neoplatonists, and hence is important to Julian as a theological cipher.

343. On the fish-god Oannes, see Berosus, *History*, who claims he taught the Babylonians the art of civilization "and thus has some analogy with the serpent of Genesis" (Wright, III, p. 366). Βῆλος is an attempt to give a Greek equivalent for Assyrian *bil*, the Baal of the Hebrew Bible.

344. In PG 176C Cyril suggests that Julian goes on to deride the accomplishments of David and Samson as being petty chiefs rather than heroes in the Greek sense.

merchants, and over time, among the Greeks, achieved the rank of a science. And these three sciences the Greeks blended in the form of music to become one, connecting astronomy and geometry through arithmetic and finding within the principle of harmony. They established rules for their music soon after, when they learned that harmony is perceived through hearing a nearly perfect agreement <in the intervals>.[345]

184B

Must I list one by one the names and contributions of each man? As for example, the individual men: Plato, Socrates, Aristeides, Cimon, Thales, Lycurgus, Agesilaus, Archidamus; or maybe I should speak of classes <of men>—philosophers, generals, artificers, lawgivers. For it can be shown that the foulest, the most brutish of these generals conducted themselves with greater justice and civility toward offenders than Moses did toward the innocent.

190C

And to what jurisdiction[346] shall I report you? Should it be to Perseus, or Aecus, or <perhaps> Minos of Crete, who rid the sea of pirates and drove the barbarians to the edge of Syria and to Sicily, extending his frontiers in two directions, and ruling not only over the islands but over the coastal peoples? For this <Minos> parceled out the care of mankind to his brother, Rhadamanthus—indeed, establishing through what he had received from Zeus laws for the whole earth, leaving Rhadamanthus the role of judge.[347]

After <Our Mother Rome's> foundation she was beset by many wars, and she won them all, prevailing over <her enemies>, ever increasing in greatness in proportion to the dangers she has faced and her need for security: so it was, then, that Zeus sent the renowned

---

345. The purpose of this digression, a lecture on the "unoriginality" of Christian teaching and story compared to the Greeks and antecedent civilizations, had become a favorite topos for pagan critics at least by the time of Celsus, who expends considerable energy attempting to show that Christianity has contributed nothing new to philosophical discussion; see *Celsus* (Hoffmann 1987), pp. 55–58.

346. Βασιλεία—in keeping with the fancy that the Christians are being tried as in a court, but have, properly speaking, no national law on their side.

347. This introduced <*apud* Cyril> a discussion of the legend of Minos, Dardanus, Aeneas, and the founding of Rome.

philosopher Numa.[348] This is the selfsame Numa, the excellent and righteous man who lived a hermit in the groves, communing with the gods in the purity of heart we know as contemplation.

193D–194B

It was Numa, chiefly, who fixed the law of the temple worship. And from this came the blessing of divine possession, and also the power which emanated from the Sibyl on the one hand, and from others who, in those days, spoke oracles in their native tongues. <And these gifts> were expressly given to the City by Zeus.

Further, <we must remember the omens of> the shield that fell from the sky[349] and the head which manifested itself on the hill, and from which the throne of mighty Zeus himself received its name.[350] Are such things to be considered the highest gifts, or merely as secondary benefits? But, do you, O deluded men, despite there being still today with us the very artifact which dropped from heaven above, sent by mighty Zeus or father Ares as sure proof, not promise, that he will always hold that shield before this city, do you cease to adore it and reverence it—You who <instead> adore the wood of the cross, trace its figure on your foreheads, draw it on your house-fronts?

194D

Who would not be right to despise the most intelligent man among <the Christians>, or feel pity for the most stupid? For these, by following you, have descended to such a pit of ruin that they have let go of the ever-living gods <of our city> in order to embrace the lifeless corpse of the Jew. <. . .> For I say nothing about the Mysteries of the Mother of the Gods,[351] and I admire Marius.[352]

---

348. Successor of Romulus, a favorite of the gods. It is not entirely clear why Julian chooses the name "philosopher" for Numa, except to tie him to a succession of philosopher kings of which he sees himself a part. Cf. Julian, Or. IV.155A.

349. Livy 1.20 (as the "shields called celestial") and *Aeneid* 8.664.

350. *Caput*/Capitoline (Livy 1.55).

351. The cult of Cybele, the "Magna Mater," was brought to Rome in about 205. Belief in eternal life was a part of the cult from its early days, and Julian seems to have suggested that the Christians borrowed the doctrine from the mysteries associated with the cult. Julian's devotion to her cult is expressed in Oration V.

352. The logic is somewhat contorted: Cyril's refutation mentions that Gaius Marius was known for his superstitious nature for his attempts to appeal to the *populares*; but he was also considered a *novus homo*, and an object of veneration.

198B

Now the spirit that comes to men from the gods is attested, but it is given rarely and to few, and it is not at all easy for everyone to share in it all at once or every time <it is present>.[353]

We are not surprised, then, that the prophetic spirit has ceased to move among the Hebrews, and is no longer known to the Egyptians. So too, we see that the ancient oracles of Greece have fallen silent[354] over the span of time. But as if to provide us with a means of enquiry sufficient to our needs, our gracious lord and father Zeus heeded our prayer for communion with the gods and gave to us a sacred art.[355]

200A

Recall the most outstanding gifts of Helios and Zeus. I naturally saved these for last. And need I say that <these gifts> are not <ones> which only we who love Rome acknowledge but also ones which we share with our Greek cousins. I mean, how Zeus fathered Asclepios from himself, placing him among the known gods, and then, through the life-giving power of Helios, revealed him to the <sons of> earth.[356] After making his visitation to the earth, Asclepios appeared in the shape of a man, alone, at Epidaurus. After this, he manifested himself in diverse ways, stretching out his saving right hand to the whole earth.[357] He came to Pergamon, to Ionia, to Tarentum, and thereafter to Rome. He also traveled to Cos, and then to Aegae. Thereafter he <was> manifested everywhere, both on land

---

353. The phenomenon of ecstatic utterance, which Julian knows both from Christian writings (cf. 1 Cor. 12) as well as from prior expressions in the Cybele *mysterion* and in the orphic and Delphic traditions, is the subject of this digression. Julian does not wish to deny the ecstatic, but to limit it to "true prophecy." Iamblichus concerned himself with the same procedure in his study of Egyptian praxis; and cf. 1 Cor. 2.4, 14.6–10.

354. Wright, III, 373, thinks that Julian here refers to unsuccessful efforts to restore the oracle at Delphi.

355. Divination.

356. Oration IV.144B: Asclepios is called σωτήρ by Julian, who in the same oration contrasts him with Jesus.

357. The phrase ἐπὶ πᾶσαν ὤρεξε τὴν γῆν τὴν σωτήριον ἑαυτοῦ δεξιάν is an attempt to relate the Asclepeian soteriology to those circulating in Christian writings: cf. Phil. 2.5–11 and especially Hebrews 3, 4.

and at sea. And though he does not take private patients, still he raises up those who are sinful and heals the sick.[358]

201E

Yet what great gift of this kind do the Hebrews say was granted to them by God?—The Hebrews who have persuaded you to desert to them? If you had only listened to what they taught, it may be you would have done better for yourselves—although worse than when you still counted yourselves among us—still, your <philosophical> position would have been tolerable, perhaps sustainable. At least you would be worshipping one God and not many; and not worshipping a man, or shall I say, many miserable men.[359] Yes, and even though you would be following a law that is vicious and hard and contains much of a savage and brutal kind—unlike our humane and gentle laws (and in other ways too would yet be inferior to us), still, <were you Hebrews> you would be more holy and more pure than your worship now makes you.

191D

Ah, but what has happened? Like leeches you have sucked the worst from <the Jews> and left the good alone. Yet the name of this Jesus who first persuaded the wretched and miserable among you[360] has scarcely been known for three hundred years. And during his lifetime, he accomplished nothing worth mention—that is, unless one should think that healing a cripple and a few blind men, or

---

358. It was a convention of anti-Christian polemicists that the Christian boast that Jesus was the divine son of a merciful God was disproved by the narrow geographical matrix of his miracles: see Celsus (Hoffmann 1987), pp. 68–69: "What god comes only to those who already look for his reappearance and is not even recognized by them?"

359. The apostles and martyrs. The growth of shrines and churches was of particular concern to Julian. Constantius had handed over church property in Edessa to the Arians, a situation Julian seeks to remedy (see Ep XL.424.C, D); and Gregory (Or.3.86D) and Sozomen (HE 5.5.) allege that Julian had begun a program of spoliation of churches and martyrs' shrines. The same worry underlies his edict on funerals (Ep. LVI).

360. Celsus (Hoffmann 1987, pp. 72–73) argues the same case on the basis of the social status of the Christians, and other pagan writers exploited Paul's description of the church at Corinth to document the inferiority of the Christians as a class (1 Cor. 6.9–11).

driving the demons from possessed men in wayside villages like Bethsaida and Bethany count as mighty works!

205E

And when the subject is purity of life, you cannot be sure that he spoke of the matter at all.[361]

You yourselves behave like the Jews who vent their rage and petulance by razing altars and destroying temples. And you slaughter us as well: not only those of us who remain true to the teachings of our ancestors, but even your own—or those you style "heretics" because they do not bewail a corpse in the manner your <teachers> demand.[362]

206B

These are your own deeds: Nowhere did Jesus or Paul pass on rules for such actions. And why? Because never could they have imagined <that their followers> would have such power as they have now. They were happy with seducing naïve women and slaves[363] and through them <their> mistresses, and men like Cornelius and Sergius.[364] (Should you show me that either of these men is recalled by any of the acknowledged historians of that time, <as> these events are said to have happened during the reign of Tiberius or Claudius, I would be happy to concede that I have misrepresented you.)

---

361. This is a central premise of Julian's critique. He seems to have in mind the disciples' breaking of the ritual and ceremonial laws of Judaism (cf. Mark 7.1–5) as reflected in the Gospels and the relative paucity of ethical teaching on Jesus' part that does not derive from Jewish law.

362. In an edict to the citizens of Bostra cited by the church historian Sozomen (5.15), Julian recalls the slaughter of heretics at Samosata, Cyzicus, Paphlagonia, Bithynia, and Galatia mandated by his predecessor, Constantius. The "heretics" in question were those who did not belong to the Arian sect. The edict itself is a call to religious tolerance, "not to become embroiled in the feuds of the clergy," the causes of which the emperor lays at the doorstep of the bishop Titus and (according to Julian) his disingenuous calls for calm and restraint on the part of the Christian community. Julian had a special dislike of Christian burial practice, which flouted the pagan practice of reserving burial until after dark in honor of the lords of the underworld; see Ep. LVI.

363. Cf. note 352.

364. The centurion and proconsul, mentioned respectively in Acts 10 and Acts 13.6–12. This allusion suggests Julian's acquaintance with the full body of the Lucan corpus, as well as his skepticism toward the historical plausibility of the episodes.

209D

I do not know how I came to speak about these things. In any case—coming back to the point from which I departed when I asked you, "Why were you so ungrateful as to desert the gods for the Jews," Was it that Rome has been allotted its sovereignty by the gods, while the Jews have been their own masters for such a short while, and ever after aliens and slaves? Look at Abraham! Was he not a stranger in a strange land? Jacob? The same, first in Syria, then in Palestine, finally as an old man in Egypt.

Or Moses, who is said to have led <the Hebrew nation> from slavery "with arm outstretched."[365] But after their rummaging about Palestine, did they not change fortune more frequently than, it is said, a chameleon changes its colors—first servants of the Judges, next slaves of foreign nations? And then they began to be governed by kings. Let me defer for a while asking about the manner of this governance, bearing in mind what <their> writings tell us[366] that God did not wish them to have kings, but <consented> only after being pressed by them and after warning them that they would be governed badly in such a way. Nonetheless, they had their little space and farmed their own ground for just over three hundred years.

213A

After that they were a subject people: first to the Assyrians, then to the Medes, later to the Persians, finally to ourselves. Jesus, who was proclaimed by you, was nothing other than one of Caesar's subjects. If you will not believe it, I shall prove it further on—but let me state it here for the record: for you yourselves teach that together with his father and mother his name was enrolled during the governorship of Cyrenius.[367]

213B

But when he was merely a man[368] what good did he do for his

---

365. Exod. 6.6.
366. 1 Sam. 8.
367. Luke 2.2.
368. Wright's translation, using Neumann's insertion—"when he became man" (p. 381) for γενόμενος ἄνθρωπος—seems to presuppose the credal formulation of 325, but it is not clear that Julian intends this allusion. Julian's sarcasm refers to the time before Jesus was elevated to divinity by his followers.

countrymen? No, say the Galileans; <the Jews> did not listen to Jesus. Indeed? Then how did it happen that this "hardhearted and stiff-necked people"[369] obeyed Moses. Yet Jesus—who commanded spirits, walked on the water, drove away the demons and, as you declare yourselves, "made the heavens and the earth"[370]—though none of his disciples dared to say such a thing concerning him, except John, and he does not say so directly or unequivocally. But for the sake of argument let us suppose that it was said: would it not then stand to reason that this Jesus might have done better for his friends and countrymen? Might he not, at least, have helped them?

218A

I shall return to this subject further on, when I take up the question of the miracles <of Jesus> and the composition of the gospels. For the present, however, answer me this: Which is the better thing, to be free without restriction and masters over the wide earth and sea for two thousand years, or to be for the same time the duty-bound slaves of others? I think no man is so lacking in self-esteem that he would willingly choose the latter. It would be as if someone chose defeat over victory in war: Is anyone as stupid as that? And speaking of <warfare>, show me in truth a single commander among the Hebrews like Alexander or Caesar? There is no such man among you. But by the gods, I cringe to think how I have insulted the valorous by asking such a question! I mention them because they are the best-known examples, and generals who are less well known would not be recognized by the masses of our people—yet the least among these deserves more admiration that all the generals ever produced by the Jews.[371]

221E

Now as to the constitution of a city, the mode of law, the governance of cities, the superiority of laws, progress in learning, the

369. Ezek. 3.7. The phrase was also current in Roman anti-Jewish polemical writing, on which see John Gager, *Origins of Anti-Semitism: Attitudes Towards Judaism in Pagan and Christian Antiquity* (Oxford, 1985), pp. 15–57.

370. John 1.3.

371. Porphyry seems also to have used heroism as a criterion for the truth of the Christian gospel. In a controversial passage, Augustine claims that Porphyry listed Jesus among the heroes; see CG VIII.12; X.21; esp. XIX.22–23. If Julian knew this tradition he does not support it.

encouragement of liberal arts—weren't these things barbarous and wretched among the Hebrews? That dreadful man Eusebius says, preposterously enough, that poems in the heroic meter can be found among the Jews—saying further that the study of logic was advanced among the Hebrews, since the word they use for logic can be heard among the Greeks![372]

But has any medical art appeared among the Hebrews, such as that the Greeks know from Hippocrates, or the schools that came after him? Can we say that their wisest man Solomon should be compared to a Phocylides, a Theognis or Isocrates among the Greeks?[373] Surely if you could compare the exhortations of Isocrates with the proverbs of Solomon you would concede, no doubt, that the heir of Theodorus is wiser far than the very wisest king <of the Hebrews>. "Ah," but they answer, "Solomon was an expert in the secret wisdom of God!" If true, is it not true as well that this Solomon, at his wives' bidding, served our gods also, which even they teach?[374] What virtue is this! What treasured wisdom! The man could not even control his passions; the murmurings of a woman led him from wisdom's path. Please call no man wise who is deluded by a woman, or if you still think him wise, then do not claim he was deluded. Say rather that he trusted his own judgement and followed his own heart, and the teaching that he received from a God who had revealed that he should serve other gods.

224E Petulance and envy should not bother the most virtuous men, for the things are distant form both angels and gods. But you <Christians> hanker after the intermediate and partial powers (which we would not be wrong in calling demonic), and in these

---

372. Eusebius, *Praeparatio Evangelica* 11.5.5: that Moses and David wrote in Hexameter.

373. Julian's choice of sages is interesting: Theognis, presumably for representing the tradition of aristocratic wisdom; Isocrates for his eloquence and reputation as the moral prophet of the Hellenistic world; Phocylides for the gnomic character of his philosophical verse.

374. 1 Kings 11.4 refers to Solomon's apostasy from the God of the Hebrews at the bidding of his wives; 1 Kings 3.1 refers to an alliance between Solomon and the king of Egypt. The point is not relevant to his argument against the Christians but is rather an accusation leveled at the Jews.

powers are pride and vanity, while in our gods there is nothing of the kind.[375]

229C And if you can be happy with reading your own books, why nibble at the learning of the Greeks? It would seem better to keep men away from <philosophy> than from the eating of sacrificial meat.[376] Speaking of this question, Paul says the one who eats is not harmed, but—O most brilliant and arrogant people!—the conscience of the brother who sees but does not eat is offended. Our own learning has caused the best and most virtuous men among you to quit impiety. So too, almost every one who has retained the virtue he was born with has quickly parted with your vanities. It is clear, then, that it would be a finer thing to keep men from learning than from sacrificial meats. Yet I suppose you know better than I what effects your writings, as distinct from ours, will have on one's intelligence. For in studying yours no man would even achieve ordinary goodness, let alone virtue, whereas from ours a man might become better than before, even if he had born with no natural aptitude for excellence. A man who has such aptitude and has added to it the benefit of our writing—that man is a gift of the gods to mankind: <such a man> can light the fire of knowledge, can write a constitution, rout his country's foes in battle, travel bravely to the ends of the earth and back again, like the heroes of old.[377]

---

375. This passage is something of a puzzle. It is not likely that Julian is talking about the intercession of the saints, as Wright (III, p. 385 n. 1) suggests. As he seems to have 1 Corinthians in view he may be referring to Paul's reference to wisdom and the rulers of the world (1 Cor. 2.6), as being derived from the tradition of solomonic wisdom. In Paul's view it is the πνεῦμα that supplies the "hidden" wisdom of God.

376. 1 Cor. 8.7–13. Paul makes the eating of meat taken from animals sacrificed to idols a matter of conscience; but he begins the chapter with an aphorism which apparently irritates Julian: "ἡ γνῶσις φυσιοῖ ἡ δὲ ἀγάπη οἰκοδομεῖ." Julian finds Paul's idea that "all of us possess knowledge" a direct attack on the Neoplatonic view that knowledge is achieved through the exercise of the intellect. It is important to distinguish Julian's view on this point from the equally anti-intellectual teachings of Iamblichus concerning the means to acquire divine wisdom, which is very distant from his argument here.

377. The Old Testament heroes are attacked next, according to Cyril. Julian also polemicizes against the Old Testament being written in a tongue unsuitable for learning and heroic tales.

229E–230A

Why not put my words to a test: Choose some from among your children. Train them in your scriptures. When they have arrived at manhood, if they have qualities any better than a slave's, then I am only grumbling out of a bad temper. But you are foolish and arrogant, so that you think those scriptures of yours are divinely inspired in spite of no man ever having become better or braver or wiser than he was before by reading them. And what of the writings whose proof is that, reading them, men do acquire wisdom and courage and justice? These you attribute to Satan and those who do Satan's bidding.[378]

235B–235C

<We say> "Asclepius heals our bodies. The Muses with the help of Asclepius and Apollo and Hermes, god of eloquence, train our souls. In war, Ares as well as Enyo fight for us. Hephaestos distributes and watches over our crafts. Athena, the virgin goddess, with the help of Zeus, presides over them all." Now consider whether we are not superior to you in every single one of these things—in art, wisdom, intelligence—not regarding whether we are speaking of the useful arts or the imitative arts whose end is beauty: Statuary, painting, household management, healing from Asclepius (with his oracles found everywhere on earth and apportioned to us at any time). With God my witness, I know that when I have been ill, Asclepius has cured me by proffering remedies.[379] And so if those of us who are not apostates from the truth do better than you do even in soul and body and worldly affairs, what reason can you give for forsaking our teachings and adopting new ones?

238A–B

And why is it that the Galileans do not accept the traditions of

---

378. See, for example, Origen's discussion of the influence of demons on poetic recitation in *De princ.* 3.3.3. On the tradition in general, see Denise Kimber Buell, *Making Christians: Clement of Alexandria and the Rhetoric of Legitimacy* (Princeton, NJ, 1999).

379. Julian's ploy at this point is a little oblique, in wanting to suggest that there are plenty of examples of miraculous intervention in the mysteries, and that even in the art of healing Asclepios surpasses the Christian God. The natural comparison would be between the healings of Jesus and those of the pagan healing god, but Julian does not make it explicit.

the Hebrews, or obey even the Law that God has given them? By rights you should have rejected our teaching more than theirs, the religion of your ancestors, the sayings of their prophets; but if any one should take the trouble to examine your religion, he will find it a wicked combination of Jewish recklessness and Greek vulgarity. You have taken the worst rather than the best, the inferior rather than the sublime from both sides and woven from it a thieve's cloak.

The Jews have exact laws concerning ritual, innumerable sacred things, observances which require the offices of a priest. And while <Moses> prohibited them from serving any gods except the one "whose portion is Jacob and Israel an allotment of his inheritance,"[380] and while he said as well, "You shall not hate the gods"[381] —but over the generations it has been thought by countless generations that the neglect of worship is a prescription for blasphemy, coming from the people's arrogance and shame. And this is the only thing you have received from the Hebrews; in all other respects you have nothing in common with the Jews. From the superstition of the Jews you have developed your attack on the gods whom we revere. But our veneration for every higher power, which typifies our religious worship—this you have set aside along with the traditions of our forefathers. Yes, you have accepted the habit of "eating all things"—even the green herb.[382]

238E

To be truthful, you have outstripped us in vulgarity—a thing that I suppose happens as a matter of course in all nations. You think you must adapt your ways to those of the lowest among you, the shopkeepers, tax collectors, the dancers and whores.[383] This is nothing new, since the Galileans of our own day are like the first to receive the teaching from Paul, who says himself that those of the earliest days were people of the vilest sort in one of his letters.[384]

---

380. Deut. 32.9.
381. Exod. 22.28 (LXX).
382. Oration VI.192D; the reference is to Christian use of Gen. 9.3 against Jewish dietary observances. Julian finds the Christian view an example of convenient interpretation.
383. Letter XXXVI, the "rescript" on Christian teachers contains the same charge, that Christians behave like salesmen.
384. 1 Cor. 6.9–11.

For I think that Paul would not have written personally concerning these matters if he had not been certain that these men committed these disgraceful deeds—written in language (even though coupled with good words along the way) that would make the writer blush. And even if the good words disguised the bad deeds, even if the good words were deserved, it does not disguise the evil—and if undeserved, if only flattery, then <Paul> should dig a hole in the ground and hide for shame for such wanton and slavish pandering. 245C

Now these are the very words Paul addressed to those who received his teaching, his precise words, to the men themselves: "Do not be deceived, for neither idolaters nor adulterers nor homosexuals, nor sexual libertines nor thieves nor the greedy nor drunkards nor extortionists shall inherit the kingdom of God. And of this you are not in ignorance, brothers, because you were these things; but you washed yourselves and you were sanctified in the name of Jesus."[385] Do you not see that he admits the men he addresses *were* these things, and then he says they were "washed" and they were "sanctified," as though water itself had acquired the power to cleanse and purify not the body only, but even the soul! But baptism does not take the sores away from the leper, or the scabs and boils, the wens and disfigurations, or gout or dysentery or dropsy, or a whitlow—in fact, <water> takes away no disorder of the body, however great or small: so shall it then do away with adultery, theft, and all of the sins of the soul? <Oh you Christians, who run from your sins like slaves from their true master, thinking that if you are retrieved, well, at least your state will be no worse than before.>[386]

253A–B

Now: as the Galileans would have us think that while they are not Jews, they are still in some sense "Israelites" because they hold to the prophets and revere Moses and his successors in Judaea above all others, let us see whether they heed these prophets. Let us, indeed, begin with the teaching of Moses himself, who, they claim, was the first to foretell the birth of Jesus who was yet to be. This Moses says

---

385. 1 Cor. 6.9–11 again, here explicit: Julian's reference point for describing the social and moral inferiority of the Christians.

386. Based on Cyril's paraphrase of an analogy made in Julian's work.

not once or twice or even three times, but repeatedly, that men should honor the one God—that is, the one men call "The Highest." He says on no occasion that they ought to honor another god. Yet he speaks about angels and lords and acknowledges <the existence> of many gods, and from them he selects a "highest" and denies rank to a second, either like or unlike him, such as you <Galileans> have invented. If from your own books you happen to possess a single word from Moses on this subject, please do submit it; for the words <you so often cite>, "The Lord your God shall raise up from among your brethren a prophet for you, like unto me and unto him shall you hearken,"[387] were certainly not said of the son of Mary.

Even if I could concede to meet you halfway, that these words were said of <Jesus>, Moses says that the prophets will be *like him*, that is, not a god, and born of men, not of a god. The words, "The scepter shall not depart from Judah, nor a leader from his loins,"[388] were certainly not spoken of the son of Mary; they apply to the royal house of David which ended with the reign of Zedekiah the king. The scripture can be understood in two ways, where it says, "Until there comes what is reserved for him," which you have mistakenly interpreted to say, "Until *he* comes for *whom* it is reserved."[389] Clearly not a single saying among these has anything to do with Jesus. He was not even from Judah. For do you not yourselves teach that he was not born of Joseph but through the Holy Spirit? In your genealogies, you trace Joseph back to Judah; but you do not even manage to create a credible line, for Matthew and Luke refute each other's genealogies with contradictions. But as I will deal with an examination of the truthfulness of these things in my second book, we shall leave it until then.[390] Even granting that he was "a scepter

---

387. Deut. 18.18.

388. Gen. 49.10, an ambiguous verse used by Jews and Christians to refer to a messianic kingdom, since the second part of the verse includes the words "nor the ruler's staff from between his feet until he comes, to whom it belongs." Julian's explanation, historically, is as good as any other.

389. In the LXX version.

390. Cyril's reply to the second book is lost. It presumably dealt in more detail with contradictions in the scriptural record, if this passage of the treatise previews some of his argumentation.

from Judah," then he is not "God born of God,"[391] as you are fond of saying, nor is it true that "By him all things were made, and without him nothing was made."[392] Ah, but you say, the Book of Numbers says, "Out of Jacob shall arise a star, a man out of Israel,"[393] but this relates only to David and his lineage, for David was the son of Jesse.

What you take from these writings, prove to me that these are at variance with my interpretation of them. Indeed, you say, Moses believed in one god, as can be proved when he speaks of the God of Israel in the Book called Deuteronomy, "So that you may know the Lord your God is one God and there in no gods beside him."[394] And he says again, "Hear O Israel, the Lord God is one Lord,"[395] and still again, "See: I *am* and there is no god beside me."[396] This is what Moses says when he proclaims that there is only one God. But of course the Galileans will say, "But we don't say that there are two gods or three gods." But I will prove that this is precisely what you do say.

262C

I call first <the evangelist> John to bear testimony,[397] when he says, "In the beginning was the Word and the Word was with God and the Word was God." This "word" is said to be with God, is it not? It makes no difference—save that I may answer Photinus <Sirmius>—whether this was the one who was born of Mary or someone else; that quibble I leave to you. But it is sufficient to point out that <John> says "with God" and "in the beginning," and how, pray, does this agree with the teaching of Moses?

"Never mind," say the Galileans, "for it conforms to the teaching of Isaiah. For Isaiah says, "Behold the virgin shall conceive and bear a son."[398] Even if this were stated of a god—and it is not so stated—

---

391. Julian here being the first pagan writer to show knowledge of the homoousion formula Nicene Creed.

392. John 1.3. Julian's broad knowledge of the New Testament canon and Christian use of the Old Testament is evident in his allusions throughout this section.

393. Num. 24.17.

394. Deut. 4.35.

395. Deut. 4.39.

396. Deut. 32.39.

397. See 1 John 5.8.

398. Isa. 7.14.

a married woman who has been with her husband before her pregnancy could hardly be called a virgin. And let us accept that it is indeed said about Mary: does Isaiah say that a god will be born to a virgin? You never refrain from calling Mary the mother of God, even though Isaiah says nowhere that the one born of the virgin is the only begotten son of God[399] or the firstborn of all creation.[400] And as for the saying of John that "all things were made by him and without him nothing that was made was made,"[401] where shall I find this among the sayings of the prophets? Yet, in quick succession, so take heed, listen to what these same prophets have to say: "O Lord our God, make us your own, for we own no other beside you."[402] And from the king Hezekiah, who is reported to have said, "O Lord God, God of Israel, you sit above the Cherubim; you are God: you alone."[403] Is there room here for a second god? If you truly believe that the Word is God born of God, of the same substance as God, why assert that a virgin is the "mother" of God. How could she—a human being—bear this god; and since God declares in plain words, "I am He and there is no one who can deliver beside me," Do you presume to call this son of hers a "savior"?[404]

290B–290C Now you may acknowledge that Moses calls the angels gods, as when he himself says "The sons of God saw that the daughters of men were fair, and they took wives for themselves as they pleased."[405] Still he writes, "And after a while when the sons of God came into the daughters of men, they bore children to them, and these became the giants of old, the renowned men."[406] It is evident that he means angels by these words, which are his own and no other, because it was not men but giants who were born from this

---

399. Alluding to John 1.18.

400. Col. 1.15.

401. John 1.3.

402. Isa. 26.13, altered by Julian.

403. Isa. 37.16.

404. This rather tedious recitation is designed primarily to show the Christian opponents Julian's virtuosity as an expounder of biblical texts; thus the punning use of the verb σώζειν, here meaning both to save and to give birth (as in the case of Mary).

405. Gen. 6.2.

406. Gen. 6.4.

union. For if mortals rather than superior beings with a higher nature and more powerful stature had been the fathers, he would not have named the offspring giants. He claims instead that the race of giants arose from the mingling of mortal and immortal.[407] So too, when Moses discusses the sons of God and says they are not men but angels, would it not be expected that [at this same moment] he would have disclosed (had he known of it) the information that Jesus Christ is the Word, or as you call him the sole-begotten Son of God?[408] 290E Is it not precisely because Moses was not thinking <of the Word> that he says specifically, "Israel is my firstborn, my firstborn Son?"[409]

But why does Moses not say this about Jesus? After all, he taught that there was one God; that he had many sons; that these were then divided into nations. As to the Word of God being the firstborn Son of God, or even God, or any of these other fabrications you have concocted, Moses knew nothing and taught nothing about them at all.

291A

So, you have listened to Moses himself and to other prophets as well. And you know that in other places Moses frequently says something of this sort: "You shall fear the Lord your God; him only shall you serve."[410] How then do the gospels teach <in defiance of this> that Jesus commanded his followers to "go into all the world teaching and baptizing men, in the name of the Father, the Son, and the Holy Spirit?"[411]

---

407. ἐκ γὰρ θνητοῦ καὶ ἀθανάτου μίξεως.

408. Julian does not challenge the normative use of prophecy, only the Christian interpretation of the Mosaic texts which were held to be prophetic. Like Porphyry, he prefers the literal meaning of texts (see the following sentence) when a clear motive for allegorical or prophetic meaning is not present. The overzealous use of prophetic prooftexts was a constant feature of anti-Christian polemic from at least the time of Celsus, the combative or propagandistic use of such texts having arisen in the early missionary preaching in times of persecution.

409. Exod. 4.22.

410. Deut. 6.13, as also in Matt. 4.10, Jesus' rebuke of Satan in the desert.

411. Matt. 28.19. Julian seems to view this as an example of unguarded tritheism, but does not develop the point in relation to Mosaic religion, which he has argued also had room for a plural concept of deity even if it had been subordinated to monotheistic practices in the course of Israel's history. Nor does he refer to the growing philosophical defenses of Nicene (homoousian) orthodoxy in the eastern Empire.

These writings speak only about serving Jesus and say nothing about serving God.[412]

Note too, if you please, how Moses speaks about the gods who fend off evil when he writes, "The man shall bring two goats from among the goats for a sin offering and a ram for a burnt offering. Then shall Aaron bring his bullock for himself and shall make atonement for himself and his household. And he shall take the two goats and present them to the Lord before the door of the tabernacle of the law. And Aaron shall cast lots for the two goats—one lot for the Lord and the other for the scapegoat. And this goat he shall let loose in the wilderness. In this way you shall send forth the goat that is the scapegoat." And of the second goat, Moses writes, "He then shall kill the goat that is meant for a sin offering for the people in front of the Lord, and gather his blood in a jar, for the blood to be sprinkled on the step of the altar <mercy seat> , making atonement for this holy place on account of the filth of the children of Israel and because of their trespasses and sin."[413] So it is clear that Moses knew the techniques of sacrifice, and did not think them impure, as <the Christians seem to,> as you will witness when you hear his own words: "But the soul that consumes the flesh of the sacrifice of a peace offering meant for the Lord, that soul incurs uncleanness and shall be cut away from the people."[414]

---

412. The meaning of this passage is unclear: Julian seems to want to say that the Christians have extended the worship of God to other "beings" through the baptismal injunction in Matt. 28.19, and so have violated their own monotheistic foundations, which are based on the exclusive worship of the God of Moses and Abraham. Cyril's summary suggests that the Greeks and the Jews have many customs in common notwithstanding the Greek worship of plural deities and their tolerance of soothsaying. He notes also the prevalence of circumcision (rejected by the Christians) among nations throughout the world and the fact that even Moses on occasion sacrificed to heathen gods.

413. Lev. 16.15. Julian's point is to suggest that Moses had learned the rites of sacrifice and found them effective in dealing with the God of Israel.

414. Lev. 7.20. It is somewhat remarkable that Julian reaches into this most arcane of Old Testament purifactory texts for arguments against Christian teaching, especially as his fascination with its description often causes him to lose sight of his central arguments against Christian practice, or to bury his grievance in reflections on the Septuagint text. The key point is that Christians have abolished the use of animal sacrifice while keeping much of the symbolism of the priestly books: Jesus is thus the lamb of God slain before the foundation of the world, an atoning sacrifice for sin. Christian symbolism, however, was remarkably fluid, as Jesus could also

Moses himself cautions you with respect to the eating of sacrificed flesh.[415]

305D

It's best to remind you of what I have already written, as it bears on the present discussion also: Why is it that after you have deserted us <Greeks> you will not accept the law of Jews nor the teachings of Moses? Of course, one of your sharper wits will say, "But the Jews do not sacrifice either."[416] But this point I can convince him is a dull one, since I can also prove that <you Galileans> fail to observe any of the customs which are observed by the Jews; moreover, that in our time the Jews continue to sacrifice—in their own homes. What they eat is always consecrated, and they pray before the sacrifice as well, giving the right shoulder of the lamb to the priests as first-fruits. But of course being deprived of their Temple, their sanctuary, they are prevented from offering these same first-fruits to God in sacrifice.[417]

But why do *you* not sacrifice? You have invented a whole new way of sacrificing that does not need Jerusalem. I suppose it is useless to ask such a question of you, since it hearkens to my earlier point—concerning my wish to show that Jews and non-Jews agree in many things, except that the Jews believe in only one God. This alone do we find unique to them and strange to us, since we have

---

be regarded as the scapegoat (released from death through resurrection, as man was released from sin); the atoning sacrifice might be regarded as a peace offering and thus not to be "eaten" by the people, who would thereby incur the guilt of having usurped a sacrifice intended for God alone. Julian's imperfect understanding of the emerging theology of the Christian eucharist is evident throughout this section, though his arguments reveal a great deal both about pagan perceptions of this theology in late antiquity as well as the relative liberty with which the Old Testament texts had been liturgically appropriated.

415. Cf. Paul, 1 Cor. 8.1–12.

416. Julian does not take notice of the historical similarity of early Palestinian Christianity and early synagogue Judaism, which emerge, following the end of the temple cult, equally as postsacrificial systems.

417. Sozomen (5.22) observes that Julian tried to persuade leading men among the Jews to resume the sacrificial cult, which they were willing to do if the Temple were restored. It is clear from his line of argumentation, which stretches the meaning of sacrifice to include ordinary meals, that Julian does not regard the Christian eucharist as bearing any resemblance to the vestiges of sacrifice in the domestic life of the Jews. For him, it symbolizes chiefly the rejection of sacrifice in the traditional sense.

much else in common with them—the temples, sanctuaries, altars, purification, even certain laws. In all these things, differences scarcely exist, except in small matters. <But it is not clear whether the Christians worship one God, or whether they worship many gods, because they have departed from the teaching of both the Greeks and the Jews in this affair.>[418]

314C

Your diet, for example: Clearly you are not as particular as the Jews, since for some reason you say we are obliged to eat everything, even as the green herb; trusting in Peter who according to the Galileans admonished them, "Do not make unclean what God has made clean."[419] And what proof do you offer that God has changed his mind, holding certain things forbidden in the past, but now <for the sake of Christian appetites> making them pure?

314D

Moses for his part, imparting the law concerning four-footed creatures, says that those with parted hooves or cloven hooves that chew the cud are pure, and others which do not fit the description are impure.[420] Ah, but now, after the visions of Peter,[421] the pig begins to chew the cud, so let us by all means <ignore Moses> and obey Peter! Is it not miraculous that following Peter's revelation the pig has acquired this skill? Yet if <Peter> lied when he disclosed that he had seen this wonderful vision, this revelation—to use your own words—in the tanner's house, why should we rush to believe him in other things? When Moses commanded you to avoid the flesh of swine, did he not also forbid you to eat things that have wings, things that swim in the seas, declaring these things unlawful and unclean according to God's law? Or is it that these rules are too difficult for you to keep?

319D

Why bother to probe these doctrines of the Galileans further when

---

418. Not quoted from Julian but paraphrased from him by Cyril.

419. Acts 10.15.

420. Lev. 11.3, the point being that even if the Jews, like the Christians, no longer observe the traditional forms of the sacrificial cult, they still respect the dietary prescriptions related to it, whereas Christians, "who have no need for Jerusalem" (the Temple), have forsaken the dietary laws pertaining to the cult as well.

421. Acts 10.9–16.

it is far more simple to examine how they work in practice? Now the Galileans will say that God had established an earlier law, but then decided on a new law.[422] They will say that the first law came about because of particular circumstances <in the life of the Jews> and was limited as to time and place, and so gave way after a while to this new law.[423] But the falsity of <their position> I can demonstrate not from ten but ten thousand different passages taken directly from the books of Moses. Moses says, for example, that the law is for all time, as you can <read> in the Exodus when he writes, "This day shall be a memorial for you, and you shall keep it throughout your generations; you shall keep this feast at my command forever; the first day you shall remove all of the leaven out of your houses."[424] There are many verses which say precisely the same thing <about the law>, but because of their great number I will not put them in evidence here to show that the law of Moses was meant to last for all time. And what will you <Galileans> answer? That there is some word of Moses to equate with Paul's rash suggestion that "Christ is the end of the Law."[425]

320B

Where does God offer the Hebrews a second law, different from the law he had <originally> set down? Nowhere—not even as much as a revised version of the original law.[426] Listen to what Moses has

---

422. δεύτερος νόμος.

423. Julian seems to have in mind passages such as Jesus' reformulation of the law in Mark 7.17–23 and Matt. 5.1–7.28.

424. Exod. 12.14–15: This Passover ordinance would seem especially flimsy given the opening flourish with which Julian introduces his evidence. According to Cyril, Julian produced other texts in support of his view that the law was not to be abrogated, but he does not reproduce them. Strangely, Julian does not quote Jesus' words to the effect that the law is established until the time of Judgment (Matt. 5.17–20), which might have been set against Paul's more Hellenistic understanding of the "provisional" or limited force of the law reflected in the passage from Rom. 10.4f.

425. Rom. 10.4, the complete verse running "Christ is the end of the Law for them that believe," being probably addressed to gentile Christian proselytes rather than Jewish Christians, but Julian takes the verse in an absolute sense.

426. Wright, III, p. 410 n. 3, cites Julian's comment in Oration V.170: "The gods, not being ignorant of their future intentions, do not have to correct their errors." It was a standard complaint among pagan critics that the Christian God seemed to lack foreknowledge and that the drama of redemption was based on the need to rectify a divine error. The criticism was also reflected in certain Christian heresies, especially the solution of the Marcionites.

said: "Add not a word nor take a single word away from what I have commanded: keep the commandments of the Lord your God which I command you this day."[427] And he says, "Cursed be every man who does not keep them all."[428] But you think it a trivial matter to add and subtract words from the law. You seem, indeed, to think it courageous and high-minded to destroy the law completely, if it suits you, and to create a revised truth that men will find attractive.

327A

But you <Galileans> are so caught up in your error that you have betrayed even the teachings passed on you by the apostles. These <writings> too have been changed for the worse and made heretical by the scribes who came later.[429] At all odds it was not Paul, nor Matthew, nor Luke, nor Mark who dared call Jesus God. No, it was the estimable John who did so, I imagine, because multitudes in the towns of Greece and Italy had already been struck down by this disease,[430] or perhaps because he had heard that the tombs of Peter and Paul were being worshiped, albeit in secret. Knowing where things stood, it was John who first presumed to call Jesus God. It was John who, giving short shrift to John the Baptist,[431] returns to proclaim <Jesus> the Word of God: "The Word was made flesh," he says, "and dwelled among us."[432]

Nor does John refer to "Jesus" or "Christ," preferring to call him the

---

427. Deut. 4.2.

428. Deut. 27.26. Julian expands his criticism, according to Cyril, by citing Acts 15.29–30, which forbids the eating of meat sacrificed to idols (cf. Paul's admonition in 1 Cor. 8.7ff., which seems to offer the opposite advice). Julian would have been unaware of the "Hellenist" crisis of the early church, which accounts for the different strata of advice concerning the law and dietary rules.

429. Julian is not offering an early theory of synoptic revision, but throughout this section he argues that the earlier gospel writers were cautious in their evaluation of the person of Jesus and that only later did Jesus come to be regarded as a god. He associates this development particularly with the Fourth Gospel rather than with Paul.

430. νόσος: Julian's standard term for conversion to Christianity; cf. Or. VII.229D, Ep. LVIII.401C (to Libanius).

431. John 1.6–8.

432. John 1.14. Julian takes it as self-evident, especially within the framework of his own Neoplatonic thought, that the reference to the incarnation of the divine Logos is an assertion of the divine status of Jesus.

Word or God[433] but then stealthily, quietly seducing our senses—saying, for example, that John the Baptist gave testimony to Jesus Christ, and that we must therefore regard <Jesus alone> as the true Word and God.

333B

I do not, of course, deny that John says these things about Jesus Christ, though certain heretics have said that Jesus Christ is distinct from the Word proclaimed by John.[434] But this is not so: The very one whom John proclaims as God the Word is the same who was recognized by John the Baptist as Jesus Christ. See how <John> cunningly, almost imperceptibly advances the action of his little stage play and in the last act, full of impiety, comes on stage to unveil this final bit of deceit: "No man has seen God at any time. But the only begotten son of God, the one who is in the bosom of the Father, he has revealed him."[435] Well then: Am I to think that the only begotten son who reclines in the Father's bosom also is the God who is the Word made flesh? Because if it is he and no other, then you *have* certainly seen God, since after all, <John> says next, "And he dwelled among you and you beheld his glory." Which makes scant sense of the verse, "No man has seen God at any time." <If John's words ring true> then you have seen God—and if not the Father, then at least God the son, the Word.[436]

But if the only begotten son is one thing[437] and God the Word something else, as I have heard it said some of the members of your

---

433. John 1.1, 18.

434. The Modalists may be in Julian's view, or the Arians, both of whom preached varieties of a separationist or subordinationist doctrine that kept the Logos unaffected by the limitations of Jesus' humanity.

435. John 1.18.

436. Julian refuses to allow the author of the Fourth Gospel any room for narrative or theological expansion, insisting that he has caught him in a contradiction brought on by his awareness that Jesus was not the Word. The order of the verses does evoke a non sequitur; but the Evangelist's point is that while no one has seen God, the Word incarnate reveals him. In Letter XLVII.434 to the Alexandrian Christians in response to their petition for the return of Athanasius from exile, Julian writes, "You dare not to worship [the gods of your fathers] and prefer instead that one you have never seen nor your fathers ever saw, namely Jesus, ought to be revered as God the Word." He enjoins them to return to the worship of Helios, "the intelligible father's living image."

437. ὁ μονογενὴς υἱός, ἕτερος δὲ ὁ θεὸς λόγος: Wright introduces the word "person" into the translation, which because of its associations with Nicene theology I have rendered simply as "thing" or "matter of concern."

sect,[438] then it seems that not even John was foolish enough to declare that <Jesus was God>.

335B

But the beginning of this wicked teaching was John's doing, and how can one begin to revile as they deserve reviling the many errors that you heap one on another, just as you heap the dead bodies of those newly martyred atop the corpses of those who died in ages past?[439]

You have filled the whole world with tombs and sepulchres, yet where in your holy books does it tell you to prostrate yourself at the tombs and pay honors to the dead?[440] But you have so far departed from the truth in this that you will not heed even the words of Jesus of Nazareth. Listen—what does he say about the gravesites? "Woe to you scribes and Pharisees, you hypocrites! For you are like whited sepulchres. On the outside the tomb appears beautiful, but within it is filled with bones of dead men and all impurity."[441] So then, if even

---

438. It is not clear what Julian means by the term "sects" or "heresies." Within the Church, the term had come increasingly to mean an illegitimate Christian minority opposed to the teaching of an orthodox bishop; for his part, Julian does not seem to think the internal doctrinal differences of the Galileans are worth pursuing except as they point up philosophical inconsistencies in doctrine.

439. Julian was exasperated by the benevolence of the Christians to the poor and their record of contributing to the welfare of the sick. In a letter to Arsacius of Galatia (Ep. XXII. 430D) he praises the Christian maintenance of graves, but, as here, he sees it within the "detestable" context of Christian veneration of the relics of the dead, which he finds an affront to pagan religion; cf. Eunapius, *Lives,* 424.

440. Julian's revulsion at Christian reverence for the tombs of martyrs is reflected in his frequent use of the word πονηρός or "depraved" to describe their activities. In recounting an expedition made ca. 354 from Nicomedia to New Ilios, Julian recalls a conversation with a Christian by the name of Pegasius, who showed him shrines to Hector and Achilles. Perplexed that even Christians in Ilios revered pagan heroes and refrained from violating their shrines, Julian is informed by Pegasius that it was natural for the people of the region to worship the brave among their own citizens "just as we also worship the martyrs." In this same letter Julian finds examples of such syncretism useful in promoting the restoration of Greek religion, observing that Pegasius was able to move about the shrines "without making the sign <of the cross> on [his] vile forehead or hissing himself. . . . For the two things are the meat of their theology, I mean hissing at demons and signing a cross on their foreheads" (Ep. XIX).

441. Matt. 23.27, though Jesus is speaking of hypocrisy and not of the veneration of tombs, which was strictly forbidden in Jewish law. Julian also seems to have cited Matt. 8.21 ("Let the dead bury their dead") to prove that Jesus commanded his followers to avoid graves.

Jesus declared that the tombs are full of uncleanness, how can you say that God can be worshiped there?

339E

With so much to condemn you, why do you persist in prostrating yourself among the tombs? If you wish to know, I will happily tell you—or rather not I but the prophet Isaiah <when he says>, "They live among the tombs and in the caves for the sake of dream visions."[442] Here you will see that this practice of sorcery was established long ago by the Jews, who are said to dwell among the tombs in order to receive dream visions. And it is certain that after the master's death your own apostles did this very thing, that is, <sleeping among the tombs>; and that they then passed on the practice to the ones who were first to practice your faith. These no doubt were able to conjure and work miracles with greater deftness than you do nowadays, displaying their abominable rites to the initiates in the secret places appointed for them so that the blasphemy might be perpetuated.[443]

---

442. Isa. 65.4 refers to the Hellenic custom of sitting among the graves in order to evoke an oracle or vision. Julian assumes the practice was initiated by apostates among the Hebrews, then illicitly carried forward into Christianity in defiance of Jewish custom.

443. The charge of witchcraft and sorcery was a polemical convention in Jewish anti-Christian propaganda but did not as such feature independently in earlier pagan polemic. The received description of Jesus as a magician and his followers as apprentices seems to have had an association with tomb ritual, which is reflected in the Lazarus tradition (John 11.1–44), in the Markan story of the rich young man, and a vestige in Mark 14.51 (the young man who flees, leaving his burial shroud behind), and in the so-called—and highly controversial—stratum of tradition known as "Secret" Mark; see M. S. Smith, *Jesus the Magician* (San Francisco, 1978), and his "Clement of Alexandria and Secret Mark: The Score at the End of the First Decade," *Harvard Theological Review* 75 (1982): 449–61. A countervailing tradition is the story of the Gadarene demoniac who is said to "live among the tombs." The presence of Jesus and his followers in a location that would have been off-limits to observant Jews would suggest a certain estrangement from Jewish tradition, as even Porphyry recognized, and it is sometimes suggested that Jesus' withdrawal to "lonely places" and even the Gethsemane account are redacted stories of cemetery rituals. Despite a flight of interpretive fancy in this verse (it is not at all clear that Christians would have utilized cemeteries for the purpose of receiving visions and revelations from the dead, though likely that eucharists were celebrated secretly at gravesites, cf. Eunapius, *Lives*, 424), the tomb tradition is a prominent religious element, beginning with the narrative of the burial of Jesus; the visitation and discovery of the empty tomb; and more to Julian's point, the extension of visitation and veneration to the graves of Christian martyrs in Rome, Antioch, and the East.

343C

So you who perform the rites which God has always hated, as we know from Moses and the prophets, you nevertheless refuse to sacrifice animals at the altar. "Naturally," say the Galileans, "because <God does not rain down> fire to consume our sacrifices, as in the time of Moses or in the days of Elijah the Tishbite, but only after a long span."[444] But I can give you proof in short order that even Moses taught that it was necessary to build the fire for sacrifices performed before him, as you may tell from story of the patriarch Abraham.[445]

And these cases can be multiplied, as when scripture says that the sons of Adam offered first-fruits to God, "And the Lord was pleased with Abel and his offerings, and so Cain was angry and looked downcast. And God said to Cain, Why are you angry and sullen? For is it not true that even if you offer what is proper but do not divide the shares properly you have sinned?"[446] And would you wish me to tell you what these offerings were? "After a long time it happened that Cain brought an offering to the Lord taken from the fruits of the earth. Abel also brought an offering from the fatted firstlings of his flock."[447]

You see! Say the Galileans, it was not the sacrifice but the division of the offering that God condemned, saying to Cain, "If you offer what is proper but do not divide the shares properly you have sinned." This is what one of your own well-read bishops has told me, though he deludes himself and deceives other men as well in thinking this way.[448] When I put to him this question: In what way

444. Lev. 9.24; 1 Kings 18.38.

445. Gen. 15.7–17. It is not clear why Julian chooses to belabor this point, especially as Christian refusal to offer animal sacrifice was tied to a particular understanding of the sacrificial death of Jesus embodied symbolically in their eucharistic celebrations, rather than to the absence of miraculous intervention.

446. Julian's use of the Septuagint of Gen. 4.4–7. It is not clear what specific relevance this quotation would have in Julian's case against Christian rejection of sacrifice unless the "bishop" he refers to in the following section had cited the passage to show that God himself rejected sacrifice, using Cain as a prototype of its inadequacy.

447. Gen. 4.3–4.

448. Aetius, "old friend and correspondent" (Ep. XV), may be the partner in this discussion, since Julian had particular delight in conversing with the bishop and refuting him in debate.

was Cain's division of the offering wrong?, he was silent and could not wriggle free of my snare with so much as a half-hearted reply. So, when I saw that I had him, I said, "God did reject the <offering>, as you say, and with justice; but the piety of the two men was equal. Both knew that they must offer gifts and sacrifice to God. But when it came to apportioning the offering, one man received praise while the other was blamed—but why? What's the reason? Because of all that exists on the earth, some things possess soul while others are soulless. And <you would agree> that things with souls are more valuable than things without souls, at least in the eyes of God who is the author of life. For that which has soul has some share in the life of God, having a life in some sense resembling his. And so, God approved of the man who offered living sacrifice."[449]

351A

To turn now to another matter, I ask why you refuse the practice of circumcision. I hear your answer when you say, "Paul teaches that circumcision of the heart rather than the flesh was imputed to Abraham because of his faith.[450] Paul was not speaking of the flesh and we should heed what he says, as well as what is said by Peter." But have you not heard that God is said to have given circumcision to Abraham as a sign of the covenant when it is written "This is the covenant you will keep between me and yourselves and your off-spring generation after generation: You shall cut away the flesh of the foreskin as a token of the covenant between us, and between me and your offspring."[451] Christ moreover instructs us that he did not come to abolish this law,[452] and teaches explicitly that it is proper to observe this law. And if he not only teaches the observance of the law but actually condemns those who violate even the least com-mandment, what can you say in your own defense—you who have

---

449. One can only imagine the reasons for the Christian bishop's silence on hearing this imaginative exegesis from his emperor.

450. Rom. 4.11, 2.22 are in view.

451. Julian's rendering of Septuagint Gen. 17.10–11. Paul's argument in Romans 4 is that Abraham himself was not circumcised "according to the flesh," and thus might be seen as a prototype of those who have faith but do not belong to the covenant people by birth or rituals associated with the ethnos.

452. According to Cyril, Julian paraphrases Matt. 5.17–19.

violated every one of them?[453] You cannot have it both ways, for either Jesus was speaking falsehood or you have failed dismally to keep the commandment: "The circumcision," Moses says, "shall be of your flesh."[454]

But the Galileans do not listen; they say instead, "Indeed, we circumcize our hearts." And well you should, for as we know there is in your little company not one evildoer and not a single sinner—so well circumcized are your hearts! And the Galileans say, "But we cannot keep the rule concerning the feast of unleavened bread, the Passover. For <we believe> Christ was sacrificed for our sake once and for all."[455] Indeed, and did he then command you himself not to eat unleavened bread? With the gods as my witnesses I count myself among those who avoid the festivals of the Jews. But I venerate without hesitation the God of Abraham, Isaac, and Jacob, <for they were> members of a sacred race, the Chaldeans, learned in the arts of divination, who became acquainted with the rite of circumcision during the time of their wandering among the Egyptians.[456] And the Jews worship a God who has always been gracious toward me, as he was <always gracious> to Abraham and those who, like Abraham, worshiped him. He is a great and powerful God, to be sure, but he is no God of yours.

356C

---

453. The logic of the argument is somewhat attenuated by Julian's tendency to rely on the apposition of the texts he is using to support his case: that as an observant Jew Jesus taught observance of the law of circumcision which Paul, in the interest of his mission to the Greeks, reinterpreted and then set aside, in violation both of Jewish teaching and practice and the example and teaching of Jesus.

454. Gen. 17.13 in Julian's rendering, "ἡ περιτομὴ ἔσται περὶ τὴν σάρκα σου."

455. A reference to the early Christian interpretation of Passover, in particular its meaning for gentile Christians not accustomed to observing Passover (Heb. 10.10). This continues Julian's routine of juxtaposing the teaching of Jesus with the theology of Paul, or in this case the epistle to the Hebrews.

456. This is typical of Julian's recognition of the Jews' zeal for tradition, whereas "[the Greeks] are in such a state of apathy as concerns religious matters that we have forgotten the traditions of our forefathers" (Letter XX.453D–454B). It is interesting that Julian here seems to complain that the Galileans reflect more of Hellenistic indifference to the forms and rules of religion. The Jewish God is worshiped "under other names" by the Greeks, but not by the Christians who have abrogated his laws (454B).

For you have nothing in common with Abraham, who built altars to <God> and worshiped him with sacrifices on those altars with burnt offerings. Like the Greeks, Abraham was accustomed to offer sacrifice daily, and he shared with us Greeks the custom of telling the future from shooting stars. And for significant things he learned to augur from the flight of birds, hiring a servant in his house who was expert in the reading of signs.[457] But someone among you may doubt this, so here are the precise words spoken by Moses to prove the point: "After this the word of the Lord came to Abraham in a night vision saying, Do not be afraid, Abraham. I am your shield, and your reward will be very great. And Abraham said, Lord, my God, what can you give me? Since I am childless, and the son of the slave-woman Masek is to be my heir. And at once the word of the Lord came to him saying, This man is not to be your heir. The one who will be born from you is to be your heir. And he brought him out and said, Consider the sky and read the stars of the heavens: can you count them all? And he said, this is how numerous your offspring shall be. And Abraham believed the Lord and righteousness was attributed to him."[458]

Can you explain to me why he was shown the stars by the one who brought him out, whether God or angel? For surely while he was yet inside the house he knew how vast the array of visible stars were shining above in the night sky? No, I think <he was brought outside> because <God> wished to show him the shooting stars as a visible sign of the promise he had made to Abraham, and to demonstrate that the fulfillment and sanction of all things can be seen in the heavens.[459]

---

457. Gen. 24.14, and an interpretation built on Gen. 24.2–43. Maimonides also seems to have seen Gen. 24.14 as an act of divination.

458. Julian has earlier examined Paul's use of this passage (Gen. 15.1–6, liberally paraphrased by Julian) in connection with the rite of circumcision; here he uses it to show that Abraham's believing in God (ἐπίστευσεν Ἀβραὰμ τῷ θεῷ) involved a reading of the stars or an act of augury. It is remarkable that Julian does not choose to mention the most famous Christian example of divination in the Gospel, the star of Bethlehem (Matt. 1.7–10) in his discussion of Hellenic customs.

459. Julian is probably guilty, and perhaps conscious, of an overimaginative piece of exegesis read back into the patriarchal narratives, stemming from his belief that the patriarchs themselves were Chaldeans and thus especially skilled in the interpretation of the skies. The idea that the stars served as a "visible pledge" might suggest that Julian is thinking of another biblical text (Gen. 9.13) where a sign is given to Noah in the heavens representing the promises of God.

358C So that no one will think my interpretation is rash, I would ask you to observe what follows in this passage, for what follows next is this: "And he said to him, I am the Lord your God that brought you out of the land of the Chaldees to give you this land as an inheritance. And he said, Lord God, how shall I know that I shall inherit it? And he said to him, Bring me a heifer three years old, a she goat of three years, a ram of three years, a turtle dove, and a pigeon. And he did as God commanded and divided them down the middle and laid each piece one against the other; but the birds he did not divide, but the birds came down on the divided carcasses and Abraham sat down among them."[460]

So you can see how even the revelation of God or an angel was supported by this use of reading the signs of the birds, how a prophecy was brought to fulfillment in a complete manner. By the offering of sacrifices, and not, as in <the case of the Galileans> an arbitrary fashion.[461] Further, he says that it was the flocking together

---

460. Gen. 15.11; lit., "drove them away." Julian according to Ammianus was especially interested in the use of birds in augury; cf. Amm., 22.12.1, who also comments on the emperor's "drenching the altars with the blood of bulls and other animals" before the Persian campaign.

461. This is yet another instance of Julian's hypogeal style of argumentation: According to his logic in this passage: The Hebrew patriarchs were Chaldeans and skilled astrologers; Abraham being a Chaldean looked to the stars for knowledge of divine things and received signs from God; these were then confirmed for him through the use of sacrifice; sacrifice is therefore a confirmation of the relationship between our knowledge of the divine and the revelations one is able to attain through observation (observation being understood to include dreaming and ecstatic states, as well as seeing). The Galileans have piecemeal taken on some of these religious customs, but so modified them that they have lost the sort of coherence which Julian thinks both the Hellenes and the Jews have preserved. Here too, however, there are noticeable silences with respect to his familiarity with earlier Christian tradition as reflected in the gospels: the Christian apocalypses (cf. Mark 13.24–27, pars.; Rev. 4–12, etc.) based on Hellenistic Jewish prototypes (1 Enoch, 4 Esdras, etc.) and Jesus' commendation of divination as a way of foretelling the coming of the heavenly son of man (Dan. 7.1–27), and Paul resorts to the same method in Rom. 1.18–20. It is reasonable to suppose that Julian's failure to mention early Christian persistence in the Hellenistic Jewish custom of divination and augury stems from his awareness that Christians had by and large given up the practice (as had the Jews) following the age of Messianic enthusiasm, ca. 70 CE. Here too, however, the receding of apocalyptic divination among the Jews is not called into question.

of the birds that proved the revelation was true. So Abraham believed the promise, saying as well that a promise that cannot be shown to be true is foolishness and stupidity.[462] For need I tell you that one cannot discern truth from mere words: there must be some sign that the words are true, some proof that everyone can see which supports the prophecy as it concerns the future. There is, I imagine, an excuse for your recklessness in this matter: the fact that you are not permitted to offer sacrifices outside Jerusalem. Yet Elijah offered his sacrifice on Mount Carmel and not in the Holy City. . . .

*   *   *

---

462. The implication is that Hebrew prophecy is supported by signs of approval, whereas Christians simply assert it to be true that their religion fulfills the Old Testament prophecies.

FRAGMENTS OF THE
CONTRA GALILAEOS[463]

FRAGMENT III:

These things have happened before, and still are happening. How can they be signs of the end of the world?[464]

FRAGMENT IV

Moses after fasting forty days received the Law. Elijah was permitted to see God face to face after fasting for the same length of time. And what did Jesus receive after fasting for just the same period?[465]

---

463. From Neumann's reconstruction, *Juliani imperator librorum contra christianos quae supersunt* (Leipzig, 1880) (with German translation). The numbering of fragments here corresponds to Neumann rather than to Wright's revision.

464. From Julian's Book II (Cyril, Book XII); derived from Theodore of Mopsuestia who wrote a refutation of Julian around 378. On the critique of Christian apocalyptic hopes as an early fixture of anti-Christian polemic, cf. Hoffmann, *Celsus*, pp. 6–12.

465. From the same source as fragment iii.

FRAGMENT VI:

Jesus was in the desert when he was [said to have been] led to the pinnacle of the Temple: how could this happen?[466]

FRAGMENT VII

Furthermore, Jesus—a "god"—requires the comfort of an angel as he prays, using language that would be humiliating even for a beggar who bemoans his adversity. And who had told this Luke[467] the story of the angel if, indeed, it ever happened, for no one was there to see the angel as he prayed, since the men had fallen asleep. So it is that when Jesus comes to them from his prayer he finds them "asleep for grief," and he says, "Why are you asleep; arise and pray with me, and so forth, until, "While he was speaking, a multitude and Judas arrived," and this is why John omits this tale about an angel, for he did not see it either.

FRAGMENT IX

Hear now this sage political advice: "Sell whatever you have and give it to the poor. Provide for yourself the purse that does not wear thin."[468] Can anyone imagine a finer piece of common sense than this? For when all men obey your command, there will be no one left to buy anything; and if this laudable teaching were carried out, what city, what nation, what family would survive? When everything has

---

466. The criticism echoes the famous comment of Origen in *De principiis* 4.3 concerning the transportation of Jesus in Matt. 4.8: "The devil is said to have taken Jesus up into a high mountain in order to show him all the kingdoms of the world and the glory of them. How could this possibly have happened literally, either that the devil should have led Jesus up to a high mountain or that with his human eyes he should have seen all the kingdoms of the world—as if they were lying close to the foot of a single mountain."

467. Luke 22.42–47.

468. Luke 12.33.

been given away, neither household nor family has aught to bargain or to buy. And it goes without saying that in a city where everything was given away [to the poor] the traders would become beggars.[469]

FRAGMENT X:

How can you say, "The Word of God takes away sin,"[470] when he causes many to commit the sin of killing their fathers and even their children?[471] So we are left with the choice, either to accept this superstition or to hold fast the traditions and the ancient beliefs which our fathers held from the beginning. Is it not the same with Moses, who was supposed to take away sin but fell prey to the charge that he caused sin to increase?[472]

FRAGMENT XV

What was written of Israel the writer Matthew transferred to Christ.[473] He does this to ridicule the naivete of those among the gentiles who believed.

---

469. Cf. Ep. XL (to Hecebolius), where Julian quotes the same passage in confiscating the property of the church at Edessa so that "their poverty may teach them virtue."

470. John 1.29, conflated with John 1.1.

471. Although many have seen this as a reference to Matt. 10.21 (the dissolution of families when confronted with the Gospel), Julian may have in view more recent divisions in household during the time of the last persecutions under Diocletian and Decius.

472. Lev. 16; cf. with Paul's argument in Rom. 5.20, which Julian seems to have in view in this passage. Julian seems to think that both Moses and Jesus failed in their purpose by creating additional opportunities for wrongdoing, Moses by imposing a law that proved too strict for the Jews, Jesus by offering unconditional forgiveness without emphasizing moral responsibility.

473. *Ad Christum transtulit.* Preserved by Jerome in his Latin *Commentary on Hosea* 3.11. The passages referred to are Hos. 11.1 and Matt. 2.15, the prophecy used by Matthew to support the tradition of the Holy Family's wandering in Egypt prior to going to Nazareth.

MISCELLANEOUS AND OCCASIONAL WRITINGS ABOUT CHRISTIANITY AND JUDAISM

INTRODUCTION

The following is a selection of Julian's occasional writings concerning Christianity and Judaism. Because of the sporadic nature of these compositions, they do not offer a consistent line of argumentation, but reflect rather the emperor's developing view of the dangers posed by the Galileans at various junctures in his reign.

Broadly speaking, the epistles fall into three categories: those written to confidants and teachers, such as those to Maximus (Ep. XII, and perhaps LIX) and Theodorus (Ep. XVI and XX); those written to deal with a particular social or religious crisis, such as those to the Alexandrians (Ep. XLVII and XLVIII) , the Bostrians (Ep. XLI), and the "people of Edessa" (Ep. XL); and those written to exhibit or to withdraw philanthropy, such as the letter to the Jews (Ep. LI) and the edict on Christian teaching (Ep. XXXVI).

1. CONCERNING CHRISTIAN TEACHERS (AD 362, WRITTEN AT ANTIOCH)[474]

The line of argumentation in this letter is straightforward: Julian accuses Christian teachers of rhetoric of hypocrisy for "thinking one thing" as

---

474. Ep. XXXVI.422A–424A (Hertlein, 36).

believers and teaching their students to respect the works of writers like Homer who were "consecrated to the gods" and the muses. The more damaging accusation is that those who profit from hypocrisy appear to be greedy and thus to violate the gospel's endorsement of poverty as the key to salvation.

A sound education, in my view, is not a hard-won command of well-proportioned sentences and glibness of tongue, but depends on a sound mind—a mind attuned to the good rather than evil, the mind that comprehends the difference between what is noble and what is base. A man who thinks in one way but teaches his pupils to think another is a failure as a teacher because he fails to be an honest man.

Now if the contradiction between what a man holds to be true and what he teaches for truth is a matter of no great significance, even though this should be wrong, still it is, I think, in some sense a minor matter. But in larger matters this is not the case: What if a man has philosophical convictions but teaches the opposite of them—what sort of behavior, but the conduct of a complete liar, should this be? A man who praises what he knows is worthless and promotes what he privately condemns is a hypocrite, a cheater, a seducer, a peddler of worthless goods. Any man who desires to teach anything must first of all be a man of virtue. Above all this means that a man <who teaches> cannot keep hidden in his soul certain ideas which clash with the ideas he openly discusses, for I believe that a teacher has a special responsibility <for the souls> of the young.

And it is for this reason that a man who teaches the young the art of speaking should be above all a man of real virtue, for it is <through this art> that the young come to understand and discuss the works of the ancients, the rhetoricians and grammarians, above all the sophists. For it will be recalled that these philosophers claimed to teach the apt use of language as well as other things, especially moral and political philosophy. I salute all who bring such high ambition with them to their teaching, of course, leaving aside for the moment any discussion of their method. Yet I cannot leave aside the fact that <there are those> who teach their students many things that do not conform to their inmost beliefs.

How can this be? Did not the gods bestow all learning on the likes of Homer, Hesiod, Demosthenes, Herodotus, Thucydides, Isocrates, Lysias? And did not these same men think themselves inspired by Hermes or one of the Muses? How terrible that the men who have the duty to expound these writers revile the gods whom these writers loved!

Now while I find this position risible, I am not suggesting that the teachers should change their views before being allowed to teach; rather I offer them a choice: either not to teach what they do not find worthy of belief, or, if they still wish to teach, require them to convince their charges that none of the writers whose works they study— Homer, Hesiod, and the rest—should be counted guilty of impiety or naivete or error with respect to the gods, as they have said.

After all, since it is by the work of these writers that they are able to make a living and receive pay, is it not the most crass admission of greed that they would sell their souls for a few drachmas? There were many reasons why, until the present time, men were terrified of being open and forthright in their private opinions about the gods and their failure to be diligent in temple worship found many excuses. But I say the gods have granted us liberty, and because this is so there is no reason for men to teach what they do not believe to be true.

If, on the one hand, they think that the men whose works they teach were wise men <and worth reading>, then their role as interpreters, indeed as prophets and wise men, would indicate they should first of all be true imitators of the poets in their piety toward the gods. But if, on the other hand, they believe our writers to have been wrong in their belief about the gods, who are most worthy of our reverence, then let them trundle off to the churches of the Galileans to expound Matthew and Luke, since the Galileans themselves commend a man who refuses to worship at the temple. As for myself, I can only hope that your ears and tongues might be, to use your expression, "born again" in accordance with the tastes of those who think and act in ways pleasing to me.

For all teachers of religion and arts let there be an ordinance to this effect: Any boy who wishes to attend a school shall not be prevented, for what sense is there in shutting the door of the true path

<of knowledge> to boys still too ignorant to know what is good for them, only to find themselves confused, overpowered <by the rhetoric of their masters>, and tricked into following beliefs that were not those of their ancestors.[475] I admit that it might be more easily done to cure these teachers as one cures the insane, against their will.

But as we grant pardon for people afflicted with the disease of insanity, we might agree that the best way to cure the insanity of Christianity is to teach rather than to punish the afflicted.

2. TO MAXIMUS (361 OR 362)[476]

This letter, written to the philosopher-theurgist Maximus, is primarily important for understanding Julian's perception of the role of gods in ordering fate and the significance of sacrifice and obedience in knowing, and responding to, the divine will. The life of Maximus is known to us from the writings of Eunapius, who reports that as a student Julian abandoned study with Edesius of Pergamon to join Maximus at Ephesus. At least part of the reason for this transfer of academic loyalty seems to have been Maximus's reputation of receiving his philosophy through oracles. In any event Julian remained faithful to his teacher, if not to every aspect of his teaching, until his dying day and the philosopher was at least unofficially the philosopher royal in Constantinople after 362 and probably sponsored Julian's initiation into the cult of Mithras. Maximus was at Julian's deathbed. Immediately following the death of his patron, Maximus's influence began to wane rapidly. Attempts to discredit his teaching as charlatanry blended with a vague charge of conspiracy which resulted in his execution, by order of Valens, in 371. In this letter Julian explains that he is determined to restore the worship of the gods "in its original purity."

My mind is a blur of confused thoughts and they well up to stop the words in my throat, so that nothing can pass from my mouth in order. Is it a psychic disturbance that causes this to happen, or some-

---

475. The biographical thrust of Julian's words in this section deserves to be underscored; see Athanassiadi, *Julian: An Intellectual Biography*, pp. 13–51. Cf. Ep. VII.236A, B, where Julian deplores the teaching of the "utterly ignorant rhetors."

476. Ep. VIII (Hertlein, 38).

thing else?[477] Oh, pray that I can relate what I must tell you in some sort of sequence—that is, after I have made due offering to the gods who, in their mercy, have commanded me to write this to you and may permit us to see each other soon. Now after I was made emperor against my will, with the gods as my witnesses—that is, having been proclaimed ruler in the usual way, I led the army against the barbarians.[478] It was only after three months on this expedition that I returned to Gaul, and after I arrived I would ask anyone who would listen to be watchful for a man wearing a philosopher's cloak or a scholar's gown <and to> report any such sighting at once. So I came to Besontio, a village recently improved a bit, and in ancient times a great city rich in temples and surrounded by strong walls as well as by the River Doub, which nature adds to its fortification. Besontio rises like a sheer cliff from the seas—towering in such a way that even the birds find it beyond reach except in a few places where the river had circled around in such a way as to create a shoreline.

As I came near to the city a man came along who, judging from his long cloak and staff, was a cynic, and when I first glimpsed him I thought, "Ah, it is my old friend Maximus!" When he came nearer, I thought, "No, not Maximus, but someone who has been sent by the teacher to speak with me." But alas! The man was a friend of mine, not the sort of thing I was hoping for, merely a frivolous dream. A bit later on I thought that you would be so busy tending to my affairs that I would scarcely find you beyond the shores of Greece. Zeus, Helios, and Athene: witness all you mighty gods and goddesses, how I did tremble for you all the way from Illyricum to Gaul, how often I supplicated the gods for some sign of your welfare—or rather, how often I asked others to ask the gods your fate since I myself could bear to hear no bad news about what might have happened to you. So others enquired for me, and the gods showed clearly that there would be trouble—though nothing fatal,

---

477. Julian implies that he is suffering from the "theurgist's disease," with the power of human speech being inadequate to convey the marvels which flow through his mind.

478. Amm., 20.10: The campaign described took place in 360, when Julian crossed the Rhine.

nothing to suggest the extent of the wicked plots that would be executed in my absence.[479]

You must forgive my passing over so much that has happened to me—especially I wish you to know that I have received revelation direct from the gods and was able to escape the death plot against me that had been perpetrated by my enemies. But escape I did, and even then I ordered no man's death, nor did I confiscate anyone's property, thinking the best punishment was prison for those whose treachery I discovered first hand. Well, I perhaps should tell you these things rather than write them down, but I know, dear friend, you will want the news and be happy to get it.

Know that I worship the gods, I worship the gods publicly, and all the soldiers returning with me do the same. I sacrifice oxen in view of all; I offer tons of thanks offerings. And why? Because the gods have revealed that it is their will that I should restore their worship in its original purity. I obey them, with absolutely no reservations. And they promise me return on my labors as long as I am solicitous of their approval and dedicate myself to them.[480]

3. TO THEODORUS, ON HIS APPOINTMENT AS HIGH PRIEST AND GUARDIAN OF THE TEMPLES (363?)[481]

The following extract illustrates Julian's concern for the operation of the temples. Theodorus, known to us only from Julian's correspondence, seems to have been a Syrian Neoplatonist and a former schoolmate of

---

479. The reference is to the parlous state of Julian's supporters in the East during this campaign and following his quarrel with Constantius.

480. Julian expresses in this and a number of other letters his conviction that the gods, especially Helios, had a direct role to play in his confrontation with Constantius, whose sudden death was seen as an act of divine intercession (see Letter X, Ἰυλιάνῳ Θεῷ) adumbrated by particular signs; cf. Ep. X, addressed to Eutherius: "I am alive and have been saved by the gods. Therefore offer sacrifices to them on my behalf as thanks offerings." It is especially irritating to Julian that the Christians have foresworn even thanks-offerings which might be expected in view of his relatively tolerant attitude toward certain churches and teachers, such as Aetius, whom he addresses (Ep. XV) as an old friend.

481. Ep. XX. 452C–454D (Hertlein, 63).

Julian. He studied under Maximus of Ephesus and may have been initi-
ated into the cult of Mithras together with the future emperor under
Maximus's tutelage. The importance of the letter consists in its clear
assertion of Julian's interest in the moral reform of the temple cults and
the priesthood, over which he asserts his rights as pontifex maximus.
While it would be too much to say that Julian is impressed with Chris-
tian concern for the poor, he recognizes charitable work as a means of
encouraging a greater asceticism among the pagan priests. Like Galen,
he regards the ethical practice of the Christians commendable while
holding their philosophical system in contempt.

. . . I am yielding to your care a trust for which I have the highest care
and concern, as it should be to all men everywhere, in the hope that
you will fulfill the task dutifully, and thereby give me comfort and
assurance of the life to come. <For dear Theodorus> I am not a man
who shares the view that the soul perishes before the body dies or
immediately thereafter. I trust no human authority in this matter but
rather believe what the gods have revealed, for is it not probable that
only they have true knowledge of what transpires <after death>, and
is it not certain that this knowledge far outweighs any human speculation of what is perfectly true. After all, we may be permitted to
speculate about such things, but the gods themselves have no need
for conjecture, for they know all there is to know.

What office do I give to you, you ask? It is the office of governor
of the temples of the East, and with it authority in each city to
appoint priests and determine their benefice. The qualities which
indicate your suitability for this task are primarily justice, kindness,
and benevolence toward all; for we know that a priest who acts in a
hateful way toward his brothers or with irreverance toward the gods
is unacceptable to all men, and that such a man must be publicly
reprimanded in no uncertain terms. I shall lay out in a separate letter
the particular requirements for priests, and this will soon be with
you,[482] while here I mean only to offer a few suggestions.

You will no doubt see the reason in obeying me in this matter,

---

482. According to Wright (III, p. 54 n. 1), these instructions are contained in
the so-called *Letter to a Priest* written after the burning of the temple of Apollo at
Daphne in 362.

for when it comes to divine things I never act rashly or offhandedly (God knows!), but always with deliberation and care. Of course I resist unnecessary change in all of life's affairs, but more especially am I cautious in matters concerning the gods. The traditions of our forefathers are always before my eyes, because they are gifts of the gods themselves; and they would not be of such incomparable value had they been dreamed up by men.

But my dear Theodorus, in our time these customs and laws have been sorely tested and violated. Love of pleasure and money has become an end in itself. Accordingly, we need to look at <these customs> afresh, with new eyes.

First, then, let us recognize that among us there is a certain indifference about the gods, and that the love of money and pleasure has suffocated our reverence for the heavenly powers. <How clear this became to me> when I observed that the adherents of the Jewish religion would sooner suffer starvation and die than compromise their faith by eating pork, or animals that have been strangled or had their life squeezed away. But what of us? We are so indifferent to religious customs that we disregard the traditions of our forebears, having forgotten whether any such rule was ever written down. But the Jews for their part are God-fearing.[483] By this I mean they worship a god who is the most powerful, most good, and rules the created order—a god who, as we recognize, is worshiped by us under different names.[484] And <the Jews> act in a way that accords with our custom when they do not abuse <our> laws. Indeed, they are in error about only one thing: they hold their god in such exclusive regard that they refuse the counsel of other gods, whom they declare to be the "gods of the gentiles only."[485] This error they have driven to such foolish extremes as only barbarians know how. But this

---

483. The standard designation: θεοσεβεῖς ὄντες.

484. Cf. CG 354b: "And we worship the God of Abraham . . . for he is great and powerful."

485. The issue of Jewish religious exclusivism on the Christian side is discussed by Paul, e.g., in Gal. 2–3, where the issue becomes whether Jews hold exclusive title to the God of Israel. Paul's view is that the God of Abraham has been "extended" to every nation (Gal 3.14) instrumentally, through faith in Jesus Christ. Presumably what follows in this letter would have been Julian's discussion of Christian abuse, as he saw it, of Jewish exclusivism.

<error is nothing> as compared to the blasphemous sect of the Galileans which spreads its disease. . . .[486]

4. TO ARSACIUS, A HIGH PRIEST OF GALATIA[487]

This letter is preserved by the historian Sozomen (5.16), who seems to think it is particularly important for understanding Julian's attitude toward Christian benevolence and charitable work. There is no good reason on the basis of language or content to question its authenticity, since elsewhere Julian offers grudging praise of Christian social practice while ridiculing aspects of their belief.

Why is it that the Greek religion does not yet flourish? It is because those who have the most to gain from its advancement are most negligent in promoting that splendid worship, that glorious ritual that puts all other forms of prayer to shame. May Adrasteia[488] excuse what I am about to say—for it will seem boastful that so much change could have been expected or even hoped for a short time ago. These atheists excel in good works to strangers, their scrupulous attention to the graves of the dead, and the feigned piety they display in their everyday lives. For my part I wish these habits could be cultivated by all—not only you but every one of the priests in Galatia. If they will not conform, then humiliate them publicly or remove them from their religious office, especially if you witness them, with their families and slaves, avoiding their duties to the gods and chasing after the teaching of the atheists.[489] If this fails,

---

486. The conclusion is lost, probably expunged by a zealous copyist "because of some disrespectful reference to Christ" (Wright, III, 61 n. 2) or, more likely, because it extolled Judaism at the expense of Christian doctrine. The reference to Christianity as νόσημα signifies plague, but also passion (thus Aeschylus, *Prometheus* 225, 265), madness (thus Sophocles, *Ajax* 338) and disorder in a state (thus Plato, *Laws* 906c).

487. Ep. XXII (Hertlein, 49).

488. Nemesis, the "goddess whom none may escape."

489. Julian's encouragement of imitating Christian practices is followed immediately by the warning to avoid Christian teaching; see Gregory Naziazen, *Against Julian*, Oration III; Sozomen, 5.16. The use of ἀθεότητα to refer to the Christians is a judicial aspersion in this instance.

then say that a priest may not enter the theater, nor carouse at taverns, nor engage in any trade that is beneath his dignity.

More than this, you should take care to hold those who take your counsel in high regard—others, throw them out. You should arrange for hostels to be erected in every city as a sign of our benevolence to those in need, and I do not mean Greeks only but those who most need our help. . . .[490] For it is a disgrace to us that no Jew has to beg, and that every Galilean is ready to provide support for our poor as well as their own, while men laugh that we cannot muster aid for our people. Tell those who hold fast the faith of the Greeks that they must provide for the downcast—offering the first-fruits to the gods; and tell those same believers that the doing of good works of this sort has been our practice from time immemorial. Does not Homer have Eumaeus say, "Stranger, I can imagine no man lower than you, but for my part even if one should come it is not permitted for me to dishonor a stranger. For all strangers and beggars come from Zeus. Every gift, however small, is precious."[491]

<As charity belongs by right to us> let us not permit others to outdo us in such service; for insofar as we are remiss in this way, so also we show dishonor to the gods. I shall be glad indeed to hear that you are carrying out these orders.[492]

5. TO PHOTINUS (CA. 362)[493]

Photinus is mentioned by Julian in Contra Galilaeos *(262C) and was bishop of Sirmium in 351 during Constantius's time in the city. His religious views were decidedly controversial and Constantius sought his deposition and banishment (Sozomen, 4.6). Photinus has the distinction of having alienated both the Arian and the Nicene parties with his theology,*

---

490. In the verses here omitted Julian itemizes the supplies of corn and wine that are to be allocated throughout Galatia.

491. *Odyssey* 14.56.

492. The remaining section of the letter contains instructions for dealing with soldiers and government officials and the reverence due to the Magna Mater (μήτηρ τῶν θεῶν) in relation to the the temples.

493. Ep. LV (Hertlein, 79), preserved in a Latin version by Facundus Hermianensis (546?); see Neumann, *Contra Christanos* (1880), p. 5.

but his insistence on the humanity of Jesus seems to have won favor with Julian. In this letter the emperor praises his views in contrast to the ideas of Diodorus, bishop of Tarsus, who held extreme consubstantiationist views concerning the divinity of Jesus. Only a portion of this letter, interspersed with its editor's stitches, can be considered authentic (see note).

My dear Photinus, you alone hold what I think is probably true and come near salvation: that one we believe to be a god cannot be brought forth from a womb. But Diodorus, the trickster priest of the Nazarenes, who tries to make a case for this ridiculous theory about the womb[494] using his flim-flam and sleight of hand <to do it> is as clever a sophist of the creed of these bumpkins as you are likely to find. . . . And if the gods and goddesses and the Muses and Fortuna will only give me their assistance, I will show that <Diodorus> is a really a deceiver, an abuser of the laws and customs of the great mysteries and the mysteries of the gods of the underworld, and that this upstart Galilean god of his, whom Diodurus calls "eternal" by preaching some preposterous fable, has surely been stripped of any divinity ascribed to him through his humiliating death and burial. . . . <For this same Diodorus> sailed off to Athens without rhyme or reason, then brashly seized on the study of philosophy, then literature, and by next becoming proficient in rhetoric, he trained his vile tongue to utter blasphemy against the gods of heaven. Ignorant of the mysteries <of our religion> he drank his fill of the degenerate and stupid nonsense preached by the ignorant and vile creed-making fishermen. [And for this he has been punished by the gods for many years, by a gradual wasting of the lungs that has now spread to his whole body. His face is now sallow, his body furrowed with scars. But I stress, this <disease> is not a philosopher's plight, as he wants it to appear when he is preaching his deceit, but rather a sign of the punishment the gods have chosen for him in direct proportion to the crime; and now he must live out his days, painfully and bitterly, a man pale and diseased.][495]

---

494. Either the view that Mary's virginity was miraculously preserved or that she is worthy of the title "god-bearer."

495. While there is no reason to challenge the central complaint of this letter as belonging to Julian, the latter portion of the epistle (bracketed) with its obvious indulgence in the physical description of Diodorus's disease suggests a sixth-century Latin provenance, and can probably be attributed to Facundus himself.

6. TO HECEBOLIUS[496]

Hecebolius (not to be confused with a sophist of the same name) was a treasury official in Edessa in northern Mesopotamia. The city had been a hotbed of heresy, especially gnosticism, since the second century. To encourage the dominance of the Arian party there, Constantius provided the sect with the basilica church of St Thomas as a trophy, which had the effect of further alienating the minority sect of Valentinian Gnostics in the city. Sozomen (6.1) suggests that Julian was particularly contemptuous of Edessa, whose Christianity seems to have been reinforced by a persecution of the non-Arian party under Valens (cf. Soc., HE, 4.18). In this letter Julian is determined to hold the Edessene Christians to their profession of poverty by rescinding the benefits which his predecessor had bestowed on the church. The epistle is also significant as being Julian's clearest expression of the benevolence he feels he has exercised toward the Galileans. In contrast, Julian asks the recipient to consider the intolerance of the Christians toward the religion of the Valentinians.

I have conducted myself with all the kindness and benevolence the Galileans deserve, not doing them violence, or dragging them into the temples, or threatening injury, or coercion of any sort. But the members of the Arian church, with all the spiteful arrogance that befits their wealth, have shown only violence to the followers of Valentinus, and have done things in Edessa of such wanton recklessness that they cannot be imagined in a well-ordered city. So I decree—because by their most excellent law they are required to sell all they have and give it to the poor so that they can fly more easily to their kingdom in the skies—and I order, in order to assist them in their noble effort, that all the funds belonging to the people of the church in Edessa be seized and distributed to the soldiers; and I order that the valuables belonging to the churches be confiscated and handed over to me. In this way, poverty will teach them good conduct, but most important, they will not be deprived of that heavenly home for which they yearn. I also order the citizens of Edessa to cease from all quarrels and disputes—for if you do not you will

---

496. The date of the letter is uncertain, but the "policies" alluded to suggest the winter of 362. Ep. XL (Hertlein, 43).

test my benevolence, and find yourselves, whether by sword or exile, paying the price for disturbing the peace of the commonwealth.

7. TO THE BOSTRIANS[497]

Bostra is described by Ammianus (14.8.13) as a large fortified city of Arabia. As in the letter to Hecebolius, Julian here expresses dismay that the Christians have yet to show gratitude for his lenient policies toward them. He is especially annoyed at threatening language used by their bishop, Titus, who has taunted Julian that Christians keep the peace because the church enjoins them to do so and not because they are ordered to do so by the emperor.

I would have expected that these leaders of the Galileans would be more grateful to me than to my predecessor for the way I have governed the empire, since in his day vast numbers of them were cast into exile, tried in the courts, thrown into prison—not to mention the congregations of those called "heretics" who were simply slaughtered—as in Samosata, Cyzicus, Paphlagonia, Bithynia, Galatia, and the villages where tribes were looted and dispersed. In my reign, none of this has happened: the ones in exile have been called home. Those whose property had been confiscated have by my own law had it restored. But <these Galileans> are so inflamed with madness and steeped in stupidity that they fault me for refusing to let them act like tyrants, <for condemning> their conduct toward one another, and toward those of us who have always revered the gods. They do everything possible to show their arrogance—turning the people toward rebellion, while they themselves deride the gods with acts of impiety. As for myself, I do not permit a single <Christian> to be dragged against his will to our altars. Indeed, I have advised that any man who wishes willingly to take part in our ceremonies and libations should first of all perform a ritual of purification and supplicate the gods who <help us to> avert evil. But far be it from me to want any of these superstitious folk to partake of sacrifices that we hold sacred,

---

497. Or, Bosrians; cited by Sozomen 5.15. Ep. XLI (Hertlein, 52).

at least until such time as he has purified his soul in the right way, through prayer to the gods and the purification of his body.

It is obvious that many people have been led astray by the clergy,[498] who advocate rebellion against us because we have taken away certain privileges. It is as if those who behaved like tyrants before now are not content with the punishments they have received, but long for the powers they used to enjoy when they sat as judges, fashioned wills, stole other men's inheritances and put it in their pocket, pulled every string to bring on disorder, and to add fuel to the fire, performed the even greater sin of actually leading the community into chaos through their wicked designs.

I have, therefore, decided to announce to citizens everywhere and by this proclamation to make it known that no one may get involved in the feuds of the clerics, or be persuaded by them to take stones in their hand and hurl them at those with authority. It is permitted for them to hold meetings whenever they wish and to offer prayers for their own well-being, as is their custom. But they must refuse if the clerics try to persuade them to take up sides on their behalf in any sort of dispute, for if they do they will no longer be free from punishment.

I have the city and people of Bostra especially in view because their bishop Titus and his clergy, according to reports I have seen, have made certain charges against other Christians. This gives the impression that when the population began to riot, it was the Christians who kept the peace and saved the state from collapse. I have added the very words <of Titus> to my decree, where he dared to write "The Christians are a match for the Hellenes in numbers, but they are restrained because of our teaching that no one must disturb the peace at any time." This is how your bishop thinks of you. Notice how he cheapens your behavior by saying it was not your choice but his words that kept you from violence against your will. So I say, use this same free will, take your accuser and cast him out of the city.[499]

---

498. The priests and teachers, especially those who are literate or those engaged in theological dispute.

499. Socrates, HE 3.25 mentions Titus still holding power in Bostra under Julian's successor, Jovian. Either Titus was restored in 363 or Julian's advice was not followed.

But by the same reasoning, live in peace with one another, let no man be quarrelsome or act unfairly. <To> those who have left the truth behind, I say do not harass those who give the gods their due in prayer and sacrifice, as we have been taught to do since earliest times. And those of you who worship the gods, do not plunder the houses of those who have erred against truth through ignorance rather than on purpose. How often have I admonished those who hold fast to true doctrine not to harm the Galileans or abuse or insult them but learn to persuade them with reason. For such men deserve pity more than scorn, since only pity is a sound response to their sad state. <And you know> that the greatest blessing is this: reverence for the gods, just as the greatest evil is irreverence. And those who have turned away from the gods in favor of corpses and relics must pay a price.[500] <By analogy> we suffer in sympathy when there are people suffering from disease, and we exult with those who are set free of their sickness by the will of the gods.

8. ON FUNERALS[501] (363)

The edict on funerals represents Julian's most explicit, if indirect, attempt to discourage Christian burial practices. His view that the Christians had "filled the world with graves and sepulchres," an allusion to the martyr cults, the celebration of anniversaries, and the practice of preserving relics and building shrines at or near the site of the graves of saints, seems to occasion the ruling. The edict is not directly aimed at Christians but includes them in its scope. The primary theme of the letter is that death harmonizes with night and rest, and that the display of the corpse during daylight is an affront to Helios. Julian ignores, or misses, the Easter symbolism which associated resurrection and sunrise in the gospel tradition. On the sources of Julian's teaching, see Eunapius, Life of Iamblichus. Julian was especially contemptuous of the displays of enthusiasm, often leading to public demonstrations, at Christian funerals, notably the interment of the bones of St Babylas in Antioch (Philostorgius 7.8; Soz. HE 5.19; Julian, Misopogon 361B).

---

500. Julian regards the cult of Christ and the martyrs as a form of perversion; cf. CG 335B; *Misopogon* 361B.

501. Ep. LVI (Hertlein, 77).

As a duty, I have decided after much reflection to confirm in law the ancient custom of our ancestors, because when these framers of wise laws, these ancestors of ours, considered the matter, they held that the difference between life and death is the greatest of differences. Accordingly, they taught that each of these states should be governed by practices and rituals appropriate to it. Now, <they taught> that death is endless rest—the "bronze sleep" sung by Homer—but waking life is different—full unequally of pain and pleasure, hardship and prosperity. And so they required that the ceremonies associated with the dead should be set apart from the business and traffic of daily life and conducted privately. They taught that the gods are the beginning and the end of all things: while we live, we belong to the gods; when we die, we return to the gods. It is not important to decide here about such matters, or to know whether both life and death are in the hands of the same gods or whether certain gods concern themselves with the living and other gods with the dead. Yet when we consider that the Sun, by being absent or present, is the cause of day and night and of winter and summer, we say that the most venerable of the gods, the one who is before all things and from whom all things proceed, allotted rulers over the living and lords over the dead. Therefore, we should give to each of these domains what is appropriate to them in their kind; and we should strive to emulate in the working of our daily lives the harmony of the gods concerning the manner in which things exist.

And so, death is a rest. Night is in harmony with rest. It is therefore fitting that the burial of the dead should be conducted at night, and that we should prohibit the business of burial, or anything associated with it, to go on during the day. Consider that <during the day> people are occupied with all sorts of business, the streets full of men on their way to the law-courts, or to or from market, or sitting at a stall plying their craft or trade, or visiting the temples to ask for a sign from the gods. Then some small mob who have just laid a body on the bier shove into the midst of those who have other things to do.[502] The situation is intolerable in every way! The ones

---

502. εἶτα οὐκ οἶδα οἵτινες. . . . Julian means the Christians who intrude on commerce to call attention to their grief.

who find themselves shoved aside are filled with disgust—some because they see it an evil omen, while for others it means they will not be able to go to the temples until they have washed themselves of the uncleanness they have incurred. <For we hold> that it is not permitted to enter the presence of the gods, the source of life and far removed from decay, after this sort of encounter.

And what can be worse than this? I shall tell you: The doors of the temples are often open, the very gates of the gods, and it sometimes happens that at the very moment someone inside is pouring libations, sacrificing or praying, behold! a procession carrying a corpse wanders by, close to the temple itself, their shrill lamentations floating even above the altar as an ill omen.

So we must understand that the activities that belong to day and night have always been separated more than other things. It is for that reason that burial has been removed from the <activity> of the day and reserved for night. And it makes little sense to ridicule the wearing of white for mourning, then to bury the dead in the full light of day. If the former practice was better because it did not offend any of the gods, this new practice[503] can only be regarded as an insult to all of the gods. For <to bury the body by day> is to ascribe death to the Olympian gods, and to deprive the gods of the underworld of their due—if that indeed is what these lords and guardians of soul are to be called. I do know that the <priests> who are expert in their knowledge of these practices say that it is right only to perform the rituals of the infernal gods at night—in no case before the tenth hour of the day. And if this is the appropriate time for the worship of these gods, we will not allow another time for ceremonies for the dead.

My words should be enough for those who choose to obey. For those in error, let them apply what they have learned and choose the better path. But if any man chooses obstinacy, such that he needs threat or punishment for persuasion, he should know that the penalty for disobedience will be of the severest kind. He shall not perform the offices of the dead before the tenth hour of the day, or

---

503. Of the Christians, but the implication is that pagans have been influenced by Christian practice as well; otherwise the edict would make scant sense.

carry the dead person through the city. These things are to be done only at sunset and before sunrise, reserving the glorious day for pure deeds and the <worship of> the shining gods of Olympus.

LETTERS CONCERNING ATHANASIUS AND THE ALEXANDRIANS

INTRODUCTION

T hree of Julian's surviving epistles concern Athanasius of
Alexandria, the teacher and bishop whose relentless stand
against the Arian heresy was both a distraction and an annoyance for
the new emperor from the start, as it had been for the Arian sympa-
thizer Constantius before him. During the years of his nominal
tenure of the see of Alexandria (326–373), Athanasius served twenty
years in exile and five times was forced into hiding: once under Constantine, twice under Constantius, once under Julian (362–363),
and lastly under Valens (himself an Arian) in 367. Valens was the
last official patron of the dying Arian cause, whose demise was
ensured by unremitting theological attacks in the east (by the Cappadocians) and by western bishops who had encountered its equal
in the form of the modalist and monarchian heresies of the third
and early fourth century. More troubling still was Athanasius's position toward the imperium, which more than any Christian writer of
his day he understood as subsumed under the divine sovereignty
and its hierarchical embodiment, the bishop-theologue.[504] In this
calculus, an emperor like Constantius can be dubbed the anti-Christ
(*Historia Arianorum*, p. 77) and the Christian bishop has the right of

---

504. See Letter LVI (Athanasius to Jovian), p. 26.813.

remonstrance against an emperor. These relatively early assertions of the episcopal prerogatives will become increasingly decisive in the contest between church and empire in the fifth century, culminating in such ruses as the eighth-century forgery known as the Donation of Constantine, which alleged a perpetual grant of sovereignty to the bishop of Rome over all the churches of the East as well as those of the west.

On December 24, 361, the Arian bishop George of Cappadocia—a hugely unpopular figure among both the orthodox and the Arians—was murdered. Initial blame fell on Athanasius who, it was said, enflamed public opinion against his enemy. The innocence of Athanasius in the affair is best supported by Julian's silence in the matter. While roundly condemning the attacks as an act of barbarism, the emperor—who detested Athanasius and repeatedly pleaded with the Alexandrians to throw off the superstitions of the Galileans and return to the faith of their political founder—does not seem to have blamed Athanasius for the death of George.[505]

Julian early in 362 proclaimed an amnesty for all non-Arian bishops who had been victims of legislation under Constantius, and Athanasius, prematurely as it worked out, returned to his see. The reasons for the amnesty are difficult to discern. It is clear that Julian had no wish to take theological sides in the debates of the Galileans, and his contempt for Alexandrian theological orthodoxy as personified in the teaching of Athanasius was consistent with his claim that he had "given up Christianity" once and for all in 350.[506] On their return, religious conflict between the orthodox ecclesiastics and their Arian opponents spread rapidly, making Alexandria the focus of sectarian violence that would last until some time after Julian's death and the solidifying of Nicene orthodoxy.

Christian writers supposed that the reason for the amnesty had been to create religious war among the Christian sects, but if this is so there is nothing in the surviving correspondence to suggest cyni-

---

505. See Socrates, HE 3.31 and Soz., HE 3.7, who also suggest that Athanasius was innocent and the victim of Arian malice. Philostorgios 7.2, however, implicates Julian directly in a conspiracy against the Arian bishop.

506. Ep. XLVII.

cism on the emperor's part. Rather, Julian, while alert to the possibility of trouble, seems to have regarded this intervention as an exercise of his role as *pontifex maximus*—if not an attempt to restore the theological balance of Constantine's day, then surely as a posthumous rebuke to Constantius and his policies. Julian first scolds the Alexandrians for their role in the death of bishop George;[507] then writes again demanding that the library of the dead bishop be dispatched to him.[508] It is thought that the tract *Against the Galileans* (composed the following winter at Antioch) was written with George's books at hand, though this is not certain, and parts of the treatise had almost certainly taken shape before Julian received George's library.

When word reached Julian of Athanasius's return to Alexandria, he immediately ordered the prefect Ecdicius Olympus to expel the bishop from his see before December 1 (Ep. XXIV). Athanasius complied by October 23, 361 ("It is but a little cloud and will pass," he is reported by Sozomen to have said.[509]), but by the autumn of 362 the Alexandrians were calling for the return of the bishop, sending a legate to Julian with a petition which the emperor ungraciously refused. Athanasius this time went into hiding near Memphis rather than into exile and resumed his duties on hearing in 363 of Julian's death—which he is reported to have greeted with a smile.

*   *   *

LETTER 21
JULIAN CAESAR, THE AUGUSTUS, TO THE PEOPLE OF ALEXANDRIA, <GREETINGS>[510]

It may be that you do not honor the memory of the founder of your city, Alexander, and that you revile the great and holy god Serapis. But how can it be that you gave no thought to your city, your human

---

507. Ep. XXI.
508. Ep. XXIII.
509. Soz., HE 5.15.
510. Hertlein, 10.

bond, your regard for the decency of your society?[511] And what of me, for I must add—you gave no thought to me, even though the gods, yes your own god Serapis among them—decreed that I should rule over the whole world. The fate of the offenders should by right have been left to me: this and only this was the right course. And yet, anger and passion led you from the right course, as often it does: "Tossing reason out the door and doing terrible things."[512]

You managed to restrain your passion at first, but then gave way to reckless passion. You tossed aside the wise decision you had made, and yes—you were not even ashamed—the lot of you to do the same abominable things you are used to seeing done by your enemies.

Tell me in the name of the most holy Serapis, what crime did you find in George that aroused such hatred in you[513] The reply, no doubt, is that he brought Constantius, now of blessed memory, to the boil: he sent an army into your blessed city, and the captain of this regiment[514] took hold of the sacred shrine of the god, stripped it of ornaments and statues, and seized the offerings from within the temples. You were right to be provoked, and right as well to try to save the treasures of the god from further insult. But Artemius was loathe to accept this—more afraid of George, I think, than of Constantius—and so sent soldiers against you illegally, unjustly, and blasphemously.[515] For

---

511. I.e., in the murder of Bishop George.

512. A fragment of Melanthius quoted by Plutarch, *On the Restraint of Anger*, p. 453.

513. Julian's suggestion that the intolerance of the pagans was as extreme as that of the Christians is also conveyed by the Church writers, notably Socrates (HE 3.2), who attributes the murder to a mob incensed at George's attempts to erect a church on the site of a Mithraic adytum: "The pagans, dragging George outside the church, fastened him to a camel, and when they had torn him to pieces, they burned him together with the camel." The invocation of Serapis seems to support Socrates' view—that the populace rather than supporters of Athanasius were to blame for the murder. In the Arian legend, later circulated throughout the Eastern church in variants, George is represented as the warrior defending truth against the dragon-wizard Athanasius.

514. The prefect of Egypt Artemius, executed in 362 by Julian's command.

515. Sozomen's balanced view is worth noting: "George compelled both parties to offer worship in the mode he decided and where opposition was made he enforced obedience by compulsion. He was hated by the rulers because he scorned them and was giving orders to the officers; and the multitude detested him on account of his tyranny and because his power was greater than all the rest. The

it was George who was keeping an eye on Artemius, to keep him, I think, from acting too moderately, too lawfully—but giving him free range to be a tyrant toward you.

So, you will say that you had reason to be outraged against George and for this reason you were entitled to desecrate the holy city yet again,[516] preferring violence to the verdict of the judges. Had you chosen the latter course, blood would not be on your hands and this would not be a case of murder and lawlessness, but a proper case at law that would leave you clear from guilt in the matter. The court would have punished an impious man for inexpiable crimes, and would have taken to task <in the same suit> all those who ignore the gods. It would have punished those who humiliate <ancient> cities and communities of men in the belief that cruel action toward others is the surety of their power.

Please recall that this letter to you is the second, and compare my words with those I used in the first, written not long ago. With what words of praise did I fête you then! Even now I want to praise you, but how can I when you have broken the law? You have torn a human being into pieces as dogs would tear a wolf, and you raised to the gods hands still steeped in his blood. And what have you to say? "George deserved it!" And well might I agree with you—perhaps he deserved even worse punishment and cruel treatment—and I might even grant you that, but when you say he deserved it at your hands, then I will not agree. You have laws, laws which must be honored by one and all, and preserved. It happens of course that on occasion an individual will break one or another of these laws, but on the whole the state is tranquil, well-ordered, because it is recognized that laws were established from the beginning in wisdom and are not to be treated with contempt.

In any case you are fortunate, men of Alexandria, that this crime happened in my time, for my reverence for the god and respect for my uncle and namesake who ruled your city and the whole of

---

pagans regarded him with greater aversion than the Christians because he prohibited them from offering sacrifice" (Soz., HE 4.30).

516. It is clear that the desecration of the city is Julian's reason for reprimanding the Alexandrians as gently as he does, not the punishment of George whose "inexpiable crimes" he acknowledges.

Egypt[517] causes me to think of you as brothers. If I dealt with you in the way a power that wishes to be respected should—that is, as a tyrannical and unswerving government would—I could never overlook the frenzied act of the mob: I would rather root it out and purge it, like a disease, with the most bitter medicine. But as I have said in this very letter, I choose instead to give you a milder tonic: the medicine of caution and argument.

And from these, if you are, as you claim, Greeks at heart, you will derive greater benefit and be more persuaded. I know and believe that to this day there remain in your blood the habits and customs, the noble imprint, of our illustrious heritage. Let this word be published throughout Alexandria.

LETTER 23
TO ECDICIUS, PREFECT
(ON THE DISPOSITION OF GEORGE'S BOOKS)[518]

While some men have a passion for horses and others for birds, and still others for beasts, for my part I have had, from my earliest days, a passion for possessing books. So it would be foolish of me to allow <these books> to be stolen by unscrupulous men who love money and gold only. Wealth cannot satisfy them, so by evil designs they plot to steal these as well. Please therefore do me the favor of locating those books which belonged to George, for so many of these in his house were on philosophy and many on rhetoric; and of course many were on the doctrines of the impious Galileans. These latter <books> I would ask to be destroyed were it not that along with them some more useful books might be destroyed as well. So let the search proceed with the greatest care. Give the job to George's secretary, and tell him that if he searches honestly and well he will have his freedom; if not, he will be put to the test and tortured. <Let him understand> that I know in many cases what books

---

517. The elder Julian (cf. *Misopogon* 365c) held office in Egypt during the reign of Constantius.

518. Hertlein, 9.

George possessed—not all, but many, for he lent me some to copy when I was in Cappadocia (which I returned).

LETTER 24
AN EDICT TO THE ALEXANDRIANS
<REGARDING ATHANASIUS>[519]

One who has been banished on so many occasions by so many emperors issuing so many decrees might have waited at least for a further edict before being so rash as to return to his own country. Instead, he has displayed again his tempestuous nature, and treated our laws as though they had never been written. We have not to this day extended to the Galileans deported into exile under our blessed predecessor Constantius the right to return to their churches; rather, only permission to enter their own countries. But the insolent Athanasius, as always, with his usual disregard for law, has again been puffed up, and again grabbed what <they call> the "episcopal seat."[520] No wonder the god-fearing people of Alexandria are worried. We solemnly warn him to leave the city immediately—on the very day he receives this grant of clemency—or else his punishment will be all the more severe.[521]

LETTER 46 TO ECDICIUS, PREFECT IN EGYPT[522]

Even though you have failed me in some matters, you should not fail me in this request: a report was to have been made on that enemy of the gods, Athanasius. That was my decree, published some time ago.[523] My decree was sworn justly before the mighty Serapis,

---

519. Hertlein, 26.

520. θρόνος.

521. In consequence of this edict Athanasius went into hiding outside Alexandria, provoking the language of Letter XLVI.

522. Hertlein, 50.

523. October 24 is the date in which Athanasius went into exile in upper Egypt; see Socrates, HE 3.14; Soz., HE 5.15. Sozomen also offers this grudging tribute to Julian's restraint: "Although Julian was anxious to advance paganism by

and it held that if Athanasius does not leave the city—rather depart all Egypt before the December kalends, I shall levy on you and your cohort a fine of one hundred pounds of gold. You know how slow I am to condemn; know then how very much slower I am to repent of what I have condemned. (*And in my own hand*) It torments me to see my orders flouted. By the gods, there is nothing that would cheer me more than to receive word that Athanasius is driven away beyond the borders of Egypt. The vile old wretch! He has the conceit to baptize even well-born Greek women during my reign—so I say: Out with him![524]

LETTER 47 TO THE PEOPLE OF ALEXANDRIA[525]

How is it that you have the nerve to ask for the return of Athanasius? Is it reasonable that you should ask this of me? Was your founder a Galilean? Did he violate the law as the Galileans have violated their own,[526] for which they now pay the price—the price of defying the very law they say they live by, the price of innovation and new teaching? No, it was Alexander who founded your city; it is Serapis whom you should worship as lord and patron, together with his fair consort Isis, the thrice blessed lady, the queen of Egypt. < > But you do not <represent> the city of Alexander, only the diseased portion that infects the whole and pretends to speak for the whole.[527]

Really, I am overcome with shame, by the gods, you men of

---

every means, yet he deemed it the height of impudence to employ force or vengeance against those who refused to sacrifice. . . . He did not even forbid them to assemble together for worship, as he was aware that when freedom of the will is called into question restraint is utterly useless."

524. It pained a copyist to read Julian's reference to Athanasius, so with Christian fervor the *Neapolitanus* MS has the following scribble: μακάριος οὗτος κυὼν μιαρὲ καὶ τρισκατάρατε παράβατα καὶ τρισάθλιε ("He is a saint, you dog of an apostate—triple cursed and thrice wretched").

525. Hertlein, 51; lacunae and editorial omissions by a Christian editor (see note 521 on the *Neapolitanus* MS) make the translation of the first section problematical. See Hertlein's notes.

526. That is, the law of the Old Testament; see *Against the Galileans* 236–37, 306ff.

527. Disease: ἀλλὰ τὸ νοσοῦν μέρος ἐπιφημίζειν . . . (437).

Alexandria, when I consider that even a single Alexandrian professes that he is a Galilean. Is it forgotten that the ancestors of the true Hebrews were the slaves of the Egyptians in days gone by? But today the men of Alexandria subject themselves to the race of men who were conquered by the founder of their city, or rather to their inferiors who have cast off the traditions of their ancestors and taught you to forsake your sacred traditions as willing slaves of superstition. And today you have no memory of the days when all Egypt had communion with the gods and when all were blessed accordingly. Yet this teaching <of the Galileans> was introduced among you only yesterday, and what good has it been to the city? Your founder was a pious man, Alexander of Macedon, who resembles the Galileans in no way, no, nor any Jews for that matter—though, to be fair, I must admit that the Jews show themselves to be far superior to the Galileans.

Was it not Ptolemy the son of Lagos who overcame the Jews[528] while Alexander himself would have been a match for the Romans any day. Then there were the Ptolemies who came after Alexander's time, those who nurtured the city as though she were their very daughter: what of them? I can tell you, it wasn't through the preaching of Jesus that you have come to be famous. Nor was it through the preaching of the detested Galileans that you learned the arts of government, in which you excel and which have caused Fortune herself to grant you favor. Now, finally, when we Romans took on the responsibility for your welfare, taking you from the Ptolemies (who had become bad rulers) it was Augustus himself who visited you and spoke to you in these words: "Men of Alexandria, I absolve this city of its sins, because I revere and honor the great god Serapis. And <also I do this> because I honor the people of this great city. And I forgive you because of the renown of Aureius, my friend." Now this Aureius was a citizen of Alexandria like yourselves, a friend of Caesar no less, a philosopher by profession.[529]

So this is the bounty which, in brief scope, the gods of Olympus

---

528. According to Josephus, *Wars*, 1.12.1, Ptolemy I took Jerusalem and then took numbers of Jews captive into Egypt.

529. Cited by Julian in his letter to Themistius as a stoic philosopher who turned down a praefecture. He is known to Philostratus and to Seneca as well; in the latter (*Dialogues* 6.4) he is said to have been a counselor to the empress Livia.

have showered on your city—and I neglect many others I could name if there were time to recount them all. But more than these are the many blessings that the known gods bestow on all of us every day—blessings confined neither to a single race nor to a few chosen people nor to a particular city,[530] but given freely to everyone the whole world over. How can you deny these? Really, are you blind to the rays that pour forth from the great god Helios? Are you simply insensible to the fact that winter and summer are his doing? Or that plant and animal life take their refreshment from him? What then do you think of the blessings showered on your city by that great goddess who is generated by him and comes through him[531]—that very Selene who is creator of the universe.[532] Oh, but you persist in refusing to adore any one of our gods, preferring to think that a man whom you have never seen (nor those before you) ought to be worshiped as God the Word—I mean Jesus. What of the god to whom the whole of humanity has looked from the very beginning, the god worshiped and acclaimed by all of us, the god who causes our devotion to prosper? I mean Helios, the living and intelligible image of the invisible god.[533] This <unseen principle> is the source of the good, for he is soul and intelligence itself < >.[534]

I beg you, do as I say: return to the straight path, that of the truth. Accept what I have to say as one who, until his twentieth year, walked the path <of error> that you now walk. But for twelve years,

---

530. A reference to the ethnocentrism of the Jews and the Christian exploitation of the theme of having been singled out by God for a special destiny.

531. τὴν δὲ ἐξ αὐτοῦ καὶ παρ᾽ αὐτοῦ δημιουργόν . . . Selene is advertised in language deliberately echoing Christian formulations of the son's generation by the father.

532. The allusion seems to be to the logos theory of John 1.1–5, which Julian seems to view as a perversion of the Helios cosmology.

533. Wright's translation diminishes the Neoplatonic thrust of Julian's allusion: The unseen Helios is νοερός—intellectual (Plato would have said an object of intellect); whereas the intelligible principle is νοητός, or "known"—a likeness or image. Julian frequently understands the celestial bodies as living likenesses of the unseen realities, which can be named differently and indeed venerated differently from region to region in the Empire (Or. IV.133C).

534. An erasure in the text, probably a Christian copyist objecting to the close resemblance between Julian's platonizing theory and the doctrine of the Fourth Gospel.

thanks to the gods, I have not swerved from the path of truth as I now know it to be.[535]

May it please you to take me at my word. I should be very happy if you did. But if you choose to continue on the course of error, drinking in the superstition and the false teachings of men of no repute, then at least spare me your craving for Athanasius. Are there not plenty of his pupils roundabout who can satisfy your itching ears, bent to hear again his mischievous words? Oh, had I had the sense to silence not only Athanasius but his wretched school as well! But as it is there are plenty of his troupe, and you will have no difficulty finding someone to fill his shoes—indeed, I should think that you could hardly do worse than to choose any man from among the mobs of the city to take his place, and he will do you at least as much good as an interpreter of scripture. But perhaps your request comes to me because you have a particular liking for the old man Athanasius, or his subtleties (I hear stories, at least, that he a clever old dog). And if this is the source of the request, then know it was for being too clever that I banished him in the first place. He is quarrelsome, and a quarrelsome man is not fit for leadership. Or is he his own man at all—perhaps rather a puppet taking orders from someone else—a recipe for disaster, and it looks as though he is courting disaster openly. It is out of my concern for your welfare that I sent Athanasius away in the first place and ordered him out of your city: now I say, Let him be sent clear out of Egypt.

This sentence is to be proclaimed throughout the city of Alexandria.

---

535. Julian's reference to his life as a Christian; see Or. IV.31A, where he "wishes this time to be forgotten."

JULIAN AND THE JEWS

J ulian's relations with the Jews have traditionally posed a dilemma for scholars. According to Sozomen (4.7.5) he reversed the policies of his predecessors, notably Gallus and Constantius, after being convinced that the Jewish community had been brutalized and subjected by degrees to a policy of economic harassment. Gallus, in an action barely mentioned by Socrates and Sozomen, had responded violently to renegade Diocaesarean Jews for incursions into the territories of Palestine (353AD) by destroying their towns and slaughtering masses of the insurrectionists. And while Constantius's attitude toward Judaism was largely driven by political necessity, Julian had at least flashes of historical interest in Jerusalem and the restorationist cause in general. For this reason, as Wright suggests somewhat anachronistically, "he may almost be called a Zionist."[536] He considerably lessened their tax burden, offered (at first in principle, and then by edict) permission for Jewish sacrifices to be restored to Jerusalem, and finally promised to rebuild the Temple and hand the city over to Jewish control. This promise, which Sozomen understands as part of a larger complex of "artful

---

536. See his discussion, III, xxi–xxii. Schwarz, Klimek, and Geffcken rejected the letter as a forgery, and Bidez and Cumont, for completely unpersuasive reasons enshrined in the European prejudices of their era, omitted it from their 1922 Paris edition (*L'empereur Julien: Ouvres complètes*, 1.2).

designs against the Christians," was interpreted by pious observers as an attempt to nullify the prophecy of Jesus (Mark 13.2) that "not one stone of the Temple shall remain upon the other." It was not for love of the Jews, argued the Christians, that Julian's largesse was evinced, but rather his hatred for the Christians:

"He hated and oppressed the Christians and showed humanity and kindness to the Jews. He wrote to the Jewish leaders and patriarchs, and even the people, asking for their prayers for him and for the empire. . . . But in so doing he was only trying to strike a blow against the Christians, who are the Jews' most determined adversaries. Or perhaps he thought that by kindness [in rebuilding their temple] he could persuade the Jews to offer pagan sacrifice, for they knew only the letter of the scripture, and could not (unlike our Christian teachers and the wisest of the Hebrews) probe the hidden meanings" (5.22.2–4).

Julian's promise, depending on whose testimony one decides to credit, fell victim either to natural catastrophe or divine intervention. Earthquakes rocked the east in the winter of 362–363. The building contract had been given to a certain Alypius, a Briton, whose men fled the work following a "shower of brimstone" that made the project impossible to carry out. Sozomen's report, the most sober, does not differ from the legendary accounts given by (among others) Philostorgius (7.9), Theodoret (3.15), and the invective of Gregory Naziazen—the last of these being probably the source of the most fantastic elements of the tradition. Sozomen says simply that Julian gave the go-ahead for work to begin and that pagans in the city cooperated with the Jews in the preparation of the building site owing to a mutual dislike of the Christians. "When they had removed the ruins of the former building, they dug up the ground and cleared away its foundation,. . . . <But> on the next day, when they were about to lay the new foundation, a great earthquake occurred, and by the turbulence of the earth stones were thrown up from beneath the ground and many Jews who were at work were injured" (5.22). Sozomen adds that the Jews were unable to interpret these signs,[537] and went back to work when the threat seemed

---

537. Which have been rhetorically adapted to the apocalyptic realization of Jesus' prophecy in Mark 13.1–2.

to have subsided. It was then that "fire burst suddenly from the foundations of the temple and consumed several of the workmen."

For all its detail, the reference to these "balls of flame" by Ammianus and Gregory seems to be a later Christian gloss of what had seemed to many Christians at the time the most audacious of Julian's attacks on the Christian teleology. That the work was not started, or postponed, or marvelously interrupted once begun, could only be seen (together with Julian's death, which followed only a few months later) as a miraculous endorsement of Christian prophecy and fulfillment. In any event, the "worst" did not happen: the temple was not rebuilt and Jerusalem was not restored to the Jews. The location of the story in one of the more providential sequences of Sozomen's History argues the unreliability of the detail: it comes as the climax in a series of *mirabilia*, which include the story of the destruction of the temple of Apollo at Daphne by fire from heaven (4.20) and the demolition of a statue of Julian erected at Paneas (in place of one of Christ) by the stroke of a thunderbolt. In this succession of miracle stories, the disconfirmation of Jewish hopes for reclaiming Jerusalem is set alongside Christian confidence that Jesus' edict concerning the temple supersedes the Emperor's promise to the Jews: a panegyric on Christ in his threefold office as High priest, final prophet, and king of kings.

For all the legendary overlay, however, there is no good reason to suppose that Julian did not actually intend to fulfill his commitment to the Jewish community. Much obviously depends on the authenticity of the letter. That such a letter was written by Julian is uniformly attested—by Sozomen, Socrates, and later tradition—and just as vigorously denied by scholars beginning with Bidez and Cumont in 1898 (1922). Its conciliatory tone has seemed at odds with Julian's muscular paganism and frustrations with the Jewish community expressed elsewhere in his writings. At the same time, it should be remembered that the use of the Jews as a counterfoil to Christian propaganda is at least as old as Celsus, and the tone of the rescript echoes Julian's perception of Judaism as being more "authentic" than Christianity—especially in its understanding of oracles and sacrifice—as recorded in the books against the Galileans.

The defense of Judaism extends no deeper than the maxim *Veritas antiqua est* (What is old, is true), just as the indictment of Christianity hinges on the opposite maxim, invoked by Suetonius: it is new, immoderate, and unapproved superstition.[538]

The arguments for including the letter in the Julianic corpus are largely circumstantial, but in the end decisive.[539] The sentiments expressed in the letter are rightly taken by Sozomen to be typical of Julian's desire to belittle Christianity: What he does, he does not out of love for the Jews but out of hostility for the more aggressive Christians, whose anti-Semitism seems to Julian a further manifestation of their impiety, disrespect for tradition, and error-strewn regard for their origins. The reference in the letter to the God of the Jews as θεὸς ὕψιστος (the most high God, a term sometimes applied to Zeus) reflects the garden variety hellenistic syncretism that Julian wished to encourage (or resuscitate, since its equivalent had flourished during the dying days of Hasmonean rule). And finally, there would be no reason for the Jews to invent such a story—or a letter to corroborate it—since the success of the building project depended on the whimsy of a man whose tenure in office was uncertain, and whose likeliest successors would hardly be expected to carry out his programs.

Further, it seems unlikely that historians such as Sozomen would allude to Julian's project as a matter of record simply in the interest of documenting the emperor's artful designs against the Christians if indeed there is not something to what Sozomen has to offer as an explanation. For this reason, the suggestion that the emperor wished to demonstrate the weakness of the Christian position by "reversing" Jesus' pronouncement on the temple remains the strongest reason for seeing the letter as coming from Julian. Some small proof of this design can be found in Socrates's description of an earlier report concerning Julian's treatment of the Christians. Departing from his original policy, which sought to win friends among influential Christians in exchange for their continuing vilification of the memory of Constantius, Julian ordered that the church of the Novatians at Cyzicus, which the Nicene zealot Euzoius had

---

538. Suetonius, *Caes.*, Nero 16.
539. And by Wright, 3:xxii.

totally demolished, should be rebuilt. The bishop Eleusius was threatened with the exaction of stiff financial penalties if he failed to carry out the construction within two months—at his own expense (3.11). Taxes previously imposed on the Jews on account of their alleged "impiety" were extracted from the Christians on a scale determined by their individual possessions in order to finance the Persian campaigns. In short, there is impressive correspondence between the benefits accorded the Jews by Julian and the penalties "transferred" to the Christians in the winter of 362/3 in advance of the Persian expedition. This will not be the last time that Julian uses the rebuilding of a preferred enemy's shrine and remission of taxes as a way of dealing with a more direct threat to his imperium—in this case the religious threat to his power and prestige represented by the growth of the Christian church. As a final point, Julian's own commitment is ambiguous in the letter: He does not actually say he intends to build the temple, but to restore the city of Jerusalem and to see it repopulated. He says that to do this, he will need to bring settlers into the city (of what religious predilection he does not say), so that "all together can once again glorify the most high God," a usage sufficiently vague as to invite doubt whether the project included replacing the Herodian temple. Julian invites the Jews to perform some duties in exchange for his promise, but all reference to them has been excised. And as to the time frame for the project, Julian seems to assume that nothing can be done until his return from the Persian frontier, which was not to transpire, while Sozomen's account assumes that preparation began prior to his departure in 363.

Taken together, the evidence suggests that Julian was attempting to curry favor with the Jews in exchange for the gift of Jerusalem. Courting Jewish opinion had the advantage of punishing the Christians, or at least doing them philosophical damage, and possibly encouraging the Jews to come to the aid of the Persian campaigns on a promissory basis—thus the reference to the folly of a religious tax imposed on a people who had limited access to their holy places, and Julian's willingness to lift it. The memory of this potential outrage was vivid in the Christian imagination, but less vibrant to the

Jews, who saw the whole affair expended within months after the letter was written from Antioch.

TO THE COMMUNITY OF THE JEWS[540]

Once upon a time you were slaves, and the most irksome thing about your slavery was that your lords bent you to their will and commands, yoked you to their laws, and then made you pay for the privilege by contributing money to their treasury. I have seen this with my own eyes, and learned more about it by examining the records and processes that have been filed against you. But when an additional burden was about to be placed on your shoulders, I stopped it, and I ordered those who delight in such obloquy to stop as well. My desk was full of transcripts of your impiety and accusations against you—and I threw the lot into the fire so that no one again might profit from charging you with disloyalty.

My brother Constantius is not entirely to blame for these reports; rather, the men he had to his table, they are the real culprits—barbarians in mind, ungodly in spirit. I seized them with my own hands, thrust them into the pit so that no memory of their wickedness might survive.[541]

My wish for you is that you should prosper. I have instructed your patriarch, the venerable Iulus, that the taxation imposed upon you should be prohibited from this time forward: no one should be able to oppress you through such measures. <I do this> to give you peace of mind throughout the extent of the Empire, and through this peace encourage you everywhere to offer heartfelt prayers on my behalf to the most high God, the creator[542] who has chosen me to

---

540. Ep. LI (Hertlein, 25).

541. It is unclear what "wickedness" Julian refers to here, unless these are survivors of the process begun in 354 following the revolt of the Jews in Dio-Caesarea (Socrates, HE 2.33). If so, there seems to have been some effort to defend the extravagant measures by documenting cases of Jewish disloyalty, a process which Julian here formally disavows. It may, however, be a reference to a conspiracy against the Jews fomented by Julian's brother Gallus, or so the language would suggest.

542. δημιουργῷ Θεῷ.

reign by the power of his immaculate right hand. For it is clear to me that when our minds are troubled, we refrain from raising our hands in prayer, but when we are free from anxiety, we happily resort to supplication, praying for my imperial person to God the all-powerful who directs my reign in all ways, according as I wish. < >[543] This you ought to do so that after I have brought the campaign against Persia to its successful completion I might restore the sacred city of Jerusalem by my own efforts—the place you have so desired to see inhabited again—settling men there so that all together, with you, may glorify the most high God in that place.[544]

---

543. The syntax is awkward: a list of requirements, possibly stipulating what the Jews must do to earn the restoration of Jerusalem and right of access, is evidently omitted.

544. Καὶ ἐν αὐτῇ δόξαν δῶ μεθ᾽ ὑμῶν τῷ κρείτονι. The project of rebuilding the Temple is not explicit but probably envisaged in the concluding sentence.

LIVES OF JULIAN

The following early histories (excerpted) of the reign of Julian are provided here as an epilogue to the effects of his reign. With the formidable exception of Constantine, no emperor who ruled between the time of Diocletian and the time of Justinian provoked such a flurry of biographies. Why this is so is not difficult to imagine: Julian was seen as the last great defender of the old Roman world, a world which Christian bishops and intellectuals like Cyril regarded as having given way, providentially, to the true doctrine of the Church. Given this perspective it is no wonder that the emperor's lectures on the superstitions of the Galileans, the irregularities of his life, the ambiguities and stratagems he employed to resuscitate the dying religious world of his ancestors invited serious attention and rebuke. The first *vita* comes from the hand of the church historian Socrates Scholasticus (ca. 379–439?), an interesting personality who had in common with Julian a love of pagan letters (he quotes, approvingly, from Sophocles, Euripides, Xenophon, Porphyry, and Libanius, among others, in his church history). The second and more expansive *vita* is taken from the church history of (Hermias) Sozomenos, an author of Palestinian background whose family was converted to Christianity in the Gaza after beholding a miracle of Hilarion. His writing covers roughly the period 323 to 439 and thus comprises some of the same detail as that treated, less expansively, by Socrates.

185

SOCRATES SCHOLASTICUS
THE EDUCATION AND PARENTAGE OF JULIAN[545]

Julian was proclaimed emperor in Constantinople, to which city he came from the western provinces around the middle of December 361, Constantius having died on the battlefields of Cilicia on the third of November during the consulate of Taurus and Florentinus. It is necessary to speak a little about the personality of this man who was so well known for his learning. In doing this there is no need for me to affect an aureate style of writing in order to do justice to my subject's great rank—just to please his admirers. My purpose in undertaking this biography is to compile a history of the Christian religion, and it requires no change in style from subject to subject for this object to be achieved. So in an orderly fashion I wish to describe his personality, his birth and education, the way he acceded to the imperial office, and to do this I must first sketch for you the essential background of Julian's career.

The emperor Constantine, who gave Constantinople his name, had two brothers, Dalmatius and Constantius. These were sons of the same father by different mothers. . . . Now <Dalmatius> had a son who took his father's name; Constantius had two sons, Gallus and Julian. When Constantine the founder of Constantinople died, the army was quick to put Dalmatius[546] to death: the lives of his orphaned sons were also in jeopardy. Gallus was saved by serious illness from being handed over to the same fate as his father. And Julian was even more fortunate, being only eight years old at the time and hence considered too young to be a threat. Constantius's jealousy seemed to have weakened, and Gallus was permitted to attend school in Ephesus—where he also had huge landholdings and estates left to him by his father.

Julian, on the other hand, when he got to be school age, followed his studies at Constantinople, indeed even going in ordinary

---

545. Socrates Scholasticus, HE, 3.1; This translation is based on the edition of the Greek text by G. C. Hansen, *Die Griechischen christlichen Schriftsteller der ersten Jahrhunderte.* Neue Folg, Bd. 1 (Berlin: Akademie Verlag, 1990).

546. That is, the younger brother of Constantius.

dress to the palace, where the schools operated in those days under the supervision of the eunuch Mardonius. He was taught grammar by Nicocles the Lacedaemonian. He learned rhetoric from Ecebolius the Sophist, who was known at the time to be a Christian—indeed his uncle had made strict provision that he should not be taught by pagan instructors, lest he fall into the superstitions of the pagans, for at the beginning, Julian was a Christian.[547]

His proficiency in letters soon became so famous that it was rumored he could run the Roman Empire on his own, and this rumor could be heard everywhere. It so unsettled the emperor that he decided to send the boy away from Constantinople to Nicomedia, but forbidding him to attend the school of the Syrian Sophist known as Libanius. This is the same Libanius who had been driven from Constantinople by a collusion among the educators, to Nicomedia, where he finally settled and opened a school and wrote diatribes against the teachers who had caused his exile.

Julian was prohibited, as I said, from mingling with the fellows of this school because Libanius was a pagan, but being resourceful he managed to get his hands on copies of Libanius's lectures, and these he read with admiration, over and over again. Julian grew ever more proficient in rhetoric, until one day the Ephesian philosopher Maximus (not to be confused with the Byzantine Euclid's father) arrived to set up shop in Nicomedia—this the same man who was later executed by Valentinian as a magician and sorcerer.[548] What brought him to Nicomedia was the fame of Julian. From this man Julian took not only elementary instruction in philosophy but religious ideas as well—and something more: the desire to rule the empire. When it was known that the emperor had got wind of what was going on, Julian—tossed between ambition and fear—was very eager to put the rumors to rest. So he began to affect the manner and style of what he once had been in truth: He had himself shaved, and pretended to live the life of a monk, publicly reading only the sacred books of the Christians, but in private following his philosophical

---

547. Ep. XLVII.434D. It is noteworthy, however, that of the teachers mentioned by Socrates, only Ecbolius is averred to be a Christian.

548. Valentinian I (364–375).

studies. He even managed to have himself installed as a lector in the Church of Nicomedia.[549] In this deceitful way Julian managed to avert the emperor's suspicions. He did this out of fear, but without abandoning ambition, telling his friends privately that the days were not far off when he would own the crown.

It was about this time that Julian's brother Gallus, who had just been created Caesar, came to visit him on the way to the East, and when not long after this Gallus was murdered, suspicion fell naturally on Julian. The emperor ordered a guard to be posted to watch him, but Julian soon found ways to avoid them and managed to slip from place to place, out of their sight, and to safety. When the empress Eusebia learned of his situation, she begged the emperor to leave him in peace and to permit him to go to Athens in order to complete his studies in philosophy. So to make short of it, that is what the emperor did: he called Julian to him and created him Caesar, also marrying him to his own sister Helen. Then he sent him off to wage war against the barbarians, for the barbarians whom Constantius had encountered when they fought as auxiliaries against the tyrant Magnentius were now on the loose and beginning to raid the Roman cities. But because of Julian's age, the emperor ordered that he should do nothing on his own without consulting the senior military men.

As it happens, these generals had become lazy with power, careless of duty, and as a result the foreign troops grew stronger with each passing day. Julian, seeing his opportunity, permitted the generals to continue in debauchery and drunkenness, while insinuating himself as the true commander of the infantry by preaching courage and offering a reward to any soldier who killed a barbarian. In this way he won the army to his side and weakened the enemy. It is said that once, as he was entering a city, a civic crown which was balanced between two columns fell on his head—which fit it perfectly. All those present shouted their approval, seeing it as an augury that one day he would be emperor in his own right. It is also said that

---

549. ἀναγνώστης : a minor office usually assigned to a young man proficient in public speaking. This would have given Julian adequate subterfuge to disguise his philosophical activities since he would be publicly in view professing Christianity.

Constantius had sent him against the foreigners because he hoped that Julian would die in the battles. I cannot know for certain whether this is true, but it seems unlikely to me that <Constantius> would first have sought an alliance with <Julian> and then, with harm to himself being the only outcome, seek to have his ally destroyed.[550] Each must decide the case for himself.

At any rate, Julian complained to the emperor that the generals had been indolent in the campaign, and this led to Constantius appointing a lieutenant more sympathetic to Julian's designs. Together they waged such an effective campaign against the foreigners that they sent him a messenger with credentials to prove that the foreigners had been ordered by the emperor himself to march into Roman territories. But [Julian] cast the messenger into prison, attacked the enemy forces, and quickly overcame them, sending their king as a prisoner to Constantius.

Upon this success, Julian was proclaimed ruler by the soldiers, and failing to find a crown at hand, one of the soldiers wound a chain he had been wearing as a makeshift crown for Julian's head. In this way, Julian became emperor. But as to the question whether he conducted himself after this day in a manner befitting a philosopher, I leave it for you to judge.[551] For Julian did not send an emissary to Constantius, nor find it in his heart to reward past favors with a recognition of his office. He set about, instead, appointing governors to the <conquered> provinces, choosing whomever he pleased for the job. Not only this recklessness, but he began to impugn Constantius everywhere by making it known that Constantius had sent letters to the foreigners. When this was learned in the marketplace, Julian had no trouble convincing the inhabitants of the cities to turn their backs on Constantius and throw their support to him.

At this point Julian had no further reason to wear the mask of a Christian. He began to style himself pontifex maximus, reopened the temples wherever he found them, and encouraged everyone to

---

550. Socrates' analysis is less fair-minded than simple: Constantius's motive for sending Julian against the invaders was that it would have acquitted him of any direct responsibility for his nephew's death.

551. Presumably Socrates means in a manner appropriate to someone educated in diplomacy and the philosophical traditions of statesmanship.

celebrate the ancient holidays. And so Julian declared war against Constantius and had no hesitation in throwing the whole empire into a state of war, his so-called philosopher's agenda being unattainable except by treason.

By God's grace, however, news of Constantius's death came just when Julian had entered Thrace, and the Empire was strangely preserved in this way from the calamity of civil war. Julian entered Constantinople in triumph, alert to the need to endear himself to the population. Accordingly, he did the following: He knew that Constantius had become an enemy of the defenders of the homoousion faith[552] by deposing their bishops and expelling supporters from the churches.

By the same token, the pagans were encumbered by laws that prohibited them from sacrifices to their gods and were eager to have their temples reopened and the old rites reinstated. Both groups harbored angry feelings toward <Constantius>, and the population in general were passionately opposed to the violence of eunuchs—especially the rapacious Eusebius, the chief of the imperial bed chamber. Julian treated each group with subtlety, hypocritical as he needed to be, patient with others, even aggrandizing some (as he was always fond of appearing benevolent), but always with an eye to the interests of the pagans.

First, then, he sought to impugn the memory of Constantius by publicizing his cruelty toward his subjects. He called the bishops out of exile and restored them to their seats. Then he commanded that the pagan temples should be opened without delay. And finally, he ordered that those who had been made victims of extortion by the eunuchs should have back their property. As for the eunuch Eusebius, he was put to death—not only because of the harm he had inflicted on others, but because Julian was convinced that <Eusebius> had ordered the death of Gallus. And so the body of Constantius he publicly honored with a royal funeral, but the eunuchs, the barbers, and the cooks he expelled from the palace: the eunuchs because Julian had resolved not to marry again following the death

---

552. The supporters of Nicene trinitarianism.

of his wife; the cooks because he stuck to a very spare diet,[553] and the barbers because he held that one will do to serve many. And in addition to these dismissals, he discharged many of the secretaries who lounged about the palace and raised the salary of those he retained. He also reformed the system of public transportation by abolishing the use of mules, oxen, and asses and decreeing that only horses were to be utilized. Some applauded his austerity, while others deplored it for bringing the dignity of the imperial office into question by reducing the amount of pomp and splendor that play so great a role in enchanting the masses.

It is even said that at night he would sit awake in his chamber composing orations to be delivered in the senate; in fact, he is the first and only emperor since Julius Caesar to make speeches in that body. And to those who were skilled in the literary arts, Julian would show the most amazing and flattering patronage—especially to professional philosophers. One saw countless beneficiaries of this sort returning from the palace showing off their palliums, many of whom can only be described as charlatans and sycophants. But those he honored had one thing in common with the emperor: a distaste for Christianity and the wellbeing of the Christians. And of course Julian was no stranger to flattery, having composed a book of his own, *The Caesars*, in which he derides the achievements and characters of all his predecessors, and another act of vanity in which he attacks the Christians.

The expulsion of cooks and barbers might be seen as an act befitting a philosopher—but not an emperor, for the latter must be above the influence of jealousy or petty dislikes. Indeed, in respect of self control and moderation an emperor may be a philosopher. But when a philosopher tries to imitate an emperor he can only stumble on his own principles.

---

553. Socrates will not allow that Julian's reason for dietary restrictions are based on Julian's Neoplatonic view of abstinence, derived largely from Porphyry (*Abst.*, 3.9.3–3.11.1).

SOZOMEN
A HISTORY OF JULIAN, CALLED APOSTATE[554]

5.1 After the death of Constantius, Julian entered Constantinople. He had already conquered Thrace when he was proclaimed emperor. It was said that the demons and fortune tellers had told of the death of Constantius and his change in fortune even before <Julian> departed for the east, and while this may have been so, the life of Julian as emperor was a short one. The power he tasted was an illusion. I think it is absurd to think that after he heard foretold the death of Constantius and his own end at the hands of the Persians in combat, he would have chosen death. . . .

After the death of Constantius a great fear of persecution arose in the church. In fact, the Christians probably suffered more from fear than from any consequences that would likely have arisen from the transition; but there had been a long and peaceful interlude. They had become accustomed to tranquility, and rumors of the emperor's hatred of Christian teaching spread rapidly, causing them to recall the misery and tortures their grandfathers had endured at the goading of other tyrants. It was <also> said that his renunciation of Christianity was so complete that he underwent the so-called renunciatory rites, which involve sacrifice and the blood of animals, in order to wash away his Christian baptism. Both secretly and then publicly he immersed himself in the observance of pagan rituals and augurs.

One day, it is said, he was examining the entrails of an animal when he saw the pattern of a cross surrounded by a crown. A number of the celebrants were terrified at the sign, exclaiming that the symbol pointed to the victory of Christianity (the circle being the symbol of that which has no beginning and no end but is of eternal duration); but the chief celebrant told Julian to interpret the sign as a favorable omen: the entrails surrounded the symbol of Christianity and impinged on it in such a way as to suggest that it would not spread or expand, but be limited by the boundaries of the circle that surrounded it.

---

554. Sozomen 5.1–6.1 (edited); translation based on the edition of the Greek text edited by Josef Bidez and G. C. Hansen, *Griechischen christlichen Schriftsteller der ersten Jahrhunderte* (Berlin: Akademie Verlag, 1960), Bd. 50.

One day, I am told, Julian was plunged into a famous pit in order to consult an oracle or to participate in an initiatory ritual. Now these rites are famous for the mechanical devices that are used to produce effects in the initiates, either to frighten or to overwhelm them, and on this occasion it was as though ghosts and spirits began to dance before him. And Julian, overcome with fear, seemed to forget those who were there with him; and even though he had long since turned away from Christ to his new faith, nevertheless he signed himself with the symbol of Christ—just as any Christian would do when confronted with dangers. As soon as he did so the apparitions disappeared and the designs were confounded. The master of the rites was amazed at first, but when he discovered what had caused the flight of the demons he said the ritual had been profaned. He told the emperor to be brave, to ignore the events, and to keep his mind away from everything Christian. Then he again conducted the rites. All of this attention to pagan custom worried and sadden the Christians, as you may imagine—and the more so because he had himself once been a Christian. He was born of pious parents, baptized in infancy, and raised according to the tradition of the church to know the scriptures. He was nurtured by bishops and Christian teachers. [Sozomen goes on the repeat and expand the main elements of Socrates' account of Julian's education.]

5.3 When Julian became unrivalled in the empire he ordered all the pagan temples reopened in the east and that those that had fallen into ruin should be restored with their altars. He set aside great sums of money for the project of reestablishing the ancient customs and ceremonies in the cities, as well as the custom of offering sacrifice.

<Julian> therefore offered libations and offered sacrifice in public. He bestowed honors of those who performed these duties. He restored the initiators and the priests, the hierophants and the keepers of images to their former status. He ratified the laws of his predecessors regarding various privileges, approving exemption from military duty and other obligations, such as had been their prerogative under previous emperors. To the temple guardians he restored their rations, but commanded them to refrain from eating

meats, and moreover to lead a life of purity by abstaining from anything which violated custom.

<Julian> also ordered that the nilometer[555] and the sacred letters and tablets should be housed again in the temple of Serapis, undoing the edict by which Constantine ordered them to be deposited in a church. He was in touch with the inhabitants of cities where he knew paganism flourished, inviting them to state what support they required <to further their cause>. But toward the Christians Julian showed only contempt. He refused to visit them or to receive their legates, those who were responsible for representing their grievances.

When the natives of Nisibis[556] supplicated for help against the Persians who were on the very brink of invading Roman territories, Julian refused all assistance on the grounds that they were wholly christianized. He refused to open their temples and shrines, saying he would not help them, receive their ambassador, or indeed even enter the city until he had assurances that they had returned to the old religion.

Similarly he accused the people of Palestinian Constantia of being attached to Christianity, and made the city subordinate to the city of Gaza. This same Constantia[557] was once Majuma, a famous port used by ships coming into Gaza. But when Constantine heard that its inhabitants had become Christian he created it a city, gave it the name of his son and an independent government—thinking that a city <of this stature> should not be dependent on a city devoted to pagan rites such as Gaza. Now when Julian became emperor, the citizens of Gaza took their case against Constantia to the court, and the emperor himself sat as judge, deciding in Gaza's favor that Constantia would henceforth be a dependent town, even though located some twenty stadia from the its capital city. . . .

5.4 <So too> Julian erased the name of Caesarea, the famous city in Cappadocia which is sited near to Mount Argeus, wiping it off the register of cities, obliterating the name that had been conferred on it by Claudius Caesar (it was known formerly as Macaza). Julian had long despised the citizens of this place because of their Christianity <and because> they had destroyed the ancient temples of Apollo

---

555. The station used for measuring the waters of the Nile.
556. Nusaybin in Mesopotamia.
557. On the Abora, also called Viransehir.

and of their patron deity Jupiter. The temple dedicated to Fortuna was left standing for a while, but then on Julian's accession it too was destroyed. When Julian got wind of this, he hated the city with a passion so intense he could hardly bear <to hear the city mentioned>. He hated even the members of the old religion, because he said—though few in number—they should have defended the temple of Fortune and suffered what befell them in its defense. So he ordered the treasury of the churches in the city and region emptied of gold—about three hundred pounds were discovered and transported to the public treasury along with other property belonging <to the churches>. Then he ordered all the clergy to register with the governor to serve in the military—a service which is regarded the most arduous and least rewarding in the Empire.

Finally, he ordered the names of all Christians to be recorded, including women and children, and he imposed taxes on them as crippling as those already imposed on the <Christian> villages. Then he ordered temples rebuilt, as quickly as possible, saying he would not be satisfied and would punish the city further if it was not done—even if not a single Galilean was left standing. For this name is the one Julian preferred to the name "Christians," and there is no doubt that he would have carried out his pledge had he not died when he did. <So> it was not out of compassion for the Christians that Julian at the beginning treated them with greater kindness than had been the case with previous persecutors. No, rather, he had discovered that their torture brought the Romans no advantage; and he knew that the Christian religion had increased because of the courage of those who died in its defense.

So Julian, envious as he was of the strength of the Christians, tried persuasion and reason to win them over to paganism rather than the tactics of his predecessors: Fire, sword, drowning, and burying-alive were eschewed in favor of other means to win them to his side, because he believed benevolence was a more efficient weapon than violence.[558]

---

558. Sozomen does not seem to recognize that the measures he is describing in relation to Palestinian Christians are the opposite of the tactics he otherwise ascribes to Julian.

The story is told that one day Julian was sacrificing in the temple of Fortuna at Constantinople when Maris, the bishop of Chalcedon, confronted him and upbraided him as a man of no religion—an atheist and apostate. In reply, Julian could say nothing by way of reproach. Maris was old, blind, and led by the hand by a child. But then Julian with his customary bile turned to the old man and said, "The Galilean, your God, will not heal you." And Maris said, "Well, I thank my God for this blindness; because of it I cannot see the one who has fallen from our faith." Julian said nothing but <left the old man in peace> thinking that by a display of patience and generosity he would advance the cause of the pagan religion.

5.5 It was for this reason Julian recalled the Christians who had been exiled under Constantius because of their religious beliefs[559] from exile to return to their cities. He returned the property that had been taken from them, and called upon the non-Christian population not to insult or injure them, but to treat them fairly and permit them to offer sacrifice freely. He said that if they wished—without coercion—to participate in the worship of the temples, they had first to expiate themselves with purifications, for the pagans believe the demons must be appeased in this way. But the clergy he stripped of the honors and immunities and stipends which Constantine had conferred. And he repealed all laws that favored the Christians while reinstating their statutory liabilities. This included requiring widows and virgins (whose poverty caused them to be reckoned among the clergy) to refund all provision that had come to them from public sources.[560]

Recall that when Constantine managed the secular concerns of the church, he made certain that a portion of the taxes raised

---

559. That is, the anti-Arians.

560. Sozomen's report should be evaluated in the light of other evidence. In Ep. XXXVII (to Atarbius, prefect of the district of the Euphrates), Julian writes: "I swear by the gods that I do not desire the death, beating, or abuse of any of the Galileans. Nonetheless, I say with conviction that the god-fearing <θεοσεβεῖς> are to be preferred to them. It is because of these Galileans that everything has been turned upside down, but through the grace of the gods everything is put right. And so let us honor the gods, as will all god-fearing people and their cities" (376C, D). Julian's standard position is that Christianity is a "disease" and that the persons afflicted are to be "treated" rather than persecuted for it; see the epistle to the Bostrians, above, XLI.438B.

throughout the Empire would be reserved for the benefit and support of Christian priests—protecting this arrangement by a law
which <reenacted after Julian's death> remains in effect to this very
day. It is said that the exactions of Julian against the clergy were cruel
and meticulous, for the collectors in charge of the process were
required to issue receipts for all the money they gained in the
process, thus proving that Constantine's generosity was fully repaid.

The emperor's hatred toward the religion was inexhaustible. And
in his spite he did all that is possible to ruin the church. He seized
property, carried away votives, sacred cups, and commanded any
guilty of destroying shrines and altars during the reign of Constantius or Constantine to rebuild them or pay for their rebuilding out
of their own pocket. But because many who were accused under the
inquiry into the disbursement of sacred money were unable to pay,
<Julian> ordered priests and clergy and others as well tortured and
thrown into prison.

So it may be seen that even if Julian shed less blood than other
persecutors of the church—if he was less severe in concocting
painful tortures—he was more cruel in some respects, because he
wanted to do incalculable harm to the church. If he recalled the
priests whom Constantius had banished, he did so because he
hoped they would at once fall into internal strife and feuding,
proving Constantius a fool and vindicating his own program
directed at the failure of the church. He reckoned that his plan
would show his predecessor in his true colors: He would favor the
pagans because he shared their values, but he would also show
mercy to those who had suffered so much in the name of Christ,
because <Constantius> had treated them so unfairly. . . .

5.6 During this time Athanasius, who had been in hiding, heard
of the death of Constantius and returned by night to the church in
Alexandria. His sudden reappearance was nothing short of aston-
ishing: He had managed to escape detection by the governor of
Egypt, who had been ordered by the emperor and the friends of
bishop George to seize him, by concealing himself in the house of a
virgin in Alexandria. This virgin is said to have been so beautiful that
everyone who saw her exclaimed that she was an apparition never

seen in nature. Men pledged to continence would avoid looking at her, lest the finger-pointers accuse them of having wicked thoughts. She was at the peak of her beauty—young, unassuming, and tender —gifts which when added to her natural loveliness enhanced her charm all the more. . . .

When I look back on the events <of Athanasius's life> I can only think that they were directed by God. His relatives might have fallen under suspicion as to his whereabouts, and might have had trouble from the authorities if they had been compelled to swear <concerning his hiding place>, but who <including his family> would have suspected that a priest would have taken refuge in the house of a beautiful virgin? She bravely took him in, and through her efforts his life was spared. She became his hostess and servant; she washed his feet, brought him food, waited on him in every imaginable way. If he needed books, she arranged for someone to bring them to her. But all during his long period of hiding, no one in Alexandria had any idea where he was.

5.7 So Athanasius, who had survived in this manner, seemed to come out of nowhere, but the people rejoiced to see him and wasted no time in restoring his churches to him. This meant, however, the expulsion of Arians from their churches, which in turn meant that they were required to hold their assemblies in private houses. They installed Lucius as supervisor of their heresy in place of <their former bishop> George. George had been murdered in an uprising of the pagans of Alexandria at the very moment it was known that Constantius was dead and Julian had been declared sole ruler. They attacked George first by shouting imprecations, then threatening to kill him on the spot. George was thrown into prison for a little while, but the instigators soon returned, rushed at the doors, seized George and slaughtered him, heaved his corpse onto the back of a camel after defiling it and subjecting it to unspeakable forms of abuse before burning it at nightfall. I am aware that the Arians allege that these things were done to George at the instigation of Athanasius. But it seems more likely to me that the perpetrators were pagans. They had good reason to hate him—more reason indeed than anyone, for he had ridiculed their temples, insulted the gods,

and prevented them from offering sacrifices or honoring the ancestors. Moreover, the influence he commanded in the palace caused
the people to despise him, and soon enough they found the flouting
of his authority insufferable.

Meanwhile, a disaster had occurred in Mithrium in an area
where Constantius had erected a church in a desert region and given
it to the see of Alexandria. George set about making way for the
church by clearing the ground in order build an oratory when an
adytum was discovered. <This adytum> was full of idols and instruments used by pagans in their rituals of initiation—strange to
behold, from the standpoint of the workers; worse, the Christians
insisted on making a spectacle of them and publicly parading them
in order to annoy the pagans. At the sight <of the procession> the
pagans formed a mob and attacked the Christians, arming themselves with rocks, with swords, with whatever came to hand. They
killed many Christians and in mockery of the faith crucified some
and wounded others.[561] This naturally brought work on the church
to a standstill, and the pagans murdered George as soon as they
heard Julian would be emperor. Indeed, the fact is admitted even by
the Emperor, who would have had more to gain if the truth had not
been so compelling, and who would have preferred to blame the
death of George on the Christians rather than the pagans, had not
truth pressed him to disclose the facts. As it is, he wrote a severe
letter[562] to the inhabitants of Alexandria on the subject, in which he
makes it clear where the blame rests. In the letter he condemns but
does not punish; he invites them to attend to Serapis, their tutelary
god, and their founder Alexander, and his uncle Julianus, who was
governor of Egypt as well as Alexandria. It was the <elder> Julian
whose hatred of Christianity was so great and love of the old faith
so strong that he remained a persecutor until his dying day. . . .

5.15 <When Julian heard> that Athanasius was using the church
of Alexandria for divine service and the teaching of catechumens,

---

561. Sozomen is the sole authority for the narrative of these hostilities. A strik-
ingly similar tale is told by Socrates (HE 5.16) concerning the destruction of a
mithreum at the behest of Theophilus of Alexandria.

562. Ep. XXIX, quoted in its entirety by Socrates, HE 3.3.

and that he had converted many from paganism in this way, he commanded him to leave Alexandria at once, on pain of death. Julian's warrant in this was to say that Athanasius had been banished by imperial decree under Constantius and had resumed his see without the approval of the reigning emperor. Julian for his part insisted that he had never intended to restore bishops exiled by Constantius to their jurisdictions in the church, but only to their homelands. On learning that he had been ordered out of Alexandria immediately, Athanasius addressed the crowds saying, "Take heart: this is a little cloud that will quickly pass away." Then he said farewell to the assembly and entrusted the church to the most courageous and loyal of his comrades, and he left Alexandria.

At this time some citizens of Cyzicus[563] sent a messenger to the emperor for the purpose of asking favors, and in particular seeking the restoration of their temples. He praised their efforts and agreed quickly to their petitions. Soon after, he expelled Eleusius, bishop of that city, who had destroyed a number of the pagan shrines and desecrated other areas, while building churches and hostels for widows, as well as houses for virgins, and having urged pagans to abandon their ancient rites. The emperor then gave word that foreign Christians were not to enter the city of Cyzicus, fearing that they might form an alliance with Christians within the city and then mount a campaign <against the pagans>. There were many sympathizers among the population who held views similar to the Christians— men who were wool makers for the state or who traded in money. They had been permitted by a succession of emperors to remain in Cyzicus with their families on condition they turn over to the state, on an annual basis, clothes for the soldiers and a supply of newly minted coin.

Now Julian was eager to ensure the triumph of paganism whatever the effort, but he was not willing to employ harsh measures to do it; he thought it unwise, for example, to use force or violence

---

563. As ecclesiastical metropolis of Hellespontus (Propontis) near Erdek, Cyzicus had a catalogue of bishops beginning with the first century; Lequien (I, 747) mentions fifty-nine. A more complete list is found in Nicodemos, in the Greek "Office of St. Emilian" (Constantinople, 1876), pp. 34–36, which has eighty-five names. Gelasius, the historian of Arianism, was born in Cyzicus.

against those who would not sacrifice[564]—and besides, there were so many Christians in so many cities that the emperor would have had trouble enough just to count them. Indeed, he did not even forbid them to come together for divine service because he realized that when freedom of the will is curtailed, coercion is never effective. So he expelled the clergy and bishops from their churches hoping that by so doing he would effectively destroy the assembly, as there would be no one left to convene it. Deprived of clergy to administer the sacred mysteries, he reasoned, <Christianity itself> would soon enough disappear. To encourage the decline of the religion, Julian caused the rumor to be spread that the clergy were fomenting rebellion among the people, and it was this pretense he used to get rid of Eleusius and his friends—though the city was far from being in rebellion against the emperor. Then Julian called upon the people of Bostra to expel Titus, their bishop, conveying in advance that he would hold Titus responsible for any act of sedition—to which Titus dutifully replied that although Christians were as numerous as pagans in Bostra, nonetheless they preferred tranquility to conflict and were inclined to remain quiet and not to rebel. Julian decided that it would do no good to incite the citizens of Bostra against Titus, so instead he composed a letter in which he slanderously suggested that the only thing preventing the Bostrians from insurrection was the intervention of Titus—not their own peace-loving inclinations. Then Julian urged them to expel Titus from the city as a traitor.[565]

In similar fashion, the Christians were subjected to trials in many places—sometimes due to commands of <Julian> and at other times due to the impetuousness of the <pagan> population, but blame should be attributed in either case to the designs of the ruler. At no time did he invoke the law against the law-breakers; instead, he settled for reprimand and scolding and the cheapness of words, while his actions goaded them on in their desire to hurt the Church. And so even though we cannot say the emperor persecuted the Christians, the Christians *were* nonetheless persecuted, fleeing from village to village, city to city.

---

564. Almost no early writer manages to square this information concerning Julian's leniency with the desire to style him a persecutor. Cf. Ep. XXXVII.

565. Ep. XLI, preserved by Sozomen.

My grandfather was born into a pagan family.[566] His own family together with that of Alaphion was the first to convert to Christianity in Bethelia,[567] a prosperous town near the Gaza, full of temples, and one which is regarded highly by the people of that country because of the magnificent design and antiquity of its temples. The most splendid among these is known as the Pantheon, built on an artificial mound commanding a view of the city. People say that the place received its name from the temple and that the original form of the name was in the Syriac language, later rendered into Greek, but retaining the meaning that it is a dwelling place for all the gods. Now it is also said that the families I have mentioned were converted because of the work of the monk Hilarion. It is said Alaphion was possessed by a devil, and neither pagan nor Jew could relive him of his suffering, no matter what prayer or incantation they tried. Hilarion, however, relieved the man's suffering simply by calling out the name of Christ. The demon had been routed, and in thanksgiving Alaphion and his whole family were converted to Christianity.

As for my grandfather, he was a man of extraordinary skill, especially in the exegesis of the holy scripture. He had a wide learning and was a competent mathematician, and he was loved by the Christians of the Gaza and Ascalon and the whole region. He was much in demand by the Christians there because of his superior training in interpreting difficult passages in scripture. <The family of Alaphion> does not need the likes of me to praise it, for the first churches and monasteries built in that country were built because of this family—and still it produces good men right down to this day. Even in my youth I knew some of them, but they were then very old. I will say more about them as my history unfolds.

5.16 The Emperor was grieved to find that his efforts to rekindle the fire of the old religion were useless, while seeing Christianity grow more famous day by day. The doors of the temples were wide open, sacrifice was offered, the old rites were restored in all the cities, but Julian was not happy. He knew that if he weakened or withdrew

---

566. It was a matter of pride among Christian intellectuals from the time of Justin martyr to boast of a pagan background and classical learning.

567. Lit., house of the gods.

the pressure <for change> his program would collapse. He was particularly unhappy that the wives, children, and servants of many
pagans had converted to Christianity, and when on examination he
decided that one of the great virtues of the Christian faith was the
moral life of those who professed it, he decided to introduce the discipline of Christianity into the temples and to create orders and
grades of ministry: teachers and lectors to give lessons in pagan doctrine, and to exhort the people to pray at certain hours. He also
resolved to create monasteries where men and women could lead a
life of philosophical seclusion. And he founded hospitals for the
poor and for the benefit of the resident foreigners, and other charitable works. Julian <even> attempted to introduce the Christian practice of penance among the pagans, related to various kinds of delib-
erate and inadvertent wrongdoing. Another custom he admired in
the Christian discipline was the practice of the bishops giving those
who travelled abroad letters of authorization, commending them to
the care and hospitality of other bishops in all circumstances. These
are the ways in which Julian attempted to graft onto paganism some
of the features of Christianity. But you need not take my word for it,
for I have in my possession the copy of a letter by Julian himself on
the subject where he corroborates these assertions.[568] . . .

5.17 Julian's artful maneuvers were designed to encourage his subjects to move from Christianity to the old faith. He was intent on rid-
ding the state of the Christian religion, but equally intent in refusing
to employ violent means which might prove embarrassing or seem
tyrannical. Nonetheless, he did everything in his power to lead his
subjects back into paganism, and he was especially persistent with the
soldiers, whom he would sometimes address personally but more
often through a commanding officer. Constantine, as I have mentioned, had made the insignia for the army the sign of the cross; Julian
commanded that this be discarded and the ancient standard of the
army be reintroduced in order to accustom the troops to the worship
of the gods. He also commissioned a painting to be displayed in

---

568. Here Sozomen reproduces Ep. XLIX (To Arsacius). While the material for
5.16 is unique to Sozomen, there is no reason to doubt on the basis of style or content that the letter put forward by Sozomen to document Julian's concern over the
perceived "moral authority" of Christianity is authentic.

public showing Jupiter coming out of heaven and presenting him with the imperial symbols—a crown or a purple robe; and also of Mars or Mercury looking intently at <Julian>, rapt in admiring his rhetoric and his military prowess. He was always certain to depict himself alongside the gods, so that in honoring the emperor they would also be seen to be worshipping the gods. But he abused the older usages and disguised his purpose from his subjects, thinking that if they accepted his sovereignty they would also be willing to obey him in every particular; and if they did not <obey him> he could then say that they were traitors to the Roman state because they had offended against custom and the dignity of the emperor. In fact, there were only a few men who saw through his scheme and refused to venerate the pictures, and the full weight of the law was brought to bear against them. The great mass of people in their childish simplicity or perhaps in ignorance simply accepted the old ways and venerated his image, and while Julian got no real advantage from this success, he was undeterred in his effort to change the religious balance.

Another measure employed by Julian was more direct and less subtle, and tested the loyalty of many soldiers assigned to the imperial household. Each year it is a custom to give a bonus of money to the troops, and usually the chosen day is an anniversary of some sort—the birthday of the emperor, the founding of a city. Julian <believed > that soldiers are naturally slow and simpleminded, and are attracted to money; so he concluded that money might be used beneficially to lure them into the worship of the gods. Fire and incense having been placed conveniently near the emperor, as each soldier approached for his bonus according to the old Roman custom, he was enjoined to offer sacrifice. A few courageously took the gold but refused to comply; others were so ignorant of the implications of what they were doing that they blindly followed habit and custom down the path to sin; still others were so hungry for gold or so afraid of the consequences if they did not comply with the pagan rites and the test in front of them that they fell into temptation, when they should have fled.

I am told[569] that a group of soldiers who had succumbed in this

---

569. This section is an example of Sozomen's penchant for creating or propagating pious fabrications.

way were at table, raising their glasses in celebration, when one among them happened to mention the name of Christ. "Strange," another said, "that you <of all people> should mention Christ when an hour ago you denied him by throwing incense into the emperor's fire." At this they all became agitated and suddenly conscious of the great wrong they had done; they rushed into the street where they publicly wailed and confessed their sin, and asked passersby to bear witness that what they had done, they had done with the hand only and not the heart—and that from that day they would live as Christians. They then presented themselves before the emperor and threw down the gold, asking him to kill them or subject them to tortures on the spot; for they said that the sin committed by their hand should be inflicted on their bodies for the sake of Christ. But the emperor, whatever he may have felt, refused to put them to death, for he wished to deprive them of the honor of martyrdom. Instead, he rescinded their military commission and expelled them from the palace.

5.18 Julian felt the same way about all Christians, and he displayed these feelings as opportunities arose. Those who refused to sacrifice to the gods risked having their citizenship revoked, though blameless in every corner of their lives—Julian would not permit them to serve as magistrates, judges, officers, or in the assemblies. He also prohibited Christian children from attending the schools and from being taught the Greek poets and writers. He detested Appolinaris the Syrian, a man noted for his skills in the science of language; as well as the Cappadocians Gregory and Basil, the greatest orators of the day, and others who were well-versed <in Greek>, some of whom defended the Nicene cause, and some of whom were followers of Arius. His real reason for excluding children of Christian parents from the study of the Greeks was that he knew such study would lead to greater skills in rhetoric and argumentation. So Appolinaris used his gifts in order to produce an epic on the antiquities of the Hebrews from the time of Saul as a substitute for Homer's poem. <Like Homer>, he divided his poem into twenty-four parts and assigned a letter of the Greek alphabet to each in turn. The same writer produced comedies in the fashion of Menander, tragedies comparable to those of Euripides, and odes like those of

Pindar. His themes came from the scripture, based on his extensive knowledge of the whole, and he <was able to do this> in a remarkably short time, producing works that, in terms of <their> style, poignancy of expression, character, and structure are the equal of the Greek literature they emulate in diversity and power.[570] I would say that if the writings of the ancients were not held so unfairly in such high regard, the writings of Appolinaris would be valued as highly. For this man was a man of copious intelligence, excelling <others> in many branches of learning, while ancient writers were usually proficient in only one. <Appolinaris> wrote, for example, a book entitled "The Truth,"[571] against the emperor and pagan philosophy; in it he shows without appeal to scripture how pagan ideas about God are falsely deduced, which Julian, upon reading it, exclaimed in a letter to the bishops, "I read it; I understood it; I condemn it."[572] To which the bishops replied, "You read it, but you did not understand, for if you had you would not have condemned it." . . .

5.19 Julian was now determined to pursue a war against the Persians, and he went to Antioch in Syria. People were saying that while goods were abundant, they came at a very high price; so out of generosity the emperor reduced prices for provisions to such a low level that the vendors fled the city. And so there was scarcity, and for this the emperor was blamed. People expressed their anger by ridiculing the length of his beard and the images of bulls which were stamped on his coins.

Some said he was butchering his people in the same way the priests were back in business butchering sacrificial animals. When these slanders were first heard, Julian was annoyed and made noises about punishing them before he went off to Tarsus. But in time he grew calm, and answered their ridicule with a finely crafted work which he called "Aversion to Beards," which he sent as a present to

---

570. No judge of literature, Sozomen here parts company with Socrates' endorsement of Greek literature and philosophy (HE 3.16). Appolinaris was widely respected by writers of the fourth century for the elegance of his style. Apart from a few fragments, all of his writings are lost.

571. Sozomen seems to attribute this work mistakenly to this Appolinaris (Apolonarius); a book by this title was written by Apollonaris of Hierapolis according to Eusebius, *Ecclesiastical History*, 1.35.

572. A letter falsely ascribed to Julian.

them. In every other respect he treated the Christians of the region in just the same way he treated them elsewhere, being sure that he did all possible to promote the spread of the pagan religion.[573] . . .

5.22 Though the emperor despised and persecuted the Christians he displayed only concern and showed kindness toward the Jews. He sent letters to the leaders and elders among the Jewish people asking them to pray for him and for the good of the whole Empire. But I am certain he did this not because he had any real affection for the religion of the Jews, which he knew was the mother, as it were, of the Christian faith, as both take their authority from the patriarchs and prophets; rather, in favoring the Jews he intended to humiliate the Christians, their most stalwart enemies. Perhaps he thought, as well, to persuade some of the Jews to accept pagan doctrines and practices, for most <of the Jews> knew only a little scripture and unlike the Christians (and the very wisest Hebrews) they did not discern the hidden meaning <of the sacred books>.

Later events proved this suspicion true, for Julian sent for the leaders of the Jewish people and adjured them to return to the observance of the laws of Moses and their ancient customs, but he was told that as the temple in Jerusalem had been destroyed it was not lawful for them to <offer sacrifice> in any other place than the ancestral city—and they had been expelled from <Jerusalem>. On hearing this Julian donated money from the treasury and commanded them to rebuild their temple, and restore the cult of their forefathers, and offer sacrifices in the old way. The Jews embarked on the project without giving a thought to the warnings of the prophets, which said the task could never be fulfilled.[574]

6.1[575] . . . [After Julian arrived at Ctesiphon, which had been

---

573. The section (5.20–21) ends with a digression on a miracle associated with the tomb of Bablas the Martyr in Antioch and the temple of Apollo at Daphne and events surrounding an order to destroy a statue of Christ in Paneas. Following sections end similarly. Sozomen relates these legends to prove that Julian by this point in his reign had incurred divine wrath, the climax of which he will see in his untimely death in the Persian campaign.

574. Sozomen continues with the legend of an earthquake sent by God as a manifestation of his disapproval of the project. When the workmen regroup, fire suddenly bursts forth from the foundations and kills the laborers.

575. Sozomen's account of the death of Julian is pieced together from a

made the imperial residence by the Persians, he had his ships anchored in the Tigris burned and began a land march of several days, guided by an old man who turned out to be an agent of the Persian army. With provisions low and the troops demoralized, the Romans were ripe for attack.] . . . The Persians chose this as the moment to wage their assault, and in the confusion an enormous wind arose occluding the sun with clouds of dust. It was in the midst of this conflict that a horseman rode swiftly toward the emperor and drove his lance clear though him. Some say the horseman was a Persian, others say he was a Saracen, and still others maintain he was a Roman who had become impatient with Julian's style of leadership and his foolishness in exposing his army to such danger. The Syrian orator Libanius, who was Julian's friend and companion, writes as follows concerning the incident: "You wish to know who killed the emperor? I do not know his name. But we do know that the killer was not a man from among the enemy—for no one came forward to claim the reward even though the king of Persia proclaimed through a herald that rewards were to be given to the one who did the deed. We are thus in the enemy's debt, for they did not claim the glory of the action for themselves, but instead have left us to look for the killer in our own ranks. Those who most wanted to see Julian dead were those who broke the law and methodically conspired to do away with him, lying in wait for the first opportunity to do it. What they wished to achieve was greater liberty than they could find under his regime, but they were also provoked by the Emperor's religious devotion to the gods, which they did not share."

6.2 As Libanius states clearly in the chapter from which I have quoted, the emperor died at the hands of a Christian.[576] I am sure this is true. It is also likely that soldiers in the army came up with the plot against him, since from the time of the Greeks down to today the murderers of tyrants have won praise for their willingness to risk death for the sake of liberty and in the defense of country, family, and friends. So no one performing this bold deed, done for the sake

---

number of sources; the outline is that of Socrates (HE 3.21), but the account is permeated with legend and improbable detail.

576. Libanius says nothing of this; in this independent chapter Sozomen is working out his own conjectures.

of God and religion, is deserving of any blame. I personally have no other information concerning the men who committed the murder other than what I have already presented, but the account itself is accepted by everyone as evidence of the divine wrath which brought about <Julian's> death.

If proof is needed, I will relate the story of a vision sent to one of the emperor's friends who was traveling to Persia with the hope of joining forces with the emperor. On his way he found himself so far from any hostel that he had to put up in a church overnight. During the night, in a dream or vision, he saw all the apostles and prophets gathered together and lamenting the injuries which Julian had inflicted on the church, meeting in council to decide what course of action should be taken. After a long discussion, two men rose from the assembly, told those remaining to take heart, and departed quickly—as though they had decided the way to deprive the emperor of his power. <When he awoke>, the soldier was so troubled by what he had seen that he did not continue his journey, but waited for news to find out how the revelation might be fulfilled; so again he fell asleep, and this time he saw the assembly convened and the two men who had left the night before sitting again in their places <at the council table>. And they told the others, "Julian is dead."[577]

---

577. Sozomen continues to relate portents, calamities, and miracles associated with the death of Julian. Socrates ends his more sober report with the information that Julian finished his life in the fourth consulate, on the twenty-sixth of June, the third year of his reign, at the age of thirty-one (HE 3.21). Theodoret provides the most famous, if unlikely, detail of Julian's death in his account (*Historia*, 3.25), that when Julian saw he was dying he "cupped his hands to fill them with blood and hurled it at the sun crying, "Galilean, you have conquered."

BIBLIOGRAPHY

Abbreviations of ancient authorities cited frequently in the notes follow the entry.

I. ANCIENT AUTHORITIES

Albinus. *Epitoma*. Edited and translated by P. Louis. Rennes, 1945.

Ammianus Marcellinus. *Res gestae*. Edited and translated by J. C. Rolfe. [In English] London, 1964. (Amm.)

Ammianus Marcellinus. *The Later Roman Empire, 354–378*. Translated by William Hamilton. London, 1986.

Aristides. *Orationes*. Edited by W. Dindorf. Leipzig, 1829.

Celsus. *On the True Doctrine*. Translated by R. J. Hoffmann. [In English] Oxford, 1987. (See below, Origen, *Contra Celsum* [CS].)

Claudius Mamertinus. *Gratiarum actio Mamertini de consulate suo Iuliano Imperatori*. Edited by C. E. V. Nixon and Barbara Satlor Rodgers. In *In Praise of Later Roman Emperors: The Panegyrici Latini*. Berkeley, 1994. (Mamertinus)

Codex Theodosiansus. Edited by Theo. Mommsen, P. M. Meyer, and P. Krueger = *Theodosiani libri XVI cum constitutionibus sirmondianis et leges novellae ad Theodosianum pertinentes*. 2 vols. Berlin, 1905. (Cod. Theod.)

Consularia Constantinopolitana. Edited by T. Mommsen. 1892. Berlin, 1961.

Cyril of Alexandria. *Contra Julianum* (*Pro Christiana religione adversus Julianum Imperatorem*). *Patrologiae Graecae Cursus Completus*, vol. 76. Edited by J-P Migne. 81 vols. Paris, 1856–61. (PG)

Ephraem Syrus. *Contra Julianum*. Edited by E. Beck. Louvain, 1957.

211

Epitome de Caesaribus. Edited by F. R. Pichlmayr and R. Gruendel. Berlin, 1961.

Eunapius Fragmenta Historicorum Graecorum. Edited and translated by R. C. Blockley. *The Fragmentary Classicizing Historians of the Later Roman Empire*. 2 vols. Liverpool, 1983. (Eunapius)

Eusebius. *Praeparatio evangelica*. Edited and translated by E. Gifford. Oxford, 1903.

———. *Vita Constantini*. Edited by F. Winkelmann. Berlin, 1975.

Firmicus Maternus. *De errore profanorum religionum*. Edited and translated by R. Turcan. [In French] Paris, 1982.

Gregory Naziazen (Nazianzos). *Orations IV—V. In Iulianum, I—II*. Edited and translated by J. Bernardi. [In French] Paris, 1983. (Greg., Or.)

———. *Historica*. PG 37.

Eutropius. *Breviarum ab urbe condita*. Edited and translated by H. W. Bird. *Translated Texts for Historians*, vol. 14. Liverpool, 1993. (Eutropius)

Corpus inscriptionum latinorum. Vol. 9. Edited by T. Mommsen. Berlin, 1883.

Gregory of Naziazen. *Orationes, IV—V*. Edited by J. P. Migne. *Patrologiae Graecae*, vol. 35. Paris, 1864. (Gregory, Or.)

Hilary. *Liber II ad Constantium*. Edited by A. Feder. *Corpus scriptorium ecclesiasticorum latinorum*, vol. 60. Vienna, 1916. (ad Const.)

Julian. *Contra Galilaeos. Juliani imp. Librorum contra Christianos quae supersunt*. Edited by K. J. Neumann. Leipzig, 1880. (CG) Note: Marginal numbers in the Greek text refer to the pagination of Spanheim's 1696 edition of Cyril of Alexandria's polemic against Julian, *Pro Christiana religione*, used by Neumann in his 1880 reconstruction of Julian's treatise.

———. *Giuliano imperatore, Contra Galilaeos*. Edited by E. Masaracchia. Rome, 1991.

———. *The Works of the Emperor Julian, I–III*. Edited and translated by W. C. Wright. [In English] London, 1913–1923.

———. *Epistulae, leges, poematia, fragmenta varia*. Edited by J. Bidez and F. Cumont. Paris, 1922. (Ep.)

———. *L'empereur Julien: Ouvres complètes, I–II*. Edited by J. Bidez, G. Rochfort, and C. Lacombrade. Paris, 1924–1964.

———. *Iuliani imperatoris quae supersunt*. Edited by F. C. Hertlein. Leipzig, 1875–1876.

Libanius. *Orationes*. Edited and translated by A. F. Norman. [In English] *Libanius: Selected Works*. 3 vols. London, 1969. (Libanius, Or.)

———. *Opera, I–XII*. Edited by R. Foerster. Lepzig, 1903–1927.

Origen. *Contra Celsum*. Translated by H. Chadwick. Cambridge, 1953.

————. *Contra Celsum.* Edited by M. Borret. Paris, 1967–76. (C. Cels.)

Orosius. *Adversus paganos historiarum libri septem.* Edited by Z. Zangemeister. *Corpus Scriptorum Ecclesiasticorum Latinorum* (CSEL), edited by the Academy of Vienna, 1866–1957. CSEL V, Vienna, 1882. (Orosius)

Panegyrici latini. Edited by R A. B. Mynors. Oxford, 1964.

Philostorgius. *Historia Ecclesiastica.* Edited by J. Bidez. GCS, XXI. Paris, 1913. (Philos., Hist.)

Plato. *Opera.* Edited by J. Burnet. Oxford, 1900–1907.

Plotinus. *The Enneads*, I–VII. Edited and translated by A. H. Armstrong. Cambridge, MA, 1966–1988. (Enn.)

Porphyry. *Adversus Christianos.* Edited by A. v. Harnack. Berlin, 1916. (Abhandlung der koen.-Preuss. Akademie der Wiss., Phil.-hist. Kl. I [fragments].)

Porphyry: Against the Christians: Fragments from the Apocriticus of Macarius Magnes. Edited and translated by R. J. Hoffmann. [In English] Amherst, NY, 1994.

Proclus. *Theologica Platonica.* Edited by H. D. Saffrey and L. G. Westerink. Paris, 1968.

Sextus Aurelius Victor. *Liber de Caesaribus.* Edited by F. R. Pichlmayr and R. Gruendel. Berlin, 1961.

Socrates (Scholasticus). *Historia ecclesiastica.* Edited by J-P Migne. PG, 67. Paris, 1864. (Socrates, HE)

————. *Historia Ecclesiastica.* Edited by R. Hussey. Oxford, 1853.

Sozomen. *Historia ecclesiastica.* Griechischen Christlichen Schriftsteller der ersten drei Jahrhunderts (GCS) (1891–). Edited by A. von Harnack and Theodor Mommsen. GCS 50 Berlin and Leipzig, 1960. (Soz., HE)

Theodoret. *Historia ecclesiastica.* Edited by G. Parmentier. Berlin, 1911. (Theod., HE)

Zosimus. *Nova Historia.* Edited and translated by François Paschoud. *Zosime: Histoire nouvelle.* 3 vols. Paris, 1971–1989. (Zosimus)

II. MODERN INTERPRETATIONS AND STUDIES

Note: This list represents a selection of works relating principally to Julian and his religious and social context, and includes works cited frequently in the notes as well as studies consulted or reviewed but not cited. Standard journal abbreviations are keyed to the abbreviations list of the University

of Toronto (Journals of Interest to Classicists: TOCS-IN) list: http://www
.chass.utoronto.ca/amphoras/tdata/inform.toc. Otherwise, the full name of
the journal is given.

Alfoeldi, A. "Some Portraits of Julian Apostata." *AJA* 66 (1962): 403–405.

Allard, P. *Julien l'Apostat.* 3 vols. Paris, 1906–1910.

Andreotti, R. *Il regno dell'imperatore Giuliano.* Bologna, 1936.

Andresen, C. *Logos und Nomos: Die Polemik des Kelsos wider das Christentum.* Berlin, 1955.

Arce, J. *Estudios sobre el Emperador Flavio Claudio Juliano.* Madrid, 1984.

Armstrong, A. H. "The Way and the Ways: Religious Tolerance and Intolerance in the Fourth Century AD." *VChr* 38 (1984): 1–17.

Athanassiadi, P. "A Contribution to Mithraic Theology: The Emperor Julian's Hymn to King Helios." *JThS* 28 (1977): 360–71.

———. *Julian: An Intellectual Biography.* London, 1992; repr. *Of Julian and Hellenism,* Oxford, 1981, with bibliographical additions.

Baldwin, B. "The Caesares of Julian." *Klio* 60 (1978): 449–66.

Balty, J. "Julien et Apamée: aspects de la restauration de l'hellénisme et de politique antichrétienne de l'empereur." *Dialogues d'histoire ancienne* 1 (1974): 267–304.

Barnes, T. D. "Poprhyry Against the Christians: Date and Attribution of Fragments." *JThS* 24 (1973): 424–42.

———. "Christians and Pagans in the Reign of Constantius." In *L'église et l'Empire au IVe siècle.* Geneva, 1989.

———. *Athanasius and Constantius.* Cambridge, MA, 1993.

Beard, M., and J. North, eds. *Pagan Priests.* London, 1990.

Benedetti, I. "Giuliano in Antiochia nell'orazione XVIII di Libanio." *Athanaeum* 59 (1981): 166–79.

Bianchi, U., and M.Vermaseren, eds. *La soteria dei culti orientali nell' impero romano.* Leiden, 1992.

Bidez, J. *La tradition manuscrite et les éditions des discours de l'empereur Julien.* Paris, 1929.

———. *La vie de l'empereur Julien.* Paris, 1930.

Blanchetière, F. "Julien: philhelléne, philosémite, antichrétien." *Journal of Jewish Studies* 33 (1980): 61–68.

Blockley, R. C. "Constantius, Gallus and Julian as Caesars of Constantius II." *Latomus* 31 (1972): 433–68.

Bouffartigue, J. *L'empereur Julien et la culture de son temps.* Paris, 1992.

Bowersock, G. W. *Julian the Apostate.* London, 1978.

———. "Emperor Julian on His Predecessors." *YClS* 27 (1982): 159–72.

———. "From Emperor to Bishop: The Self-conscious Transformation of Political Power in the Fourth Century." *CP* 81 (1987): 235–51.

Bradbury, S. G. "Innovation and Reaction in the Age of Constantine and Julian." PhD dissertation, Berkeley, 1986.

Braun, R., and J. Richer, eds. *L'empereur Julien: de l'histoire à la légende*. Paris, 1978.

Brock, S. P. "A Letter Attributed to Cyril of Jerusalem on the Rebuilding of the Temple." *BSOAS* 40 (1977): 267–86.

Browning, R. *The Emperor Julian*. London, 1976.

Caltabiano, M. "Il comportamento di Giuliano in Gallia verso i suoi funzionari." *Acme* 32 (1979): 417–42.

Calza, R. *Iconografia romana imperiale da Carausio a Giuliano*. Rome, 1972.

Cameron, Av. *Christianity and the Rhetoric of Empire*. Berkeley, 1991.

Chauvin, P. *A Chronicle of the Last Pagans*. Cambridge, MA, 1990.

Cinnock, E. J. *A Few Notes on Julian and a Translation of His Public Letters*. London, 1901.

Cracco-Ruggini, L. "The Ecclesiastical Histories and Pagan Historiography: Providence and Miracles." *Ath.* 55 (1977): 107–26.

Croke, B. "The Era of Porphyry's Anti-Christian Polemic." *Journal of Religious History* 13 (1984): 1–15.

———, and J. Harries. *Religious Conflict in Fourth Century Rome*. Sydney, 1982.

Cumont, F. *Sur l'authenticité de quelques lettres de Julien*. Gand, 1889.

Daly, L. "Themistus' Plea for Religious Tolerance." *GRBS* 12 (1971): 65–81.

———. "In a Borderland: Themistus' Ambivalence to Julian." *Byz. Zeitschr.* 73 (1980): 1–11.

Di Maio, M., and W. H. Arnold. "Per vim, per caedum, per bellum: A Study of Murder and Ecclesiastical Politics in the Year 337 AD." *Byzantion* 62 (1992): 158–91.

Dillon, J. *The Golden Chain: Studies in the Development of Platonism and Christianity*. London, 1900.

Downey, G. "Philanthropia in Religion and Statecraft in the Fourth Century." *Historia* 4 (1955): 199–208.

———. "Themistius and the Defence of Hellenism." *HThR* 50 (1957): 259–74.

Drachman, A. B. *Atheism in Pagan Antiquity*. London, 1922.

Drinkwater, J. F. "The Pagan Underground: Constantius' II's Secret Service and the Survival and Usurpation of Julian the Apostate." In *Studies in*

Latin Literature and Roman History, edited by C. Deroux, III:348–87. Brussels, 1983.

Dvornik, F. "The Emperor Julian's Reactionary Ideas on Kingship." In *Late Classical and Medieval Studies in Honor of A. M. Frend,* edited by K. Weitzmann, 71–81. Princeton, NJ, 1955.

Ensslin, W. "Kaiser Julian's Gesetzgebungswerk und Reichsverwaltung." *Klio* 18 (1923): 104–109.

Festugière, A-J. "Julien à Macellum." *JRS* 47 (1957): 53–58.

Fornara, C. W. "Julian's Persian Expedition in Ammianus and Zosimus." *JHS* 111 (1991): 1–15.

Fortin, E. L. *Ad Adulescentes in Neoplatonism and Early Christian Thought.* London, 1981.

Geffcken, J. *The Last Days of Graeco-Roman Paganism.* Translated by S. MacCormack. Amsterdam and New York, 1978.

Gibbon, E. *Decline and Fall of the Roman Empire.* Edited by J. B. Bury. London, 1909.

Gilliard, F. "Notes on the Coinage of Julian the Apostate." *JRS* 54 (1964): 135–41.

Gleason, M. "Festive Satire: Julian's *Misopogon* and the New Year at Antioch." *JRS* 76 (1986): 106–19.

Gregory, T. "Julian and the Last Oracle at Delphi." *GRBS* 24 (1983): 355–66.

Guida, A. "Frammenti inediti del Contra i Galilei e della replica di Theodoro de Mopsuesta." *Prometheus* 9 (1983): 139–63.

———. *Un anonimo panegyrico per l'Imperatore Giuliano: Introduzione, Testo Critico, Commento.* Florence, 1990.

Halsberghe, G. *The Cult of Sol Invictus.* Leiden, 1972.

Harl, K. "Sacrifice and Pagan Belief in Fifth and Sixth Century Byzantium." *Past and Present* 128 (1990): 7–27.

Hunt, E. D. "Christians and Christianity in Ammianus Marcellinus." *CQ* 35 (1985): 186–200.

Kaegi, W. E. "Emperor Julian's Assessment of the Significance and Function of History." *Proc. Amer. Phil. Soc.* 108 (1964): 29–38.

———. "Research on Julian the Apostate: 1945–1964." *CW* 58 (1965): 229–38.

King, C. W. *Julian the Emperor: Containing Gregory Naziazen's Two Invectives and Libanius' Monody with Julian's Extant Theosophical Works.* London, 1888.

Labriolle, P. *La Réaction paienne. étude sur le polemique antichrtienne du Ier au VIe siècle.* Paris, 1934.

———. "Julian the Apostate." In Palanque, Bardy, Labriolle, et al. *The Church in the Christian Roman Empire*, translated by E. C. Messinger, 1:229–39. London, 1949.

Lacombrade, C. "Julien et la tradition romaine." *Pallas* 5 (1960): 155–64.

———. "L'empereur Julien, émule de Marc-Aurèle." *Pallas* 14 (1967): 9–22.

Lane Fox, R. *Pagans and Christians*. Harmondsworth, 1986.

Liebeschuetz, J. *Continuity and Change in Roman Religion*. Oxford, 1979.

Lieu, J., J. North, and T. Rajak, eds. *Jews among Pagans and Christians*. London, 1992.

Lieu, S., ed. *The Emperor Julian: Panegyric and Polemic*. Liverpool, 1986.

MacDonald, D. "Another Representation of the Sasanid Triumph Over Julian." *JNC* 28/29 (1978–79): 32–33.

Macmullen, R. *Paganism in the Roman Empire*. New Haven, CT, 1981.

Malley, W. J. *Hellenism and Christianity: The Conflict between Hellenism and Christian Wisdom in the* Contra Galilaeos *of Julian the Apostate and the* Contra Julianum *of St Cyril of Alexandria*. Analecta Gregoriana, vol. 210. Rome, 1978.

Mau, G. *Die Religionsphilosophie Kaiser Julians*. Leipzig, 1907.

Meredith, A. "Porphyry and Julian against the Christians." *ANRW* II.23.2, 1119–49.

Millar, F. "Jews of the Graeco-Roman Diaspora between Paganism and Christianity, AD 312—438." In J. Lieu et al., *Jews among Pagans and Christians*, 97–123. London, 1992.

Momigliano, A., ed. *The Conflict between Paganism and Christianity in the Fourth Century*. Oxford, 1963.

———. *On Pagans, Jews and Christians*. Middletown, CT, 1987.

Neander, A. *The Emperor Julian and His Generation*. Translated by G. V. Cox. London, 1850.

Negev, A. "The Inscription of the Emperor Julian at Ma'ayan Barukh." *Israel Expl. Journal* 19 (1969): 170–73.

Nillson, M. *Geschichte der griechischen Religion, II*. Munich, 1962.

O'Donnell, J. "The Demise of Paganism." *Traditio* 35 (1979): 45–88.

Paschoud, F. "Trois livres recents sur l'empereur Julien." *REL* 58 (1980): 107–23.

Pack, E. *Staedte und Steuern in der Politik Julians*. Brussels, 1986.

Rendall, G. H. *The Emperor Julian: Paganism and Christianity*. London, 1979.

Ricciotti, G. *Julian the Apostate*. Rockford, IL [ET]. 1999; Italian original, *L'imperatore Giuliano l'Apostata*, Verona, 1956.

Richer, J., ed. *L'empereur Julien: de la legende au mythe*. Paris, 1981.

Ridley, R. "Notes on Julian's Persian Campaign." *Historia* 22 (1973): 317–30.

Rostagni, A. *Giuliano l'apostata: Saggio critico con le operette politiche e satiriche tradotte e commentate.* Turin, 1920.

Rothrauff, C. M. "The Philanthropia of the Emperor Julian." PhD dissertation, University of Cincinnati, 1967.

Sacks, K. S. "Meaning of Eunapius' History." *History and Theory* 25 (1986): 52–67.

Salaman, M. "La conception de l'empereur Julien l'apostat pour la réorganization du monnayage romain." *Wiadomosci Numiizmatyczne* 23 (1979): 20–30.

Scheda, G. "Die Todesstunde Kaiser Julians." *Historia* 15 (1966): 380–84.

Schwartz, W. *De vita et scriptis Iuliani Imperatoris.* Bonn, 1988.

Sciolone, S. "Le accezioni dell'appellativo 'Galilei' in Giuliano il Apostata." *Aevum* 56 (1982): 71–80.

Sihler, E. G. "The Emperor Julian and His Religion." In *Augustus to Augustine: Essays and Studies Dealing with the Contact and Conflict of Classic Paganism and Christianity,* edited by E. G. Sihler, 190–217. Cambridge, 1923.

Simpson, W. D. *Julian the Apostate.* Aberdeen, 1930.

Smith, A. *Porphyry's Place in the Neoplatonic Tradition: A Study in Post-Plotinian Neoplatonism.* The Hague, 1974.

Smith, R. *Julian's Gods: Religion and Philosophy in the Thought and Action of Julian the Apostate.* London, 1995.

Thompson, E. A. "The Emperor Julian's Knowledge of Latin." *CR* 58 (1944): 49–51.

———. *The Historical Work of Ammianus Marcellinus.* Cambridge, 1947.

Truempelmann, L. "Triumph über Julian Apostata." *JNG* 25 (1975): 107–11.

Vogt, J. *Kaiser Julian und das Judentum: Studien zum Weltanschauungskampf der Spätanike.* Leipzig, 1939.

Wallace-Hadrill, A. "The Emperor and His Virtue." *Historia* 30 (1981): 298–323.

Wallis, R. T. *Neoplatonism.* London, 1972.

Warren-Bonfante, L. "Emperor, God and Man in the Fourth Century: Julian and Ammianus Marcellinus." *PP* 19 (1964): 401–27.

Wilken, R. *The Christians as the Romans Saw Them.* New Haven, CT, 1984.

Wirth, G. "Julians Persekrieg: Kriterien einer Katastrophe." In R. Klein, *Julian Apostata,* 455–507. Darmstadt, 1978.